Innovation in City Governments

Structures, Networks, and Leadership

Jenny M. Lewis, Lykke Margot Ricard, Erik Hans Klijn, and Tamyko Ysa

 Routledge
Taylor & Francis Group

NEW YORK AND LONDON

First published 2017
by Routledge
711 Third Avenue, New York, NY 10017

and by Routledge
2 Park Square, Milton Park, Abingdon, Oxon OX14 4RN

First issued in paperback 2018

Routledge is an imprint of the Taylor & Francis Group, an informa business

© 2017 Taylor & Francis

The right of Jenny M. Lewis, Lykke Margot Ricard, Erik Hans Klijn, and Tamyko Ysa to be identified as authors of this work have been asserted by them in accordance with sections 77 and 78 of the Copyright, Designs and Patents Act 1988.

Library of Congress Cataloging in Publication Data
A catalog record for this book has been requested

ISBN 13: 978-1-138-61721-6 (pbk)
ISBN 13: 978-1-138-94231-8 (hbk)

Typeset in Sabon
by Apex CoVantage, LLC

Innovation in City Governments

"If you are interested in how social structure can deeply influence social innovation outcomes, or in jump-starting social innovation in your city, this
book will provide clear insights about how the way we lead, organize, and
interact affects the way we innovate as a society".
— *Michael W-P Fortunato, Sam Houston State University, USA*

Innovation has become an important focus for governments around the world over
the last decade, with greater pressure on governments to do more with less and expanding community expectations. Public sector innovation is related to creating new
services that have value for stakeholders (such as citizens) in terms of the social and
political outcomes they produce.

Innovation in City Governments: Structures, Networks, and Leadership establishes
an analytical framework for innovation capacity based on three dimensions:

1   Structure—governance structures and societal traditions, political and socio-
    economic context
2   Networks—informal structures that shape and constrain actors and their ability
    to implement new ideas, connections outside the organization
3   Leadership—the qualities and capabilities of senior individuals within the
    organization.

Each of these is analysed using data from a comparative an EU research project that
compared Barcelona, Copenhagen and Rotterdam.

The book provides major new insights on how structures, networks, and leadership
in city governments shape the innovation capacity of cities. It provides groundbreak-
ing analyses of how governance structures and local socioeconomic challenges are
related to the innovations introduced by these cities. The volume maps and analyses
the social networks of the three cities and examines brokerage and boundary spanning within and outside of the cities. It also examines what leadership qualities are
important for innovation.

Innovation in City Governments: Structures, Networks, and Leadership combines
an original analytical approach with comparative empirical work, to generate a
novel perspective on the social innovation capacity of cities and is critical reading
for academics, students and policy makers alike in the fields of Public Management,
Public Administration, Local Government, Policy, Innovation and Leadership.

Jenny M. Lewis is a Professor of Public Policy and Director of The Policy Lab,
School of Social and Political Sciences, at the University of Melbourne, Australia.

Lykke Margot Ricard is Senior Adviser on Innovation at the Faculty of Health and
Medical Sciences, University of Copenhagen, Denmark.

Erik Hans Klijn is professor at the Department of Public Administration and Sociology, Erasmus University, Netherlands.

Tamyko Ysa is an Associate Professor, Department of Strategy and General Management, and in ESADE-Gov: Center for Public Governance, ESADE Business School,
Spain.

Routledge Critical Studies in Public Management

Edited by Stephen Osborne

For a full list of titles in this series, please visit www.routledge.com

The study and practice of public management have undergone profound changes across the world. Over the last quarter century, we have seen

- increasing criticism of public administration as the overarching framework for the provision of public services,
- the rise (and critical appraisal) of the 'New Public Management' as an emergent paradigm for the provision of public services,
- the transformation of the 'public sector' into the cross-sectoral provision of public services, and
- the growth of the governance of inter-organizational relationships as an essential element in the provision of public services

In reality, these trends have not so much replaced each other as elided or co-existed together—the public policy process has not gone away as a legitimate topic of study, intra-organizational management continues to be essential to the efficient provision of public services, whilst the governance of inter-organizational and inter-sectoral relationships is now essential to the effective provision of these services.

Further, whilst the study of public management has been enriched by contribution of a range of insights from the 'mainstream' management literature, it has also contributed to this literature in such areas as networks and inter-organizational collaboration, innovation and stakeholder theory.

This series is dedicated to presenting and critiquing this important body of theory and empirical study. It will publish books that both explore and evaluate the emergent and developing nature of public administration, management and governance (in theory and practice) and examine the relationship with and contribution to the overarching disciplines of management and organizational sociology.

Books in the series will be of interest to academics and researchers in this field, students undertaking advanced studies of it as part of their undergraduate or postgraduate degree and reflective policy makers and practitioners.

Social Accounting and Public Management

Unbundled Government
A critical analysis of the global trend to agencies, quangos and contractualisation
Edited by Christopher Pollitt and Colin Talbot

Innovation in City Governments
Structures, Networks, and Leadership
Jenny M. Lewis, Lykke Margot Ricard, Erik Hans Klijn, and Tamyko Ysa

Contents

vi   *Contents*

Boxes, Figures and Tables

Boxes

Figures

Tables

Acknowledgements

The research was part of a project on innovation in the public sector "Learning from Innovation in Public Sector Environments", which was funded by the 7th Framework Program of the European Union (N. 320090). The empirical study contained within this book would not have been possible without this funding. We would like to thank our colleagues in this project for their support. In particular, we would like to thank Adrià Albareda, who worked on the Barcelona case, and Sanne Grotenbreg, who worked on the Rotterdam case. We would also like to thank Phuc Nguyen, who provided invaluable help with the references.

Part I
Innovation Capacity
A Framework for Analysis

1   The Public Sector Innovation Puzzle

Governments around the globe have a responsibility to solve the pressing needs of citizens and ensure sustainable developments. Along with changes in society, politicians and public administrators are experiencing an increase in the complexity of problems that society is wrestling with, while having to manage these within tight fiscal constraints. These problems need innovative policy solutions and public sector organizations that are capable of creating and delivering them. However, there is a significant lack of understanding in relation to how collective action produces innovation and how innovation can be supported from *within* public sector organizations. This book aims to address this gap by focusing on public sector innovation capacity.

Innovation in the public sector has become an important focus for governments around the world over the past decade, as they try to solve intractable policy and societal problems, such as changes in demography and social inequity in health and education. Particularly since the last global financial crisis, policy makers have begun to realize that policy instruments for balancing markets are expensive (Pyka and Hanusch 2013). Consequently, 'innovation' has become a hot political topic in the field of governance (Hartley 2005, 2013, 2014; Osborne and Brown 2011; Osborne, Radnor and Strokosch 2016). The almost explosive pressure on municipalities 'to do more with less' in response to shrinking budgets, combined with increasing community expectations to deliver high quality services at a much faster pace, has led to a greater need to understand how the public sector manages change and innovation (Bartlett and Dibben 2002). With governments in many nations now portraying innovation as the way forward for their economies, it has become essential for public administrators to engage with the concept.

However, until quite recently, most government policy has been directed at the role of governments (including municipal governments) in boosting the innovation capacity of the private sector, or at least not 'crowding out' the private sector. Hence, there has been an emphasis on public procurement, subsidies and taxes (exogenous factors) and less emphasis on building innovation capacity within public organizations (endogenous factors). As Schumpeter (1934, 63) phrased it when writing about the fundamentals of economic development: *"By "development", therefore, we shall understand only such changes in economic life as are not forced upon it from without but arise by its own initiative, from within"*. Taking this as our starting point, our goal was to understand what contributes to the innovative capacity of public organizations. We are interested not in how the public sector can help the private sector to innovate, but what kind of arrangements support public sector innovation.

Calling for an innovative public sector is easier said than done: Innovation as a process in the public sector is said to be a contradiction in terms, because of its complexity and the centrality of discontinuity in innovation processes (Hartley 2006; Osborne and Brown 2011). Innovation inside public sector organizations challenges existing routines and practice. Thelen (2003, 224) has called public innovation 'a game changer' which breaks with path dependencies (Voorberg, Bekkers and Tummers 2015). This special feature of innovation has deep roots in classic discussions in the organizational literature about the competency struggle between path creation versus path dependency. Path dependency relates to routinization (Garud and Karnøe 2001) and is seen as a particularly strong characteristic of public organizations. This is because public organizations are often equated with the formal hierarchical structures of Weberian bureaucracy, and they are generally characterized as heavily institutionalized. Innovation, conversely, has very different features: it involves risk-taking and often a process of experimentation, and it may result in costly failures (Kobrak 1996).

Notwithstanding the problematic nature of the term innovation, with its contested place in government administration and its strongly normative positive overtones, research on the topic of innovation in the public sector has gained traction in recent years (Osborne and Brown 2011; Walker 2014; de Vries, Bekkers and Tummers 2015). Some of this literature uses the term 'social innovation' (Phills, Deiglmeier and Miller 2008), relating innovation to the process of producing a public good (Pyka and Hanusch 2013) or defining it as creating new services that have value for stakeholders (such as citizens) in terms of the social and political outcomes they produce (Harris and Albury 2009). This term is, however, in many cases linked to the field of social entrepreneurship and so, for the purposes of this book, we deploy the term 'public sector innovation', to refer to innovation that occurs *in* public sector organizations. We do, of course, recognise that innovation inside organizations relies on the external environment within which they are located.

In short, this book addresses the question: *"What supports innovation in public sector organizations?"* To answer that, we first describe different perspectives on innovation, and in particular, what it means in a public sector context. We then examine a number of different factors that are thought to be related to innovation capacity and which we use to construct a conceptual framework for the analysis that follows.

Four Perspectives on Innovation

Innovation has primarily been researched as an economic phenomenon in the economic and business literature, which tends to be focused on the private sector. However, it is also relevant for innovation in the public sector. Four perspectives stand out in the classic innovation literature as offering particularly useful insights for our purposes here. First, we have the well-known perspective of innovation as 'creative destruction'. Schumpeter borrowed this idea from Marx, who wrote of the accumulation and annihilation of wealth leading to revolution. Schumpeter (1942, 82–83) turned this idea into a theory of economic innovation and business cycles, and claimed that innovation is a "process of industrial mutation that incessantly revolutionizes the economic structure from within, incessantly destroying the old one, incessantly creating a new one". At that time, he had witnessed the revolution of the new manufacturing and production technology and how these inventions contributed to the puzzle of why certain industrial and service sectors grow more than others.

This perspective was grounded in evolutionary economics rather than in mainstream economics, which Schumpeter regarded as not focused enough on the economic value of innovation and entrepreneurship (as endogenous factors). Creative destruction includes creating more effective production techniques that could produce more for less. Schumpeter's idea was in contrast to general equilibrium theory: Entrepreneurs are not seen to create economic balance between demand and supply, but as individuals who are restlessly searching for information and opportunities to do things smarter, thereby creating a competitive advantage (Foster and Metcalfe 2012). In evolutionary economic terms, profitable techniques tend to replace less productive ones (Nelson 1993). Following Schumpeter, innovation has commonly been defined as a means to find new ways of producing more for less, more efficiently or in new ways that create greater value or better outcomes. This perspective offers a view of innovation as a rather disruptive creative force breaking with exiting production methods, routines and practices and challenging the status quo.

The second perspective is that user engagement in innovation produces better outcomes. This idea may be traced back in history to Adam Smith's (1776) notion that greater productivity arose from the division of labour and from technical innovations invented by the users of machines. He used the example of the boy who was hired to work on a ship to manually work the fire engine. In order to do less work, this boy introduced communication between the boiler and the cylinder by simply tying a string between them. This invention was later seen as a radical improvement to the development of the steam engine (Lundvall 2007). This user-driven innovation perspective was later developed by Eric von Hippel's (1988) 'Sources of Innovation' and the idea of open innovation in 'Democratizing innovation'.

This perspective is particularly salient to researchers of organizational studies, because it focuses on the power and value of involving users in the innovation process. In contrast with earlier notions that technology advances come from the R&D departments of large firms, it pays attention to user communities (often revolving around computers and information communication technologies). These communities often share information and develop their own products and new services, and freely share their open source innovations with others. They are seen as trendsetters, and manufacturers may pick up their innovations and implement them for commercial purpose (von Hippel 1988). This perspective stresses the value of the producers' connectivity with users in/during the innovation process and an interdependent relationship through two mechanisms, one that focuses on the role of lead users for consumer products or services, and one that pays attention to the learning aspects between the users (demand) and producers (supply). Lundvall (2007) also saw the later idea as a precondition for the learning aspect of innovation.

The third perspective extends the second perspective to the idea of innovation systems. It builds around connectivity and focuses on network of agents interacting in specific areas or sectors in terms of the exchange of knowledge and competence flows (Lundvall 1992, 2007). In contrast to simple market theory, where agents meet purely to exchange goods and services (Lundvall et al. 2002), this perspective emphasizes the complexity of innovation. Originally, it emerged as a corrective to the OECD's R&D measures used for comparison between countries, as these favour a linear innovation model, overlooking feedback mechanisms from the market and R&D systems (Lundvall 2007; Freeman and Soete 2009). Freeman argued against the linear innovation model, pointing to the empirical evidence of numerous case studies that support the fact that innovation involves many entities and the knowledge flows between them (Ricard 2016). In this perspective, innovation is more than new technology: It might be a product, a technology, a service, a new type of production, a new process or a new form of collaboration (Kline and Rosenberg 1986).

The innovation system idea has since become widespread and applied at national and regional levels and in different sectors. It revolves around both user-producer connectivity and systems thinking, to critique the linear innovation model, while pointing to the importance of knowledge flows between mutually dependent actors to stimulate innovation. It embraces earlier ideas about innovation, but introduces them in a network context: Lundvall (1988) wrote about user-producer interactivity and Freeman (1995, 30) related the process of innovation to "the importance of information flows to and from sources of scientific and technical knowledge and of flows to and from users of products and processes". In this perspective, the idea is that system failure in the network flow, rather than market failure, is the reason why otherwise promising technology fails to reach the market (Ricard 2015). 'System failure' is based on the problem of missing information, missing knowledge or even missing actors. This perspective also emphasizes that firms do not innovate in isolation. It moves away from the individual entrepreneur and towards the embeddedness of entrepreneurs, where behaviour and institutions are constrained by ongoing social relations (Granovetter 1985).

The fourth perspective that is important for our study is the concept of dynamic capabilities. This refers to the capabilities needed for organizations to adapt to changes in the environment. It serves as an add-on to the resource-based view of the firm. While the term capabilities relates to certain skills that have become routine or practice, dynamic capabilities relates to skills that are needed to learn new things (Barney 2001). From an innovation management perspective, Teece (2007) claims it is the ability to sense changes in the environment, seize the entrepreneurial opportunities and redirect resources in time. This perspective develops in situations where new technologies emerge quickly and where the outlook shapes the competition between firms and large corporations. Like the first perspective we outlined, this one also has strong roots in evolutionary economics and relates to the idea of creative destruction. It also relies on the notion that new knowledge can generate new opportunities and on Israel Kirzner's claim that entrepreneurial skills are required to take advantage of existing information (Teece, Pisano and Shuen 1997; Teece 2007).

None of these four perspectives on innovation would regard the public sector as a natural environment for supporting innovation. But their ideas have been applied to public sector innovation in some different variants. We discuss these in the next section.

Public Sector Innovation

There is a widespread belief, but little empirical evidence, that people who work in the public sector are less innovative than those who work in the private sector (Rainey 1999, 2009). This tends to be purely based on stereotypes (Bysted and Hansen 2015). People who work in the private sector are regarded as more innovative because they are thought to be driven by competition, while people who work in public organizations are seen as less innovative because the nature of their work causes them to be risk-averse in taking chances with public money (Hartley 2005) or in failing to attract personal political esteem. In contrast, it may be argued that high innovation potential is present in public organizations, because of an assumed greater willingness to share ideas, information and knowledge: Private leaders may be more reluctant to share information because of the risk of giving away competitive advantage (Hartley 2013). The first argument is related to Schumpeter's idea about creative destruction, and particularly, to the destructive side of innovation being a risky business, while the second relates to knowledge sharing, organizational performance and organizational capabilities (Barney 1991, 2001) or even the concept of dynamic capabilities in a broader interpretation (Harvey et al. 2010).

Because innovation has become an imperative for public services, the literature has grown in scale and also in scope. Even though most of the public sector innovation literature is found to be conceptual, some of it is normative and little of it is based on empirical research (de Vries, Bekkers and Tummers 2015), it is becoming much broader in its conceptual perspective. It now includes efforts to empirically research specific types of innovations and their diffusion, as well as examine the organizational capacity to stimulate innovations from within local governments (Harvey et al. 2010). However, in general terms, the empirical evidence remains scant in regard to public sector innovation.

Understanding Public Sector Innovation Capacity

In the following sections, we describe what the extant literature claims in relation to some key organizational elements that either close down or open up pathways for innovation capacity in public sector organizations.

User Involvement and Co-Production

The user involvement perspective is seen as an important aspect of public sector innovation. New Public Management (NPM) reforms intended public sector organization to engage with users (customers), to better understand their needs and priorities and to improve management design (Harvey et al. 2010). It was these reforms that identified innovation as a primary goal to improve performance and increase public value (see, for example, Mulgan and Albury (2003)). Later reforms introduced the idea of co-production between governments, citizens and business (Bovaird 2007). This advance in the literature is strongly related to the idea of innovation models in the business economics literature, which assume that there will be learning (knowledge spill-overs) through feedback mechanisms. The information from these quasi-market-like environments feed back into the communication system with (presumed) direct impacts on organizational performance (Bryson, Ackermann and Eden 2007; Harvey et al. 2010). Public administration scholars agree that taking aspects of implementation into consideration at an early stage of the innovation process may indeed contribute to the creation of more robust solutions (Sørensen and Torfing 2011).

These directions are central in the New Public Governance (NPG) literature on public sector innovation. Here, the user-centred orientation in innovation plays a key role. It is claimed that the development and efficiency of public service delivery systems requires input from public service officers, service users and wider local community stakeholders (Radnor et al. 2014; Osborne, Radnor and Strokosch 2016). Another, more advanced NPG form of co-production is where a user orientation serves as a political instrument to achieve legitimacy for innovation as a public good (Bekkers, Edelenbos and Steijn 2011). This perspective on public sector innovation is prominent in the NPG literature, regarding it as a promising tool to reduce the democratic deficit caused by governments ignoring citizens and their needs.

The Dynamics of the Organization's External and Internal Environment

Public sector environments are changing rapidly. Some claim that the public sector is more exposed to changes than the private sector, due to the frequent changes that often occur in policy-making (Pablo et al. 2007). This naturally opens the door to the resource-based view of the organization and the broader concept of dynamic capabilities (Piening 2013), which is focused on how organizations adapt to rapidly changing environments. Innovation in the public sector and its place within a rule-bounded culture emphasizes the importance of knowledge processes from an organizational learning perspective: "What an organization learns depends on what it already knows and on the development stage of its organizational routines" (Salge and Vera 2013, 160). This is what is termed an organization's 'absorptive capacity', which mediates between organizational performance and knowledge processes relating to the resource-based view of the firm (Cohen and Levinthal 1990).

Absorptive capacity arises from the idea of dynamic capabilities in a broad sense (Harvey et al. 2010; Hartley 2013). Although there are many propositions regarded as likely to be related to a public organization's absorptive capacity, e.g., the effect of the dynamics of the local environment it operates in, its public tasks, its investment in knowledge processes etc., these have not often been researched empirically. Basically, this is the idea of fitness in evolutionary economic theory, which suggests some sort of 'adaptive skills' that are further explored in the public management literature on organizational performance (see: Harvey et al. 2010; Piening 2013).

The literature claims that managing and measuring the performance of public organizations is still underdeveloped, and the best available measures are "individual performance indicators" and "functions undertaken by the organization, and the inspection of an organization's governance and management by an independent regulator" (Harvey et al. 2010, 80–81). Empirical studies have shown that some public organizations have a better institutional fit to changes in the environment than others. Harvey et al. (2010) provide an overview of such studies, summing up that earlier studies of underperforming public organizations have shown that one causal factor is a failure of learning (McKiernan 2002), often by senior managers who were introspective (Fulop, Scheibl and Edwards 2004) or out of touch with reality, e.g., when data reveal a gap between actual and perceived performance (Filochowski 2004).

Recent studies of underperforming local governments have provided a more managerial explanation for the fact that some organizations are more institutionally 'fit' to respond to signs of declining performance, evoking some sort of self-regulating mechanism to turn around the performance curve. Here, tools like strategy, vision and the adoption of a new corporate paradigm are mentioned as better management controls (Jas and Skelcher 2005; Harvey et al. 2010). The idea of performance and adaptive capacity is transferable to the idea of innovation capacity. Here, the organization's dynamic capabilities, which enable it to adapt to the surrounding environment, can be related to government's responsibility for delivering effective policies and the need for governments to adapt to changes in their (local) environment to innovate where it is needed the most.

Innovation and Governance

Acknowledging the work on the sources of innovation, and those aspects of it that have inspired the literature on public sector innovation (user orientation and internal/external dynamics), most of the perspectives discussed above do not discuss factors that support public sector innovation capacity. The literature on the public sector theorizes that the capacity to learn and understand the needs and priorities of local environments, and the translation of this into actual innovations and productivity, are both important for public sector innovation. And, it should be acknowledged that public organizations inhabit more complex environments than their private sector counterparts. They are multi-level governance systems and politically driven organizations based on leaders being democratically elected periodically as representatives of the people. As noted by several scholars (e.g., Borins 2001; Hartley 2005; Damonpour, Walker and Avellaneda 2009; Goffin and Mitchell 2010), this makes the diffusion of innovation—the degree to which the innovation is understood and implemented (Rogers 2003)—more complex and perhaps more difficult (Torugsa and Arundel 2016). However, it has also been argued that governments might have an advantage, because a centralized bureaucracy is able to implement innovation at a larger scale and more efficiently than private firms or agents (Hartley 2014).

Perhaps, as Bartlett and Dibben (2002) claim, it really is a question about how public sector organizations manage change and innovation. An example is a recent study by Munro (2015), who interviewed public officials (politicians, managers and employees) about accelerating innovation in local councils in the UK. This study echoed earlier assumptions about barriers and constraints that prevent innovation in the public sector, such as the short-term horizon of politicians, the risk-averse culture and the challenges of reaching agreement in complex political organizations. These constraints were also found in a study by van Buuren and Loorbach (2009) in the Dutch context. But it also shows how to turn these barriers into drivers; it stresses the importance of leadership to fostering innovation by clearly communicating the innovation strategy and specific priorities, as 'innovation' simply is too broad a term to manage in practice. Leadership culture at the organizational level was also seen as important. Time and resources must be devoted to developing priorities by listening and communicating with managers and employees, from the start of an innovation until its implementation has been achieved (Munro 2015). Again, engagement is highlighted as a way to ensure that innovation is understood and implemented.

Not all innovations are equally important. It has been stressed that most innovation implemented in the public sector is not novel but, more often, adopted from others (Torugsa and Arundel 2016). But the entrepreneurial skill of taking advantage of existing knowledge from elsewhere might represent a significant innovation when it is implemented in a new context. For this study, we are interested in the structures that evolve around individuals inside the organization, making it possible for significant innovations to occur in public organizational contexts. We are therefore curious about how collective action works within organizations, even when it draws on outside sources of knowledge, and how organizations manage innovation. In other words, we are interested in the organizational capacity to turn economic and societal challenges into innovation opportunities and then implement them.

Innovation, Networks and Governance

The idea of a network can be simply conceived of as a concern with interactions between actors (both individuals and organizations). In a network perspective, it is emphasized that policy processes and service delivery results from joint interactions between interdependent actors. Networks are considered as a suitable vehicle for tackling complex problems, because they can connect the various involved actors, provide an infrastructure for gathering information and provide a possible opportunity for innovation. Networks are especially viewed as suitable for gathering more and better information, because they enable access to the information needed to develop innovation (Lewis 2010) and also connect actors (like local citizens and community leaders but also external collaborators, firms etc.) into a set of relationships. However, such networks need active managerial effort if they are to achieve the desired results. To achieve the advantages that are supposed to, leaders must be able to set frames, intervene and solve emerging problems (van Wart 2013a).

As noted earlier, NPG stands in contrast to NPM as it entails a new perspective on citizens as associates in the innovation process, rather than service-receivers (Osborne 2010; Osborne, Radnor and Strokosch 2016). It includes the idea of co-production processes, where the creation of solutions occurs together with the involvement of citizens (Bovaird 2007; Osborne 2010; Voorberg, Bekkers and Tummers 2015). This form of governance focuses on the interdependence of the many stakeholders that the solution to a complex problem requires; combining different perspectives of the problem, different interests and different ideas about the most desirable solution to it (Koppenjan and Klijn 2004; McGuire and Agranoff 2011). Notably, an NPG perspective on public administration has focused heavily on the context of governance traditions and on the adaptive capabilities of public organizations in enabling innovation. Contextual factors that we know have a positive impact on the innovation capacity of public sector organizations are a decentralized state, corporatist traditions and a strong civil society (Bekkers, Edelenbos and Steijn 2011).

The importance of networks in facilitating innovation and shaping innovation pathways at the organizational, sectoral and national levels has long been recognized within the private sector innovation literature. For example, in a cross-country case study of innovation in electronic identification data management systems, Huijboom (2010) showed that the characteristics of the people involved (e.g., expertise and position), their ties (strength and levels of trust) and network structures (closure, heterogeneity and brokerage) generate certain network dynamics which affect innovation strategy, decisions, output and impact.

Previous research on innovation inside local governments has shown that innovators and innovations create an institutional space—partly formed by formal positions and informal networks (Considine and Lewis 2007). In particular, the innovative capacity of local governments has been shown to be linked to the presence of strong internal and external networks, where networks are viewed as the prime means to facilitate information exchange and hence to diffuse innovative ideas and practices (Walker 2006; Lewis, Considine and Alexander 2011).). Previous empirical studies show that innovation in local governments occurs in the spaces between the formal structures and informal networks, although governance structures shape and constrain opportunities for informal interactions. Having spaces where individuals can meet each other without the burden of formal responsibilities, positions and rules is seen as crucial to innovation (Nooteboom 2006; Considine, Lewis and Alexander 2009; van der Voort et al. 2011).

In summary, network studies of regional and local governments have shown that innovation takes place within particular environments and within particular structures and networks that either have a positive or negative impact on innovation capacity. The network characteristics that are postulated to be positively related to innovation capacity are organizational slack, network diversity, external focus, recognition of dependency, higher levels of trust, openness and equally distributed costs and benefits (Bekkers, Edelenbos and Steijn 2011; Lewis, Considine and Alexander 2011).

The Framework of This Book

The overarching goal of this book is to better understand what supports innovation in public sector organizations. The specific cases that we focus upon are city governments. Clearly, there are a multitude of different factors that could be considered relevant for such an investigation. We cannot hope to study everything, so we have reduced the important factors to three: Many scholars agree that the context and the environment in which an organization is situated, its capacity to collect and absorb information (informal networks) and the skills or activities required of its leaders are all vitally important. Therefore, our analytical framework for examining innovation capacity is based on these three dimensions:

- Structure—governance structures and societal traditions, political and socioeconomic context;
- Networks—informal structures that shape and constrain actors and their ability to implement new ideas, connections outside the organization; and
- Leadership—the qualities and capabilities of individuals within the organization.

These are briefly outlined here but the theoretical foundation for each dimension is described in greater detail in Chapters 2, 3 and 4.

Structures

The innovation capacity of any public sector organization is related to the environment within which it is located. Therefore, an important first set of considerations has to do with the formal structures within which each municipality is located. What kinds of governance structures have an impact on public sector innovation? Previous work has shown that the political and administrative context, the legal culture of the public sector, state and governance traditions and resource arrangements can either trigger innovation or constrain it. The theory behind this is described in more detail in Chapter 2. Boundary spanning, which relates to working across and outside of formal governance structures, is also examined in this chapter.

Networks

Innovation capacity is expected to be linked not only to contextual factors such as those discussed above, but also to informal social structures. Social networks based on interpersonal communication generate embedded resources such as social capital and trust relations. The importance of networks in facilitating innovation and shaping innovation pathways at the organizational, sectoral and national levels has long been recognized within the private sector innovation literature, and networks are now also increasingly being acknowledged as crucial in the public sector (Lewis, Considine and Alexander 2011). Of particular interest here are interpersonal networks based on communication between individuals. They consist of a set of nodes (people) connected to other nodes by interpersonal ties of some kind (e.g., friendship, work relationships, advice seeking). Social network analysis enables us to test complex theories of collective action in innovation, as well as to explore how public sector environments shape and constrain people and their ability to implement new ideas. The theory linking social networks to innovation is examined in Chapter 3.

Leadership

In addition to structures and networks, the third important component for this study is leadership. The link between leadership and innovation in the public sector is not yet well developed. Much research on innovation from a New Public Management perspective has focused on the role of individual entrepreneurship in pushing for change, while the Network Governance or New Public Governance version emphasizes 'co-creation' as producing innovation through new government-society interactions. We argue that innovation in the public sector is related to the leadership qualities both of politicians and senior administrators, and we develop a model for measuring different leadership types. The theory on leadership and innovation is described in detail in Chapter 4.

Each of these three components of our framework is important for innovation in its own right, but we postulate that the components are also interrelated. Thus, we expect that formal structures will have an impact on the formation of social networks and that particular leadership styles might be associated with networks and formal hierarchical positions. These overall sets of expected relationships are shown in the conceptual model provided in Figure 1.1. Each of these are unfolded within the theoretical

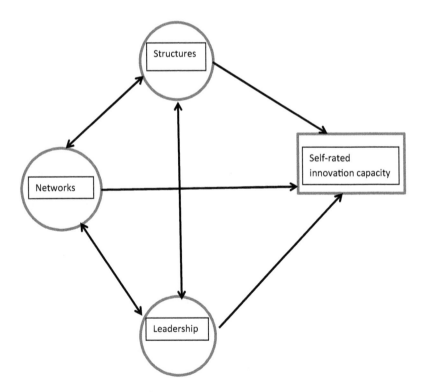

Figure 1.1 Conceptual Model Linking Structures, Networks, Leadership and Innovation Capacity

and empirical chapters in Parts I and II of the book. This model guides the analysis contained in the individual chapters and then is finally examined as a whole in Chapter 9. This brings us to the choice of cases for the empirical component of our study.

City Governments as Our 'Cases'

While much of the focus of contemporary research on public sector innovation is on innovation cases—meaning examples of innovations that have been implemented in public sector organizations to address particular problems—our study uses three city governments (municipalities) as cases. We regard these cities as innovation environments that shape a municipality's capacity for innovation.

We chose municipal governments for a variety of reasons. First, they are the level of government that is closest to the citizenry and the most likely to have ongoing interactions with them, making them a likely site for innovation. Second, this level of government has taken on an increasingly important role in many nations, as service delivery functions in keys areas such as health, human services and community development have been devolved from higher levels of government over the past three decades. Municipal governments are now often responsible for delivering a range of services and programmes to local communities. One particularly salient study of innovation in municipal governments in Australia demonstrated how networks contribute to an understanding of innovation inside government organizations and showed that whether or not a person is regarded as an innovator depends on how innovation is defined, what formal position the person holds and who s/he communicates with (Considine and Lewis 2007; Considine, Lewis and Alexander 2009; Lewis, Considine and Alexander 2011Lewis, Considine and Alexander 2011; Lewis, Alexander and Considine 2013). This study substantially informed the framework for this book, but we extended the idea to a cross-national comparison and focused exclusively on relatively large cities.

Studying the municipal governments of reasonably large cities in different nations has a number of advantages: There is now a good deal of attention being directed towards cities as places where major societal challenges arise, because so much of the populace lives and works in cities. Cities are also places where a lot of innovation occurs, because the needs are so pressing. In addition, cities are generally centres for activities associated with the new service and knowledge economy, including numerous educational institutions, tourist sites, sporting arenas and creative arts venues. Hence, they are solid 'cases' of public sector organizations faced with multiple challenges and the need to innovate. The cross-national comparison allows us to evaluate the impact of different national governance contexts on local structures—both formal and informal. It provides an interesting source of variation in analysing the interactions between our three dimensions of governance, networks and leadership.

Three European cities were compared. These were Copenhagen in Denmark, Rotterdam in the Netherlands and Barcelona in Spain. These three reflect different geographical areas and different state and society traditions which are likely to influence innovation environments. We expected that each of these cities would be facing a set of relatively common global challenges (such as the global financial crisis), as well as a unique set of local challenges. More detail about each of these cities can be found in Chapter 5. In each case, a number of different methods were used to gather the information on the cities, but a major component of this study was an online survey of senior administrators and politicians in each of the cities.

The Survey Methods

First, and in order to help with sampling for the survey, we conducted a document analysis of the formal organizational structure of each municipality, mainly by using their websites, but also by directly asking them questions for clarification. This information was used to develop an inventory of both the political and administrative structures and the functional divisions in each city government, and to ascertain the number of staff employed in the different divisions and at different levels in the hierarchy. We then used these data to develop the sampling framework for the survey.

As noted earlier, the major empirical component of this study was a survey of senior administrators and politicians in each of the municipalities, which was administered online. Some politicians were interviewed in lieu of completing the survey online, but the same set of questions was used in both cases. We received a total of 419 responses. Most of these were from administrators, but 18 were from politicians. More details about the numbers of respondents in each case can be found in Chapter 5.

In addition to the first survey of people inside the municipal governments, we conducted a shorter survey with people outside the municipalities, who were identified in the first survey as being innovators in the community. These interviews included a small subset of the questions used with politicians and administrators, and the results are described in Chapters 5 and 6.

Because we have a small number of politicians, most of the analysis includes only the administrators. The exceptions to this are Chapter 7 on networks, plus the politicians' answers are included in the assessments of socioeconomic challenges and significant innovations in Chapters 5 and 6.

For the survey, respondents were given the following definition of innovation: *"the process from ideas to successful implementation of these, which makes a substantial difference to an organization's understanding of the needs it is addressing and the services it delivers"*.

The survey contained questions on each of the following:

• Innovation environments (significant innovations in the municipality, what helps and hinders innovation, socioeconomic challenges in the municipality, self-rated innovativeness of the municipality);

- Networking (number of external contacts, boundary spanning activities, membership of organizations and boards, conference attendance, leadership training, excursions);
- Social networks and associated resources (interpersonal communication about work projects and to obtain strategic information, trust and importance);
- Leadership for innovation; and
- Background information (job title, division, time in position, education, gender).

An English version of the questionnaire was created first, and then the questions were translated into Catalan, Danish and Dutch for use in (respectively) Barcelona, Copenhagen and Rotterdam.

The Structure of the Book

The book is divided into three parts. As described already, Chapters 2 to 4 (which, along with the current chapter, comprise Part I) address the theoretical aspects of our framework for studying innovation. In each of these chapters, we summarize the extant literature and demonstrate why these particular dimensions are important for public sector innovation capacity.

Part II of the book is centred on the empirical data gathered from the survey and the interviews. Chapter 5 examines the innovation environment of the three cities (national governance structures, background and context on the municipalities and socioeconomic challenges). Chapter 6 explores innovation drivers and supports, significant innovations and self-rated innovativeness. In Chapter 7, we map and analyse two different types of social networks, namely work and strategic information networks. Chapter 8 analyses leadership qualities in relation to innovation.

Part III of the book draws the strands together and attempts to answer the question: What supports innovation in the public sector? Chapter 9 links together structures, networks, leadership, and innovation, and draws out second order conclusions based on the interactions between each of the three components of our framework and their relationship to innovation capacity. It also uses these findings to suggest which governance conditions are likely to best support innovation. Our final chapter provides a synthesis and some further reflections on our findings, and looks to the future of public sector innovation studies.

References

Alexander, Damon, Jenny M. Lewis, and Mark Considine. 2011. "How politicians and bureaucrats network: A comparison across governments." *Public Administration* 89(4): 1274–92.

Barney, Jay. 1991. "Firm resources and sustained competitive advantage." *Journal of Management* 17(1): 99–120.

Barney, Jay B. 2001. "Resource-based theories of competitive advantage: A ten-year retrospective on the resource based view." *Journal of Management* 27(6): 643–50.

Bartlett, Dean, and Pauline Dibben. 2002. "Public sector innovation and entre-preneurship: Case studies from local government." *Local Government Studies* 28(4): 107–21.

Bekkers, Victor J.J.M., Jurian Edelenbos, and Bram Steijn, editors. 2011. *Innovation in the public sector: Linking capacity and leadership*. Basingstoke: Palgrave Macmillan.

Borins, Sanford. 2001. "Encouraging innovation in the public sector." *Journal of Intellectual Capital* 2(3): 310–19.

Bovaird, Tony. 2007. "Beyond engagement and participation: User and community coproduction of public services." *Public Administration Review* 67(5): 846–60.

Bryson, John M., Fran Ackermann, and Colin Eden. 2007. "Putting the resource-based view of strategy and distinctive competencies to work in public organiza-tions." *Public Administration Review* 67(4): 702–17.

Bysted, Rune, and Jesper Rosenberg Hansen. 2015. "Comparing public and pri-vate sector employees' innovative behaviour: Understanding the role of job and organizational characteristics, job types, and subsectors." *Public Management Review* 17(5): 698–717.

Cohen, Wesley M., and Daniel A. Levinthal. 1990. "Absorptive capacity: A new per-spective on learning and innovation." *Administrative Science Quarterly* 35(1): 128–52.

Considine, Mark, and Jenny M. Lewis. 2007. "Innovation and innovators inside government: From institutions to networks." *Governance* 20(4): 581–607.

Considine, Mark, Jenny M. Lewis, and Damon Alexander. 2009. *Networks, innova-tion and public policy: Politicians, bureaucrats and the pathways to change inside government*. Basingstoke: Palgrave Macmillan.

Damanpour, Fariborz, Richard M. Walker, and Claudia N. Avellaneda. 2009. "Combinative effects of innovation types and organizational performance: A longitudinal study of service organizations." *Journal of Management Studies* 46(4): 650–75.

de Vries, Hannah, Victor Bekkers, and Lars Tummers. 2015. "Innovation in the public sector: A systematic review and future research agenda." *Public Adminis-tration* 94(1): 146–66.

Filochowski, J. 2004. "All fall down." *Health Service Journal* 114: 5888, 28–30.

Foster, John, and J. Stan Metcalfe. 2012." Economic emergence: An evolutionary economic perspective." *Journal of Economic Behavior & Organization* 82(2): 420–32.

Freeman, Chris. 1995. "The national system of innovation in historical perspec-tive." *Cambridge Journal of Economics* 19(1): 5–24.

Freeman, Christopher, and Luc Soete. 2009. "Developing science, technology and innovation indicators: What we can learn from the past." *Research Policy* 38: 583–9.

Fulop, Naomi, F. Scheibl, and N. Edwards. 2004. *Turnaround in health care provid-ers*. London: London School of Hygiene and Tropical Medicine.

Garud, Raghu, and Peter Karnøe. 2001. *Path dependence and creation*. New York: Lawrence Erlbaum Associates.

Goffin, Keith, and Rick Mitchell. 2010. *Innovation management: Strategy and implementation using the Pentathlon framework.* Basingstoke: Palgrave Macmillan.

Granovetter, Mark. 1985. "Economic action and social structure: The problem of embeddedness." *American Journal of Sociology* 91(3): 481–510.

Harris, Michael, and David Aldbury. 2009. *The innovation imperative.* London: NESTA.

Hartley, Jean. 2005. "Innovation in governance and public services: Past and present." *Public Money & Management* 25(1): 27–34.

Hartley, J. 2006. *Innovation and its Contribution to Improvement. A Review for Policy-makers, Policy Advisers, Managers and Researchers.* London: Department for Communities and Local Government.

Hartley, Jean. 2013. "Public and private features of innovation." In *Handbook of innovation in public services,* edited by Stephen Osborne and Louise Brown, 44–59. Cheltenham: Edward Elgar.

Hartley, Jean. 2014. "New development: Eight and a half propositions to stimulate frugal innovation." *Public Money & Management* 34(3): 227–32.

Harvey, Gill, Chris Skelcher, Eileen Spencer, Pauline Jas, and Kieran Walshe. 2010. "Absorptive capacity in a non-market environment." *Public Management Review* 12(1): 77–97.

Huijboom, Noor. 2010. "Joined up ICT innovation in government: An analysis of the creation of eIDM systems from an Advocacy Coalition and social capital perspective." PhD diss., Erasmus University.

Jas, Pauline, and Chris Skelcher. 2005. "Performance decline and turnaround in public organizations: A theoretical and empirical analysis." *British Journal of Management* 16(3): 195–210.

Kline, Stephen J., and Nathan Rosenberg. 1986. "An overview of innovation." In *The positive sum strategy: Harnessing technology for economic growth,* edited by R. Landau and N. Rosenberg, 275–305. Washington, DC: National Academy Press.

Kobrak, Peter. 1996. "The social responsibilities of a public entrepreneur." *Administration & Society* 28(2): 205–37.

Koppenjan, Joop F.M., and Erik-Hans Klijn. 2004. *Managing uncertainties in networks.* London: Routledge.

Lewis, Jenny M. 2010. *Connecting and cooperating: Social capital and public policy.* Sydney: UNSW Press.

Lewis, Jenny M., Mark Considine, and Damon Alexander. 2011. "Innovation inside government: The importance of networks." In *Innovation in the public sector: Linking capacity and leadership,* edited by V. Bekkers, J. Edelenbos, and B. Steijn, 107–33. Houndsmills: Palgrave McMillan.

Lewis, Jenny M., Damon Alexander, and Mark Considine. 2013. "Policy networks and innovation." In *Handbook of innovation in public services,* edited by Stephen Osborne and Louise Brown, 360–74. Cheltenham: Edward Elgar.

Lundvall, Bent-Åke. 1988. "Innovation as an interactive process: From user producer interaction to the national system of innovation." In *Technical change and economic theory,* edited by G. Dosi, C. Freeman, R. Nelson, G. Silverberg, and L. Soete, 349–69. London: Pinter.

Lundvall, Bent-Åke. 1992. *National systems of innovation: Towards a theory of innovation and interactive learning.* London: Pinter Press.

Lundvall, Bengt-Åke. 2007. "National innovation systems—Analytical concept and development tool." *Industry and Innovation* 14(1): 95–119.

Lundvall, Bent-Åke, Björn Johnson, Esben Sloth Andersen, and Bent Dalum. 2002. "National systems of production, innovation and competence building." *Research Policy* 31(2): 213–31.

McGuire, Michael, and Robert Agranoff. 2011. "The limitations of public management networks." *Public Administration* 89(2): 265–84.

McKiernan, P. 2002. "Turnarounds." In *The oxford handbook of strategy. Volume II: Corporate strategy*, edited by D.O. Faulkner and A. Campbell, 267–318. Oxford: Oxford University Press.

Mulgan, Geoff, and David Albury. 2003. *Innovation in the public sector*. London: Cabinet Office.

Munro, Joan. 2015. "Accelerating innovation in local government." *Public Money & Management* 35(3): 219–26.

Nelson, Richard R. 1993. *National systems of innovation*. Oxford: Blackwell.

Nooteboom, Sibout Govert. 2006. *Adaptive networks: The governance for sustainable development*. Delft: Eburon.

Osborne, Stephen P., editor. 2010. *The new public governance?* London: Routledge.

Osborne, Stephen P., and Louise Brown. 2011. "Innovation, public policy and public services delivery in the UK: The word that would be king." *Public Administration* 89(4): 1335–50.

Osborne, Stephen P., Zoe Radnor, and Kirsty Strokosch. 2016. "Co-production and the co-creation of value in public services: A suitable case for treatment?" *Public Management Review* 18(5): 639–53.

Pablo, Amy L., Trish Reay, James R. Dewald, and Ann L. Casebeer. 2007. "Identifying, enabling and managing dynamic capabilities in the public sector." *Journal of Management Studies* 44(5): 687–708.

Phills, James, Kriss Deiglmeier, and Dale Miller. 2008. "Rediscovering social innovation." *Stanford Center for Social Innovation Review* Fall. 6(4): 34–43.

Piening, Erk P. 2013. "Dynamic capabilities in public organizations." *Public Management Review* 15(2): 209–45.

Pyka, Andreas, and Horst Hanusch. 2013. "Social innovations in the perspective of comprehensive Neo-Schumpeterian economics." In *Social innovation—New forms of organization in knowledge-based societies*, edited by Ruiz Viñals Carmen and Parra Rodríguez Carmen, 29–43. London/New York: Routledge.

Radnor, Zoe, Stephen P. Osborne, Tony Kinder, and Jean Mutton. 2014. "Operationalizing co-production in public services delivery: The contribution of service blueprinting." *Public Management Review* 16(3): 402–23.

Rainey, Hal G. 1999. "Using comparisons of public and private organizations to assess innovative attitudes among members of organizations." *Public Productivity & Management Review* 23(2): 130–49.

Rainey, Hal G. 2009. *Understanding and managing public organizations* (4th edition). San Francisco, CA: Jossey-Bass.

Ricard, Lykke Margot. 2015. "Coping with system failure: Why connectivity matters to innovation policy." In *The evolution of economic and innovation systems (part of the series Economic Complexity and Evolution)*, edited by Adreas Pyka and John Foster, 251–76. Switzerland: Springer International Publishing.

Ricard, Lykke Margot. 2016. "Aligning innovation with grand societal challenges: Inside the european technology platforms in wind, and carbon capture and storage." *Science and Public Policy* 43(2): 169–83.

Rogers, Everett M. 2003. *Diffusion of innovations* (5th edition). New York: Free Press.

Salge, Torsten Oliver, and Antonio Vera. 2013. "Small steps that matter: Incremental learning, slack resources and organizational performance." *British Journal of Management* 24(2): 156–73.

Schumpeter, Joseph A. 1934. *The theory of economic development.* Cambridge, MA: Harvard University.

Schumpeter, Joseph A. 1942. *Capitalism, socialism and democracy* (5th edition 1976). London: George Allen and Unwin.

Smith, Adam [1776] 1982. *The wealth of nations.* Harmondsworth: Penguin.

Sørensen, Eva, and Jacob Torfing. 2011. "Enhancing collaborative innovation in the public sector." *Administration & Society* 43(8): 842–68.

Teece, David J. 2007. "Explicating dynamic capabilities: The nature and microfoundations of (sustainable) enterprise performance." *Strategic Management Journal* 28(13): 1319–50.

Teece, David J., Gary Pisano, and Amy Shuen. 1997. "Dynamic capabilities and strategic management." *Strategic Management Journal* 18(7): 509–33.

Thelen, Kathleen. 2003. "How institutions evolve: Insights from comparative historical analysis." In *Comparative historical analysis in the social sciences*, edited by James Mahoney, and Dietrich Rueschemeyer, 208–40. New York: Cambridge University Press.

Torugsa, Nuttaneeya, and Anthony Arundel. 2016. "Complexity of innovation in the public sector: A workgroup-level analysis of related factors and outcomes." *Public Management Review* 18(3): 392–416.

van Buuren, Arwin, and Derk Loorbach. 2009. "Policy innovation in isolation?" *Public Management Review* 11(3): 375–92.

van der Voort, Haiko, Joop Koppenjan, Ernst ten Heuvelhof, Martijn Leijten, and Wijnand Veeneman. 2011. "Competing values in the management of innovative projects: The case of the RandstadRail project." In *Innovation in the public sector: Linking capacity and leadership*, edited by Victor Bekkers, Jurian Edelenbos, and Bram Steijn, 134–54. Houndsmills: Palgrave McMillan.

van Wart, Montgomery. 2013a. "Lessons from leadership theory and the contemporary challenges of leaders." *Public Administration Review* 73(4): 553–65.

von Hippel, Eric. 1988. *The sources of innovation.* Oxford: Oxford University Press.

Voorberg, William H., Victor J.J.M. Bekkers, and Lars G. Tummers. 2015. "A systematic review of co-creation and co-production: Embarking on the social innovation journey." *Public Management Review* 17(9): 1333–57.

Walker, Richard M. 2006. "Innovation type and diffusion: An empirical analysis of local government." *Public Administration* 84(2): 311–35.

Walker, Richard M. 2014. "Internal and external antecedents of process innovation: A review and extension." *Public Management Review* 16(1): 21–44.

2   Structures and Innovation

The first of the three components of our framework for examining innovation capacity is structures. We use the term 'structures' to refer to governance structures, including both formal national structures of governance, and modes of governance that reflect how governance actually happens in contemporary societies. These can be seen as the 'hard' formal structures, and the more open but still managed structures, that enable and constrain action within institutions, in contrast to the 'soft' and informal networks, which are discussed in Chapter 3.

Governance Structures

The innovation capacity of any public sector organization is related to the environment within which it is located. What kinds of contextual factors could we expect to have an impact on public sector innovation capacity? Based on an analysis of the literature, Bekkers, Tummers and Voorberg (2013) found that the following aspects of the environment could function as important drivers and barriers of innovation:

- The social and political complexity of the environment in which public organizations operate, which leads to specific demands that function as an external 'trigger' for innovation;
- The characteristics and degree of the legal culture in a country or policy sector, which shapes the level of formalization and standardization and the degree of rule-driven behaviour;
- The type of governance and state tradition in a country or policy sector, which affects the amount of discretion that public sector organizations have to explore and implement new ideas; and
- The allocation of resources, resource dependency and the quality of relationships between different (public and private) organizations at different levels, which all have an impact on how well innovation practices are supported.

More specifically, there is a set of governance structures that has an impact (positive or negative) on innovation capacity (Bekkers, Tummers and

Voorberg 2013). These are political and administrative triggers such as crises and competition (positive effect); a strong, formalized, centralized, rule-bound and silo-bound legal culture (negative effect); and a decentralized state, corporatist governance traditions and strong civil society (positive effect).

In addition to the formal and contextual factors such as those discussed above, the importance of networks in facilitating innovation and shaping innovation pathways at the organizational, sectoral and national levels has long been recognized within the private sector innovation literature (Lundvall 1992; Nelson 1993; Jones, Conway and Steward 1998; Jones and Beckinsale 1999; Love 1999). These 'soft structures' are examined in detail in Chapter 3. While the internal governance structures for each of the three cities included in this study are described in more detail in Chapter 5, there are also some important national-level governance structures and traditions that are likely to have an impact on innovation capacity. These are briefly examined for each of Denmark, the Netherlands and Spain in the following section.

National Culture in Spain, the Netherlands and Denmark

There is a broad consensus that there are (cultural) differences between northern European and southern European countries. Denmark and the Netherlands are good representatives of the northern countries and Spain for the southern countries (see: Skelcher at al. 2010). While culture is an ambiguous and multi-faceted concept, one approach to differentiating between national cultures that is widely used is the work of Hofstede (Hofstede 1983; Hofstede and Bond 1998). This is employed here to provide an overview of the similarities and differences between these three nations.

Hofstede uses five different measurements: power distance (PDI), individualism (IDV), masculinity (MAS), uncertainty avoidance (UAI) and long-term orientation (LTO). These dimensions are defined as follows (taken from Hofstede.com):

- Power distance is the degree to which the less powerful members of a society accept and expect that power is distributed unequally. This dimension is about how a society handles inequality. A low degree of power distance indicates a society that strives for equality, while a society with a high power distance is more hierarchical;
- Individualism refers to a preference for a loosely knit social framework in which individuals are expected to take care of themselves and their immediate families. Its opposite, Collectivism, represents a preference for a tightly knit society in which individuals can expect their relatives or members of a particular in-group to look after them in exchange for unquestioning loyalty;
- Masculinity represents "a preference in society for achievement, heroism, assertiveness and material reward for success. Society at large is

more competitive. Its opposite, femininity, indicates a preference for cooperation, modesty, caring for the weak and quality of life. Society at large is more consensus-oriented."

• The uncertainty avoidance dimension in the Hofstede scale expresses the degree to which the members of a society feel uncomfortable with uncertainty and ambiguity. Countries exhibiting strong UAI maintain rigid codes of belief and behaviour and are intolerant of unorthodox behaviour and ideas. Weak UAI societies maintain a more relaxed attitude in which practice counts more than principles; and

• The long-term orientation dimension is related to a society's search for virtue. Societies with a short-term orientation generally have a strong concern with establishing the absolute truth. They are normative in their thinking. They exhibit great respect for traditions, a relatively small propensity to save for the future and a focus on achieving quick results. In societies with a long-term orientation, people believe that truth depends very much on situation, context and time. They show an ability to adapt traditions to changed conditions, a strong propensity to save and invest, thriftiness and perseverance in achieving results.

The Hofstede scores on these five cultural items for the three countries are shown in Figure 2.1. Spain scores much higher on the power distance score (57) than Denmark (18) and the Netherlands (38). The same picture can be observed with masculinity (Spain: 42, the Netherlands: 14 and Denmark: 16) and individualism (Spain: 51, the Netherlands: 80 and Denmark: 74). Hence, Denmark and the Netherlands are characterized by more individualization than Spain. Compared to Spain, the other two countries also have a higher score on femininity (where achievement and reward are less valued

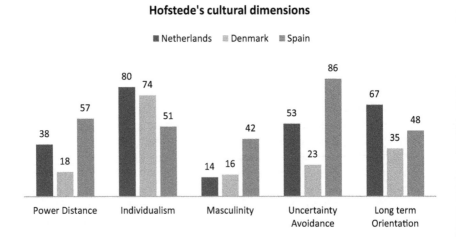

Hofstede's cultural dimensions

■ Netherlands   ▨ Denmark   ■ Spain

Figure 2.1 Comparison of Hofstede Scores for Denmark, the Netherlands and Spain

and consensus is more important). Spain is the nation most inclined towards uncertainty avoidance, and the Netherlands has the strongest long-term orientation. Denmark has the lowest score of the three countries in regard to both uncertainty avoidance and long-term orientation.

Political and Societal Structures in Spain, the Netherlands and Denmark

If we compare the three countries on their political and societal structures, we again get a picture where Denmark and the Netherlands are quite similar, while Spain is more different. A well-known distinction in political structures is the one made by Lijphart (1999), who distinguished between majority and consensus patterns of democracy. Majority democracies show a power structure that is concentrated in representative institutions and work through a majority system of political power. Consensus democracies have more dispersed power, not only within representative institutions (coalition governments), but also between representation institutions and societal groups (interest organizations, social movements etc.). Denmark and the Netherlands are examples of consensus democracy, while Spain is an example of a majority democracy (see: Lijphart 1999; Skelcher et al. 2010).

Another way of viewing this is to examine social capital. As Robert Putnam (1995) argued, the nature of civic community is important, because it tends to foster values and actions that are supportive of democracy (equity, tolerance etc.). In accordance with Skelcher et al. (2010), we call this strong or weak associationalism, which is indicated by the number of intermediate organizations in a country and the number of citizens that are members of these organizations. In general, Denmark and the Netherlands are characterized by strong associationalism, while Spain is characterized by weaker associationalism (see: Skelcher et al. 2010). Countries with stronger associationalism could also be expected to have a stronger tradition in regard to the importance of network governance. For confirmation of this for Denmark and the Netherlands, see Skelcher et al. (2010) and Torfing and Triantafilliou (2011). This also fits with the more consensualist democracy of these two countries.

Given this, one might expect, based on the earlier observations by Bekkers, Tummers and Voorberg (2013), that the Netherlands and Denmark have slightly better conditions for innovation in the public sector: These two nations have more pluralistic environments, stronger civil society and a stronger tradition for negotiation and reaching out to societal organizations through more horizontal governance networks. The cultural features of less power distance, less masculinity and less uncertainty avoidance should also help to reinforce this. On the other hand, Spain has been hit much harder by the financial crisis of 2008 and so has experienced a stronger external trigger that might lead to a greater emphasis on the need for innovation in that country.

Linking governance structures to innovation seems incongruous from the perspective of those who see innovation as running counter to existing structures, where "frustration with the status quo" is a major source of innovation. There are also observers who find innovation to be an individual rather than collective property, or simply observe on the basis of the case study literature that "innovative ideas spring up from all over the place" (Walters 2001, 9–11). However, for public sector innovation, these structures are crucially important, providing the institutional hardware that creates a particular set of possibilities for change.

The formal institutions of the state described above are supplemented by a myriad of temporal and structural governance networks in which mutually dependent actors and actor-coalitions struggle for objectives, problem definitions and the organization of collective action (Kickert, Klijn and Koppenjan 1997). As such, the role of governmental agencies has evolved from unilateral control and strategic planning towards new forms of governance. These are described in the next section.

Innovation and Public Governance Forms

In the previous chapter, we argued that innovation involves a major discontinuity with existing practice and routines. This usually does not happen by itself but needs some form of (public) governance, processes of guidance through which outcomes are achieved. In general, three forms of public governance are distinguished: hierarchical or traditional Public Administration, market governance, which has been represented by the New Public Management perspective, and network governance (Levi-Faur 2012; Klijn and Koppenjan 2016). Table 2.1 provides an overview of these three forms of public governance.

Table 2.1 Three Forms of Public Governance

	Traditional public administration (hierarchy)	New public management (market governance)	Network governance (networks)
Focus	Differentiation and coordination within bureaucracy	Internal functioning of governmental bodies and contractual relations	Relations between governments and with other actors (inter-organizational focus)
Objectives	Production of effective and uniform policies and services according to principles of equality, legitimacy and legality	Improving effectiveness and efficiency of public service delivery and public organizations	Improving inter-organizational coordination and quality of policy-making and service delivery

	Traditional public administration (hierarchy)	New public management (market governance)	Network governance (networks)
Core ideas/ management techniques	Using hierarchy and command and control; line management; building on rule following, loyalty and a public service orientation of civil servants; policy cycle as control mechanism	Using business and market instruments (modern management techniques, market mechanisms, performance indicators, consumer boards) to improve service delivery	Using network management: activating actors, organizing research and information gathering (joint fact-finding), exploring content, arranging, process rules and so forth
Politics	Politicians set goals that are being implemented by the executive in a neutral way. Both civil servants and elected administrators are held accountable by representative bodies of elected politicians	Politicians set goals (separation of policy formation and implementation). Policy implementation/ service delivery done by independent agencies or market mechanisms on the basis of clear performance indicators	Goals are developed and negotiated during interaction processes, with no sharp distinction between formation, implementation and delivery of policies and services. Politicians are part of these processes or facilitate these processes
Innovation	Not very much attention to innovation. Innovation stems from central coordination and charismatic leaders who change the organization and its processes	Innovation achieved by giving implementers space for innovations and by competition among implementers. Only steering on output performance. Market incentives to govern implementing units	Innovation stems from variety in knowledge confrontation and connecting various resources and knowledge available by various actors

Adapted from Klijn and Koppenjan 2016.

Hierarchical Governance

Hierarchical governance has several characteristic features, such as stan-dardized rules and procedures, a chain of command, centralized structure and management, heavy reliance on supervision and neutral administrative procedures. The classical image of hierarchical governance is the Weberian Bureaucracy, with its reliance on rules and an impartial civil service (Con-sidine and Lewis 1999, 2003; Pierre and Peters 2000). Private firms are sometimes characterized by strong hierarchical governance structures too (see, for instance, the classical management theories).

Standardized rules and procedures explicitly guide the key decisions affecting individual tasks and provide substantially identical services to cli-ents with similar needs. A centralized chain of command results in close supervision, where subordinates rely on their supervisors when encounter-ing situations undefined by rules and procedures. Not surprisingly, individ-ual supervisors are acquainted with their subordinates' day-to-day activities. Performance and outcomes are necessary consequences of an adherence to standardized rules and procedures in a hierarchical system (Hughes 2012). Thus, the key to performing tasks under this mode of governance is to fol-low the right procedures for getting things done.

Innovation in this governance model is driven from the top down: Public sector innovation in this model results from decisions by leaders who have the ability to change the organization, how it functions, and what it delivers. Senior leadership in such organizations is likely to be transformational, with charismatic leaders who make a difference (see Chapter 4).

Market Governance

Market coordination works through the mechanisms of prices, demand and supply. Prices and competition create an 'invisible hand' which secures co-ordination. The only conditions are a set of rules and regulations that need to be enforced (property rights, legal safeguards etc.) in order to ensure that the competition is fair.

In the model of public governance through markets that is generally asso-ciated with the New Public Management (NPM), competition is assumed to make governments smart and skilful buyers. They control the production costs of service providers, because contracts are contestable, and so govern-ments should pay less for the services it buys in, rather than providing these itself (Hood 1991; Kettl 2000). Service providers might be private firms or consortia, non-profit organizations or even hived-off separate parts of the public administration (agencies or other separate bodies). This requires a clear separation of the setting of policy goals from policy implementation.

Because of this separation, monitoring is important to protect against the potential for self-serving behaviour. After all, the contractor might have an incentive to exert less effort in order to increase its profits (Williamson

1996; Deakin and Michie 1997). Opportunism becomes more important as actors become more dependent on each other due to specific investments (Williamson 1996). Safeguards in the contract are often used to protect oneself against the opportunistic behaviour of other actors. But monitoring and including safeguards in the contracts assumes that interactions can be monitored and that behaviour can be foreseen, at least to some extent.

Under market governance, innovation emerges because of competition between actors/firms and their desire to be the first mover in introducing new products. Innovation is connected to a great amount of uncertainty (actors do not know what the end result of innovation will be) and may be subject to opportunistic behaviour by the partners. Some neo-institutionalists emphasize the importance of trust relations to overcome opportunistic behaviour and mitigate the risks in the case of innovation (see: Lane and Bachman 1998; Nooteboom 2002). From a market governance perspective, innovation results from both competition between possible implementing actors and from the fact that while outputs are specified, the means to achieve these are not.

Public sector innovation in this model is driven by competition. Supervisory roles are minimal, so long as individual staff are focused on results and costs (Considine and Lewis 1999, 2003), and innovation is deemed to arise from the 'hot breath of the market'. Leadership under this form of governance is likely to be transactional and characterized by rationality, or entrepreneurial (see Chapter 4).

Network Governance

Network governance has gained popularity as a form of governance that deals more effectively with complex policy problems. Proponents contend that networks promote better decision-making by building collaborative relationships that match the growing interdependence between clients, suppliers and producers who share resources and the authority to make decisions (Rhodes 1997; Pierre and Peters 2000). Collaborative networks are loosely coupled multi-actor arrangements that emerge out of interdependencies between actors. As such, they are capable of connecting various actors and resources (including information), but are also characterized by complex interactions and the need for coordination.

While the source of rationality and form of control behind hierarchical governance is law and rules, and for market governance it is competition and contracts, network governance relies on interaction and relationships (Considine and Lewis 1999, 2003). Individuals working under this governance mode have a high level of flexibility to co-produce services with actors in other agencies, and sometimes, with the clients of those services. Leadership under this mode of governance is networked and interpersonal (see Chapter 4).

This book has a major focus on networks, because of their presumed importance to innovation, including in the public sector (Lewis, Considine and Alexander 2011). Hence, network governance and innovation are described in more detail in the next section.

Network Governance and Innovation

Much of the literature on network governance stresses the complexity of the governance process and emphasizes that networks can provide new and innovative solutions for societal problems and can improve implementation (Koppenjan and Klijn 2004; Skelcher, Mathur and Smith 2005; Sørensen and Torfing 2007). Although innovative policy solutions are needed, network governance does not necessarily make them easy to achieve, because various actors favour different, often conflicting values and policy solutions. These problems are referred to in the literature as 'wicked problems' (see: Rittel and Webber 1973). Wicked problems are policy issues that involve many actors who might disagree about the nature of the problem and the desired solution. In addition, there is usually insufficient or controversial information surrounding these problems, which makes it difficult to interpret them and to find appropriate solutions. Wicked problems are difficult to resolve as they almost always involve conflicts between values and scarce resources.

This is very clear in the list of problems mentioned by the politicians and administrators who responded to our survey (see Part 2 of this book): The most important socioeconomic challenges they nominated (poverty, integrated services, citizen collaboration, improving education levels and so on) are all problems that require the effort of a number of actors, but are also plagued by quite different views on what the problem is and what the desirable solutions might be.

Resource Dependency

Crucial to the emergence and existence of networks are dependency relations among actors (Hanf and Scharpf 1978). Resource dependencies around policy problems or policy programs require actors to interact with one another and create more intensive and enduring interactions (Mandell 2001; Agranoff and McGuire 2003). Hence, network governance is characterized by patterns of interactions between actors and a set of (emergent) institutional rules (Lewis 2011). These network characteristics, in turn, influence decision-making and service provision. In this sense, the institutional characteristics create some stability and shared expectations.

At the same time, actors, in concrete decision-making and service provision processes in networks, have different perceptions about problems and may choose different strategies, thereby making interactions less predictable and more complex (Rhodes 1997; Agranoff and McGuire 2003). Network governance thus manifests itself in concrete policy interactions, which can be seen as policy games that are played by the various actors. During these games, the actors attempt to influence policy issues, partly by re-interpreting the available information and the informal and formal rules that were previously generated. In short, these networks can be characterised by intense dynamism and a high degree of complexity (Teisman et al. 2009), which make them very difficult to manage (Klijn and Koppenjan 2016).

Conflicting Values and Trust in Networks

The interactive nature of networks and the different values of the involved actors make it necessary to attempt to combine the values of various parties. Creativity is essential to the generation of new solutions. Most of the solutions initially available for consideration are developed by parties advocating their own point of view and their own particular values. For the network to be useful, it has to be able to generate new, innovative solutions that combine information arising from different actors and their resources. But the act of sharing information and resources and of working cooperatively toward an innovative solution is often seen by individual actors or interest groups as risky. None of the actors can fully predict the form that the solution will eventually take. Exchanging information with other actors can lead to a situation in which other actors use the information for their own benefit.

This situation presents a classic mix of the challenges associated with collective decision-making, strategic games and risk taking (Axelrod 1984; Williamson 1996). Trust is important to achieve innovative solutions which require information exchange between actors. This is even more the case when the actors have opposing perspectives on the nature of the problem, which values are relevant and the nature of desirable solutions. Networks, which build durable connections and relationships between actors (Lewis 2010), have the potential to serve as a viable means for developing trust between actors that help to achieve outcomes. But trust does not naturally arise from networks: It must be built through interactions (Huxham and Vangen 2005). As has been observed in theories of social capital and social networks, networks provide strategic options for reaching actors, acquiring information and organizing collective action (Lewis 2010). But that also has to be activated, guided and nurtured.

Network governance is considered to be especially important for achieving public sector innovation. There are numerous reasons for this, the most important of which are:

- Networks provide a means for connecting different points of view (diversity);
- Networks enable the mobilization and connection of various necessary resources (resource mobilization);

- Networks are loosely coupled and enable information collection and exchange (flexibility); and
- Networks are a vehicle to build interactions and potentially trust relations which are seen to be important for innovation (trust).

We discuss each of these briefly, in turn.

Diversity

Innovation occurs when different perspectives confront each other (Nooteboom 2002). Network governance has a great advantage over hierarchical control in this sense because hierarchies tend to breed uniform ideas and visions and force actors to act according to preformed roles. Networks have the potential to provide diversity through interactions between actors with different perceptions of the problem and possible solutions. This is often considered as one of the possible contributions of networks to solving complex problems, according to the literature (see: Fischer 2003; Klijn and Koppenjan 2016). If various actors with different problem perceptions are included, a more varied and complete problem definition can be formed. Where different ideas for solutions are proposed, a better and more encompassing (and more innovative) solution to the problem can be created (Ansell and Gash 2008; O'Leary and Bingham 2009). Thus, it is precisely the potential of interaction between a variety of actors with different views that provides a solid foundation for innovation.

Resource Mobilization

It is clear that for innovation, whether it is new solutions for wicked problems or innovation in (for instance) service delivery, resource mobilization is crucial. After all, it is only when resources are combined that innovation can be realized (and implemented). Networks can be suitable vehicles for activating the necessary actors and resources, as has been argued in inter-organizational theory (see: Scharpf 1978; Aldrich 1979; Rogers and Whetten 1982). They provide the relationships to channel resources and organize them for innovation. Of course, resources can also be mobilized by hierarchies (or markets). But hierarchies can only activate resources within the structure of the organizational units that are directly under their control, and markets can only do so within the confines of the contract. Innovation often requires resources from organizational units that can only be controlled horizontally, through interaction.

Flexibility

Loosely connected networks have greater flexibility than formal organizational units. Unlike organizational hierarchies, which are strictly regulated and steered by central control mechanisms, networks generally do not have such strict rules and organizational structures. This makes it more difficult to organize collective action but also easier to horizontally connect different actors together when they are not willing to function as subordinate units. It can generate a sense of informality and openness that is not apparent in either hierarchical or market governance structures.

Trust

Networks are potentially vehicles for the creation of trust. Building interaction patterns in networks enables trust to develop, which is, as much of the literature emphasizes, an important condition for innovation. Trust can be defined as actors' more or less stable, positive perception of the intentions of other actors, that is, the perception that other actors will refrain from opportunistic behaviour (Rousseau et al. 1998; Edelenbos and Klijn 2007). Because trust is a perception about intentions, it can be distinguished from institutional characteristics such as rules and norms, which often serve to facilitate trustworthy behaviour. Trust can further be distinguished from actions that are the result of trust. It develops in action, or to put it more precisely, through interactions amongst actors (Ring and van der Ven 1992; Lane and Bachman 1998; Huxham and Vangen 2005).

An important argument in the literature about trust is that it stimulates the exchange of information and knowledge. Access to knowledge increases the problem solving capacities of governance networks through the 'bundling' of knowledge sources (e.g., different fields of expertise) (Huxham and Vangen 2005; Provan, Huang and Milward 2009). Knowledge is partly tacit and sometimes only available in the form of human capital (Nooteboom 2002), so it requires intensive and repeated interactions between actors for this knowledge to be exchanged. Trust can facilitate this. A similar observation is made about learning (Lane and Bachmann 1998). Learning and discovery, too, require knowledge exchange and intensive interaction, and trust plays an important role in these types of interactions, for example, causing trusting actors to be more open towards each other (Zand 1972), which facilitates learning processes (Miles and Snow 1986; Ring and van der Ven 1992; Parker and Vaidya 2001). Another aspect of this is the psychological safety that arises with trust. This is described in Chapter 3.

Network Conditions for Innovations

The list of potential advantages of networks that we dealt with in the previous section are not always gained very easily. Networks are loosely coupled 'soft structures' containing many actors with different perceptions. Controversies about different interests and conflicting strategies are often found in networks and can hinder collaboration, trust building and the achievement of innovation. In this section, we discuss some of the important conditions needed to create and foster innovation in networks.

Knowledge Management

Managing knowledge is very important to realizing the possible advantages of networks. Knowledge has multiple manifestations, and this gives rise to various forms of conflict and fragmentation in governance processes. Here, knowledge management strategies include not only the building of a coherent body of knowledge that policy makers can use to pinpoint a problem and gauge the efficacy of measures, but also the organization of a consensus-building process in which actors come to a shared understanding of both the problem and the optimum solution. Actors' different perceptions can also lead to varying interpretations of knowledge and to strong conflicts about knowledge if every actor in the network fosters his/her own research and facts (Ansell and Gash 2008; Klijn and Koppenjan 2016).

Knowledge management in the context of controversial governance processes is not easy, because knowledge is normally dispersed among the various actors within a network (Koppenjan and Klijn 2004). Moreover, actors have conflicting bodies of knowledge, leading to miscommunication, controversy and conflict. Such fragmentation and divergence can be explained by differences in actors' underlying ways of knowing (Feldman et al. 2006; Feldman and Khademian 2007). Reconciling the inevitable tensions can be achieved by using inclusive management (Feldman et al. 2006). This builds communities of participation in which actors share their individual perspectives in order to achieve mutual comprehension and a broadly shared ambition for collective action (Ingram and Schneider 1990).

Taming the Institutional Complexity of Networks

Networks are also characterized by complexity. We can define institutions roughly as sets of rules regulating behaviour (Ostrom 1990; Scharpf 1997). Networks as enduring relationships between actors are also characterized by the emergence of sets of rules that are developed in interactions between actors. Each network will have a unique set of rules, partly constrained by formal structures and partly created during interactions. Network rules may reduce complexity and enhance cooperation, because they make the behaviours of actors more predictable. However, network rules may also compete with other sets of rules stemming from informal groups, specific professional roles, organizations, national laws etc. (March and Olsen 1989; Scott 1995).

When the number of rules grows, become inconsistent, opaque and not well understood, this may generate complexity instead of predictability. Because many policy problems cut across existing demarcations between organizations, administrative levels and functional areas, inconsistencies and institutional complexity are very likely. As a result, interactions can become more difficult because their behaviour will be guided by different rules and frames of reference, causing complexity and lack of mutual understanding. In this case, actors will have different routines and speak diverse professional languages (Ostrom 2007; Baumgartner and Jones 2009). This may cause stagnation in interactions or even prohibit interactions within networks.

On the other hand, rules can also become too rigid and form an obstacle for innovation: Rules may become fixed and leave no scope for new behaviour, new interactions or new products. Of course, both of these problems—institutional rigidity, and complexity and uncertainty—can be present simultaneously.

Network Management

Knowledge management is not enough to facilitate innovations in networks. Because cooperation and the coordination of goals and interests and connecting interactions and strategies of actors do not occur on their own accord, it is necessary to steer interactions in policy games within networks. The (implicit) assumption in the literature is that a satisfactory outcome is often impossible without network management (Gage and Mandell 1990; Agranoff and McGuire 2001).

Network management then is seen as the deliberate attempt to govern processes in networks (Gage and Mandell 1990; Kickert, Klijn and Koppenjan 1997; Meier and O'Toole 2001). Network management aims at initiating and facilitating interaction processes between actors (Friend, Power and Yewlett1974), creating and changing network arrangements for better coordination (Scharpf 1978; Rogers and Whetten 1982), creating new content by exploring new ideas, for instance (Koppenjan and Klijn 2004), and guiding interactions (Gage and Mandell 1990; Kickert, Klijn and Koppenjan 1997).

Various network management strategies have been identified in the literature. In general, most of the strategies that have been mentioned can be categorized either as strategies of process management or of institutional design (Gage and Mandell 1990; Koppenjan and Klijn 2004). Process management strategies attempt to facilitate interactions between actors in policy games. What is crucial in these types of strategies is that although they are indirect in the sense that they try to facilitate interactions and the actions of other actors, they consider the structure of the network (the rules, positions of actors and resource division) as a given. They are thus direct strategies aimed at actors and interactions (hands-on strategies; see: Sørensen and Torfing 2007).

If management strategies are aimed at altering the institutional characteristics of the network (like changing actor positions, entry rules or other more drastic ways to intervene in the structure of the network), they can be labelled as institutional design strategies (Koppenjan and Klijn 2004).

Institutional network management strategies may be suitable to cope with the institutional complexity and rigidity which has been described in previous sections. Chapter 4 elaborates leadership styles, and we examine network and other management strategies in more depth in that chapter.

Boundary Spanning Activities

Another condition that has often been mentioned in relation to innovation is the presence of boundary spanning. To link internal and external networks, that is, the organization to its surrounding networks, boundary spanners are considered to play an important role in solving complex public issues (Williams 2002; Voets and de Rynck 2008). Boundary spanners manage the interface between organizations and their environment, and they are people who are able to link the organization they represent with its environment (Tushman and Scanlan 1981; Levina and Vaast 2005).

Clearly, boundary spanning has some overlap with notions like 'collaborative public management' and 'collaborative public managers' coined by O'Leary and Bingham (2009), and 'network manager' (van Meerkerk and Edelenbos 2014). Boundary spanners are engaged in three main and interrelated activities Aldrich and Herker 1977; Williams 2002):

• Connecting different people and processes on both sides of the boundary;
• Selecting (and interpreting) relevant information on both sides of the boundary; and
• Translating this information to the other side of the boundary.

Aldrich and Herker (1977) emphasize the importance of boundary spanners in selecting and filtering relevant information, and the possibility they provide for an organization to adapt to its environment and maintain its legitimacy to important client groups. They assume that stable environments need less boundary spanning than turbulent environments. If the observation of many governance scholars is correct and the environment of governments has become more complex, with greater dependencies between many actors (Kickert, Klijn and Koppenjan 1997; Pierre and Peters 2000), then we can expect that boundary spanning activities are important for governments and for innovation.

Recent network governance literature often emphasizes the importance of boundary spanners. Network and collaboration theorists emphasize several functions of boundary spanners (Williams 2002; Huxham and Vangen 2005; van Meerkerk and Edelenbos 2014). Firstly, they make the necessary connections between actors in a network, and because actors are dependent on each other's resources, this is crucial. Secondly, boundary spanners facilitate the flow of information between actors and thus generate the conditions for innovative solutions (van Meerkerk and Edelenbos 2014; Klijn and Koppenjan 2016). Thirdly, they enhance the level of trust between actors in the network by intensifying interactions and creating mutual benefits (see Williams (2002) and van Meerkerk and Edelenbos (2014) for empirical evidence). Trust in turn facilitates the flow of information and innovation (Lane and Bachman 1998).

There is empirical evidence to support the idea that boundary spanners generate organizational outcomes, such as innovation (Tushman 1977), financial performance (Dollinger 1984) and strategic decision-making (Jemison 1984). There is also evidence that boundary spanning enhances trust and performance in networks (van Meerkerk and Edelenbos 2014). Accordingly, we expect that the presence of boundary spanners is positively associated with innovation in the public sector.

Conclusions

Public sector innovation is not achieved in a vacuum: It is underpinned, and fundamentally affected by, a set of governance structures. We have briefly elaborated a set of governance structures that is regarded as important for innovation capacity in this chapter. And we also discussed some of the social, political and cultural characteristics of the three nations from which our three city governments are drawn in order to provide some background information on their innovation capacity in terms of these contextual factors.

We have also examined three public governance forms: hierarchical, market and network governance, and have shown why network governance (and boundary spanning) is considered to be supportive of innovation. We have also discussed some of the problems and necessary conditions for innovation in network governance. This is linked to the discussion of networks in the next chapter, although that has a more specific focus on social networks and their importance for innovation. This chapter contributes the first component of the framework that underpins our approach to analysing innovation capacity in city governments. The next two chapters describe the other two components: social networks (Chapter 3) and leadership (Chapter 4).

References

Agranoff, Robert, and Michael McGuire. 2001. "Big questions in public network management research." *Journal of Public Administration Research and Theory* 11(3): 295–326.

Agranoff, Robert, and Michael McGuire. 2003. *Collaborative public management: New strategies for local governments.* Washington, DC: Georgetown University Press.

Aldrich, Howard. 1979. *Organizations and environments.* Englewood Cliffs, NJ: Prentice-Hall.

Aldrich, Howard, and Diane Herker. 1977. "Boundary spanning roles and organizational structure." *The Academy of Management Review* 2(2): 217–30.

Ansell, Chris, and Alison Gash. 2008. "Collaborative governance in theory and practice." *Journal of Public Administration Research and Theory* 18(4): 543–71.

Axelrod, Robert M. 1984. *The evolution of cooperation.* New York: Basic Books.

Baumgartner, Frank R., and Brian D. Jones. 2009. *Agendas and instability in American politics.* Chicago: The University of Chicago Press.

Bekkers, Victor J.J.M., Lars G. Tummers, and William H. Voorberg. 2013. *From public innovation to social innovation in the public sector: A literature review of relevant drivers and barriers.* Rotterdam: Erasmus University Rotterdam.

Considine, Mark, and Jenny M. Lewis. 1999. "Governance at ground level: The front-line bureaucrat in the age of markets and networks." *Public Administration Review* 59(6): 467–80.

Considine, Mark, and Jenny M. Lewis. 2003. "Bureaucracy, network or enterprise? Comparing models of governance in Australia, Britain, the Netherlands, and New Zealand." *Public Administration Review* 63(2): 131–40.

Deakin, Simon, and Jonathan Michie. 1997. "Contracts and competition: An introduction." *Cambridge Journal of Economics* 21(2): 121–5.

Dollinger, M.J. 1984. "Environmental boundary spanning and information processing effects on organizational performance." *Academy of Management Journal* 27(2): 351–68.

Edelenbos, Jurian, and Erik Hans Klijn. 2007. "Trust in complex decision-making networks: A theoretical and empirical exploration." *Administration and Society* 39(1): 25–50.

Feldman, Martha S., and Ann M. Khademian. 2007. "The role of the public manager in inclusion: Creating communities of participation." *Governance* 20: 305–24.

Feldman, Martha S., Ann M. Khademian, Helen Ingram, and Ann S. Schneider. 2006. "Ways of knowing and inclusive management practices." *Public Administration Review* 66: 9–99.

Fischer, Frank. 2003. *Reframing public policy: Discursive politics and deliberative practices.* Oxford: Oxford University Press.

Friend, John K., J. M. Power, and C. J. L. Yewlett. 1974. *Public Planning: The Inter-Corporate Dimension.* London: Tavistock.

Gage, Robert W., and Myrna P. Mandell, editors. 1990. *Strategies for managing intergovernmental policies and networks.* New York/London: Preager.

Hanf, Kenneth I., and Fritz W. Scharpf, editors. 1978. *Interorganizational Policy Making: Limits to Coordination and Central Control.* London: Sage.

Hofstede, Geert. 1983. "National cultures in four dimensions: A research-based theory of cultural differences among nations." *International Studies of Management & Organization* 13(1–2): 46–74.

Hofstede, Geert, and Michael Harris Bond. 1998. "The Confucius connection: From cultural roots to economic growth." *Organisational Dynamics* 16(4): 5–21.

Hood, Christopher. 1991. "A public management for all seasons." *Public Administration* 69(1): 3–19.

Hughes, Owen. 2012. *Public management and administration: An introduction* (4th edition). Basingstoke: Palgrave Macmillan.

Huxham, Chris, and Sev Vangen. 2005. *Managing to collaborate: The theory and practice of collaborative advantage.* London: Routledge.

Ingram, Helen, and Anne Schneider. 1990. "Improving implementation through framing smarter statutes." *Journal of Public Policy* 10(1): 66–87.

Jemison, David B. 1984. "The importance of boundary spanning roles in strategic decision-making." *Journal of Management Studies* 21(2): 131–52.

Jones, Oswarld, and Martin Beckinsale. 1999. *Analysing the innovation process: Networks, micropolitics and structural change.* Research Paper 9919. Birmingham: Aston Business School. Accessed 7 July 2016. http://citeseerx.ist.psu.edu/viewdoc/download?doi=10.1.1.200.2735&rep=rep1&type=pdf.

Jones, Oswald, Steve Conway, and Fred Steward. 1998. "Introduction: Social interaction and innovation networks." *International Journal of Innovation Management* 2(2 Special issue): 123–36.

Kettl, Donald F. 2000. *The global public management revolution: A report on the transformation of governance.* Washington, DC: Brookings Institution Press.

Kickert, Walter J.M., Erik-Hans Klijn, and Joop F.M. Koppenjan, editors. 1997. *Managing complex networks: Strategies for the public sector.* London: Sage.

Klijn, Erik Hans, and Joop F.M. Koppenjan. 2016. *Governance networks in the public sector.* Oxon: Routledge.

Koppenjan, Joop F.M., and Erik-Hans Klijn. 2004. *Managing uncertainties in networks.* London: Routledge.

Lane, Christel, and Reinhard Bachmann, editors. 1998. *Trust within and between organizations: Conceptual issues and empirical applications.* Oxford: Oxford University Press.

Levi-Faur, David, editor.2012. *The Oxford handbook of governance.* Oxford: Oxford University Press.

Levina, Natalia, and Emmanuelle Vaast. 2005. "The emergence of boundary spanning competence in practice: Implications for implementation and use of information systems1." *MIS Quarterly* 29(2): 335–63.

Lewis, Jenny M. 2010. *Connecting and cooperating: Social capital and public policy.* Sydney: UNSW Press.

Lewis, Jenny M. 2011. "The future of network governance research: Strength in diversity and synthesis." *Public Administration* 89(4): 1221–34.

Lewis, Jenny M., Mark Considine, and Damon Alexander. 2011. "Innovation inside government: The importance of networks." In *Innovation in the public sector: Linking capacity and leadership*, edited by Victor Bekkers, Jurian Edelenbos, and Bram Steijn, 107–33. Houndsmills: Palgrave McMillan.

Lijphart, Arend. 1999. *Patterns of democracy.* New Haven, CT: Yale University Press.

Love, James H. 1999. *Patterns of networking in the innovation process: A comparative study of the UK, Germany and Ireland.* Research Paper 9913. Birmingham: Aston Business School. Accessed 7 Jul 2016. http://citeseerx.ist.psu.edu/viewdoc/download?rep=rep1&type=pdf&doi=10.1.1.195.4317.

Lundvall, Bent-Åke. 1992. *National systems of innovation: Towards a theory of innovation and interactive learning.* London: Pinter Press.

Mandell, Myrna P., editor. 2001. *Getting results through collaboration: Networks and network structures for public policy and management.* Westport, CT: Quorum Books.

March, James G., and Johan P. Olsen. 1989. *Rediscovering institutions: The organizational basis of politics.* New York: Free Press.

Meier, Kenneth J., and Lawrence J.O'Toole. 2001. "Managerial strategies and behaviour in networks: A model with evidence from U.S. public education." *Journal of Public Administration and Theory* 11(3): 271–93.

Miles, R.E., and Charles C. Snow. 1986. "Organization: New concepts for new forms." *California Management Review* 28(3): 62–73.

Nelson, Richard R. 1993. *National systems of innovation.* Oxford: Blackwell.

Nooteboom, Bart. 2002. *Trust: Forms, foundations, functions, failures and figures.* Cheltenham: Edward Elgar.

O'Leary, Rosemary, and Lisa Blomgren Bingham, editors. 2009. *The collaborative public manager.* Washington, DC: Georgetown University Press.

Ostrom, Elinor. 1990. *Governing the commons: The evolution of institutions for collective action.* Cambridge: Cambridge University Press.

Ostrom, Elinor. 2007. "Institutional rational choice: An assessment of the institutional analysis and development framework". In *Theories of the policy process*, edited by Paul A. Sabatier, 21–64. Boulder, CO: Westview Press.

Parker, David, and Kirit Vaidya. 2001. "An economic perspective on innovation networks." In *Social interaction and organisational change: Aston perspectives on innovation network*, edited by Oswald Jones, Steve Conway, and Fred Steward, 125–63. London: Imperial College Press.

Pierre, Jon, and B. Guy Peters. 2000. *Governance, politics and the state.* Basingstoke: Macmillan.

Provan, Keith G., Kun Huang, and H. Brinton Milward. 2009. "The evolution of structural embeddedness and organizational social outcomes in a centrally governed health and human service network." *Journal of Public Administration Research and Theory* 19(4): 873–93.

Putnam, Robert D. 1995. "Tuning in, tuning out: The strange disappearance of social capital in America." *Political Science and Politics* 28(4): 664–83.

Rhodes, Rod A.W. 1997. *Understanding Governance: Policy networks, governance, reflexivity, and accountability.* Buckingham: Open University Press.

Ring, Peter Smith, and Andrew H. van der Ven. 1992. "Structuring cooperative relations between organizations." *Strategic Management Journal* 13(7): 483–98.

Rittel, Horst, and Melvin Webber. 1973. "Dilemmas in a general theory of planning." *Policy Sciences* 4(2): 155–69.

Rogers, David L., and David A. Whetten, editors. 1982. *Interorganizational coordination: Theory, research, and implementation.* Ames, IA: Iowa State University Press.

Rousseau, Denise M., Sim B. Sitkin, Ronald S. Burt, and Colin Camerer. 1998. "Not so different after all: A cross discipline view of trust." *Academy of Management Review* 23(3): 393–404.

Scharpf, Fritz W. 1978. "Interorganizational policy studies: Issues, concepts and perspectives." In *Inter-organisational policy making: Limits to coordination and central control*, edited by Kenneth Hanf and Fritz W. Scharpf, 345–70. London: Sage.

Scharpf, Fritz W. 1997. *Games real actors play: Actor-centred institutionalism in policy research.* Boulder, CO: Westview Press.

Scott, W. Richard. 1995. *Institutions and organizations.* Thousand Oaks, CA: Sage.

Skelcher, Chris, Erik-Hans Klijn, Daniel Kübler, Eva Sørensen, and Helen Sullivan. 2010. "Explaining the democratic anchorage of governance networks: Evidence from four European countries." *Administrative Theory & Praxis* 33(1): 7–38.

Skelcher, Chris, Navdeep Mathur, and Mike Smith. 2005. "The public governance of collaborative spaces: Discourse, design and democracy." *Public Administration* 83(3): 573–96.

Sørensen, Eva, and Jacob Torfing, editors. 2007. *Theories of democratic network governance*. Houndmills: Palgrave Macmillan.

Teisman, Geert R., Arwin van Buuren, and Lasse M. Gerrits, editors. 2009. *Managing complex governance systems: Dynamics, self-organization and coevolution in public investments*. London: Routledge.

Torfing, Jacob, and Peter Triantafillou, editors. 2011. *Interactive policy making, metagovernance and democracy*. Colchester: ECPR Press.

Tushman, Michael L. 1977. "Special boundary roles in the innovation process." *Administrative Science Quarterly* 22(4): 587–605.

Tushman, Michael L., and Thomas J. Scanlan. 1981. "Characteristics and external orientation of boundary spanning individuals." *Academy of Management Journal* 24(1): 83–98.

van Meerkerk, Ingmar, and Jurian Edelenbos. 2014. "The effects of boundary spanners on trust and performance of urban governance networks: Findings from survey research on urban development projects in the Netherlands." *Policy Sciences* 47(1): 3–24.

Voets, Joris, and Filip de Rynck. 2008. "Exploring the innovative capacity of intergovernmental network managers: The art of boundary scanning and boundary spanning." In *Innovation in the public sector: Linking capacity and leadership*, edited by Victor Bekkers, Jurian Edelenbos, and Bram Steijn, 155–75. Houndsmills: Palgrave McMillan.

Walters, Jonathan. 2001. *Understanding innovation: What inspires it? What makes it successful?* Arlington, VA: PricewaterhouseCoopers Endowment for the Business of Government. Accessed 8 Jul 2016. http://unpan1.un.org/intradoc/groups/public/documents/un/unpan011090.pdf.

Williams, Paul. 2002. 'The competent boundary spanner.' *Public Administration* 80(1): 103–24.

Williamson, Oliver E. 1996. *The mechanisms of governance*. Oxford: Oxford University Press.

Zand, D.E. 1972. "Trust and managerial problem solving." *Administrative Science Quarterly* 2: 229–39.

3   Social Networks and Innovation

Networks are a prime means to facilitate information exchange and hence to diffuse innovative ideas and practices. They are, therefore, expected to play a vital role in shaping innovation capacity. This is the starting point for this chapter, which theorizes the link between network structures and innovativeness. We introduce social network concepts and the structural approaches that are considered relevant for examining the innovative capacity of public sector environments. Networks are the second component of our analytical framework.

It is only in recent years that networks have been recognized as important for innovation in public sector environments. However, their importance in facilitating innovation and shaping innovation pathways at the organizational, sectoral and national levels has long been recognized in the private sector innovation literature (Lundvall 1992; Nelson 1993; Conway 1995; Jones, Conway and Steward 1998; Jones and Beckinsale 1999; Love 1999). In this literature, social networks are widely regarded as underpinning firms' capacity to benefit from the environment and social capital around them.

The research that links firms' networking behaviour with their innovative capacity has shown that networks are opportunities for risk sharing and for providing access to complementary skills and external knowledge bases (Pittaway et al. 2004). But while innovation in the private sector is about competitiveness and new business opportunities, innovation in the public sector is more closely linked to the ability to respond to changes or needs in society. Networks are extremely relevant for public sector organizations, because they are challenged by having formal hierarchical organizational structures that can be slow in sensing changes in the environment. In contrast, networks are thought to be more dynamic, fluid and open. They are therefore crucial to public sector innovation capacity.

More practically, the innovative capacity of local governments has been linked to the presence of strong internal and external networks (Newman, Raine and Skelcher 2001). At the organizational level, social networks are expected to play a key role in shaping innovation capacity, as they are a prime means to facilitate information exchange and hence diffuse innovative ideas and practices. An approach based on social network analysis was previously applied to examining innovation in municipalities in Australia (Considine, Lewis and Alexander 2009; Lewis, Considine and Alexander 2011; Lewis, Alexander and Considine 2013). This study provides solid evidence that the networking patterns of innovators in the municipal context differ from those who were not recognized as innovators (Lewis, Alexander and Considine 2013). Clearly, networks contribute significantly to an explanation of innovation inside government. This chapter reviews the most important literature on the topic and delves into a number of social network concepts that help us to understand innovation capacity.

Social Network Research

Social networks can either be understood as cognitive perceptions by organizational members or as opportunities that either facilitate or constrain actions (Balkundi and Kilduff 2006; Kilduff, Tsai and Hanke 2006). Social networks are based on analyses of interpersonal connections between individuals, which consist of a set of nodes (people) connected to other nodes by interpersonal ties of some kind (e.g., kinship or close friendship). While there is much research into those relations that are considered to be relatively stable, more dynamic relationships are still underexplored in the literature (Spiro, Acton and Butts 2013). Examples of dynamic relations are work relations that are more informal (e.g., advice networks, collaboration networks or strategic information-seeking networks) than those amongst people belonging to the same organizational division or people formally assigned to work on projects together. While the latter type of relations can be found by looking at organizational charts and project lists, more informal relations have to be uncovered by asking people about their relations or by observing interactions. A common method for doing this is to use a name generator to gather names of alters (their contacts) from each respondent for a limited number of alters (Merluzzia and Burt 2013). This is further described in Chapter 7.

When asking relational questions, we may decide on whether to ask about one-to-one relations—for example: Who do you go to for advice in relation to important managerial decisions? (an ego to alter relation which is either present or absent)—or to ask about frequency or emotional closeness (an ego to alter relation which has different values or levels of strength). This can be sensitive information to be asking respondents about, and when making a survey, a choice must always be made regarding which strategy will generate data that is detailed enough but that will not impose too much of a burden (of time and energy) on respondents and hopefully achieve an acceptable response rate.

Empirical research into the benefit of networks and network advantages in organizational studies is growing (see: Brass et al. 2004; Burt et al. 2005; Burt, Kilduff and Tasselli 2013); the research methods are becoming more refined as the research base grows (Merluzzia and Burt 2013) and so are the software programmes (Borgatti, Everett and Freeman 2002) and the statistical modelling approaches (Robins, Lewis and Wang 2012). For instance, it is well documented that managers with non-redundant network structures (alters that are not connected to each other) have an advantage over those with redundant network ties (alters that are interconnected) (Burt, Kilduff and Tasselli 2013). It is also argued that a diversity of knowledge matters with regard to managerial innovativeness (Rodan and Galunic 2004). But maybe the combination of redundant versus non-redundant ties is different in public organizations, where individual competition is less important than collaboration? Perhaps too many entrepreneurs within organizations are not effective in ensuring internal knowledge-sharing processes? The New Public Governance literature on network management shows that the recognition of mutual dependency is a fundamental factor that supports the sharing of resources, capacities and capabilities across boundaries (Klijn and Koppenjan 2016). Recognition of interdependency implies that actors are able and willing to explore whether their interests can support each other instead of competing with each other (van Buuren and Loorbach 2009). So, what is the right prescription? This is central to the discussion of network theory and linking network structure with innovation capacity in a public sector context.

First, we introduce the research programme perspectives that form the core principles of social network analysis. Extensive literature reviews on organizational network research (see: Kilduff, Tsai and Hanke 2006; Balkundi and Kilduff 2006) suggest that at least four of the core social network research perspectives (or interrelated principles) found in the organizational network studies are relevant here, where innovation is a core mechanism that links network structure and performance together. Table 3.1 provides an overview of these four core research programmes, based on Powell (1990), Burt (1992, 2000, 2005), and Balkundi and Kilduff (2006).

Table 3.1 Four Core Perspectives in Social Network Studies

	1 *Relations*	2 *Embeddedness*	3 *Utility*	4 *Structure*
Core ideas:	Relations between individuals, organizational members or organizations (support)	Human behaviour is embedded in interpersonal relations, i.e., shaped by social environment (constraint)	Social relations generate trust and certain forms of value (social capital)	Patterns in which organizational members connect and create ties (structural holes, structural equivalence)
Innovation:	Innovators need informal relationships in order to govern in formal organizations	Innovators are constrained by their local environment	Innovators have a set of social connections that provide potential access to resources	Innovators actively focus on shaping their ego networks (creating ties that are diverse)

Relations

In this first perspective, the emphasis is on the importance of relations between organizational members, where it is social relations between individuals and not just individual attributes that are important explanatory factors (Granovetter 1983). As our ambition is to come one step closer to a systematic theory of public sector innovation (Teske and Schneider 1994), we are not only interested in individuals, but in their network interactions. Using this perspective, social network studies focus upon the creation of ties between people, and their individual organizational attributes (e.g., seniority in the hierarchy, membership of particular divisions), because these are likely to shape tie formation choices. Hence, innovators' ego networks within an organization are important focal points that direct us to other organizational factors, such as the importance of formal structures and positions.

Embeddedness

The second perspective is derived from the first and is termed embeddedness—i.e., human behaviour enmeshed in social network relations (Granovetter 1985). The idea of embeddedness was introduced by Karl Polanyi (1944) in his book *The Great Transformation* and later adopted by Granovetter (1985) in his work on the problem of embeddedness. It proposes that economic relations between firms, organizations and/or individuals are embedded in social relations and not necessarily formalized in abstract markets. Social networks are based on interpersonal communication that generates embedded resources such as social capital and trust relations. In other words, peoples' perceptions, how they see others, their beliefs, their trust in others and their world perspectives are *"reflected through the sets of embedded ties within which people are located"* (Balkundi and Kilduf 2006, 420). The idea of embeddedness is central to the idea of social networks, bringing with it the idea of constraints and obligations. Hence, would-be innovators cannot act alone, because they are surrounded and constrained by their networks.

Utility

The third driving social network research programme perspective is that networks generate social capital, and highlights the benefits of being connected to specific people who can provide access to desired resources (Lewis 2010). This perspective relates to the utility of particular connections (Burt 1992) or even to some form of economic return on the investment from a social relation to an individual (Burt 2000). At the organizational level, the social interaction of trust and interdependence between individuals creates resource 'capacity' or social capital. In this context, we may even talk about innovation capital. Connectivity in networks is important for successful innovators, but we know little about the social roles that they play (informally), which may potentially enable or constrain actions that spur innovation.

Structure

Finally, the fourth perspective is the structural approach, which is where network researchers look for patterns in order to understand the underlying structure, showing which people create network ties (Balkundi and Kilduff 2006, 421). Those who pay close attention to targeting their networks in order to extend their abilities (by seeking diverse ties in their relationships) are regarded as entrepreneurs, or innovators. Our study is premised on an assumption that a closer examination of ego networks (particular individuals and those people they are directly connected to) will contribute to understanding the relationship between these network structures and the public sector's innovative capacity. From the structural perspective, ego networks around important actors within an organization are a focal point for locating network structures that are likely to be related to innovation capacity.

We relied on these core network research perspectives to create the design of the social network analysis component of our study. In particular, and following the structural perspective, we used Ron Burt's (1992, 2000, 2005) and James Coleman's (1988) work. Burt's 'structural holes' is based on the idea that ego (the focal individual) benefits from brokering between disconnected alters. The concept of network closure, where ego is embedded in very dense, local structures (Coleman 1988), was also used. Coleman argues that a high number of linkages in a densely connected ego network is important to outcome performance; it lowers the risk of dependence as there are redundant ties, and more possible knowledge channels create visibility. We regard cohesion as important for innovation because it makes it easier to mobilize resources and diffuse new ideas. On the other hand, innovation emerges in environments where there is a high degree of openness and variety. Openness and diversity can be difficult to manage, and diversity (heterophily) might be hard to achieve within an organization or an organizational network that is rather homogeneous (Rogers 2003; Mulgan 2009). It seems that some kind of balance needs to be struck.

Ron Burt's work on constraints in networks suggests that a high level of redundancy within a group (internal closure), combined with a low level of redundancy beyond the group (external diversity), results in maximum performance in networks. However, there is no guarantee that a combination of internal closure and external diversity will actually achieve maximum performance, because structures only represent the potential associated with a particular network configuration. As Boari and Riboldazzi (2014) point out, the individual attributes, experience and motivations of people are important in shaping how they actually behave while occupying a specific position. Different actors in an identical network position (such as a structural hole, for example) might use that position to exploit their superior knowledge, or to broker relationships between actors who are not connected or to do neither of these things.

In this section, we have discussed some of the core principles of social network research. But the most important consideration for this book is to consider those concepts that have been shown to be mechanisms linking network structure to managerial performance, such as the innovativeness of individuals and groups.

In the social network literature, much empirical work shows a robust relationship between social network structure and individual leadership performance (Burt 1992, 2000). Network structure is surely important to innovativeness within organizations. Many senior public administrators recognize the importance of networks and actively take part in managing network relations, but there is a limited amount of research into the social structure of opportunities that facilitate and constrain action by managers in the public sector. This is one of the gaps that we sought to fill with our study. What kinds of network structures are likely to support innovation?

In summary, the network positions held by senior public administrators are likely to be crucial to innovation capacity. These positions might give them good access to diverse resources through their network ties, such as brokerage positions which would (according to Burt) enable them to innovate. Alternatively, they might occupy positions that have high levels of redundancy, and this will constrain their actions. Yet, close relationships that enable actors to work together have been acknowledged as important in the public administration literature. Network governance describes (and sometimes attempts to prescribe) how policy-making and governance occurs in contemporary societies where relationships between people/organizations are necessary in order to govern in fragmented and multi-level situations (Lewis 2011). Hence, the inclusion of an analysis of social networks is vital in regard to understanding innovation capacity.

Innovation Capacity and Networks

Innovation capacity in local governments is conceived of in this book as being related to structure, networks and leadership, as outlined in Chapter 1. The first two of these components—structure and networks—are distinguished between on the basis that the first of these refers to overarching governing structures and political and socioeconomic contexts, while the second refers to interpersonal interactions. Numerous aspects of structure and context are related to innovation capacity and these were discussed in Chapter 2. Network characteristics, a set of which are postulated to be positively related to innovation capacity (such as organizational slack, network diversity, external focus, recognition of dependency and higher levels of trust and openness) are the focus in this chapter. Furthermore, it has been argued that innovative ideas can come not just from those who are most central in the networks, but also from those who play brokerage roles across 'structural holes' (Burt 2000). We are especially interested in how networks contribute positively to shaping an organization's innovation capacity.

Grandori and Soda (1995) have argued that personal networks consist of exchanges of information that have hidden economic value. These networks are chosen by people and are often used to exchange confidential information. Granovetter (1985) studied such personal networks, arguing that they mobilize social capital, creating *"a pool of trusted contacts to choose from when needed"* (Moritati 2013, 17). Personal networks are fundamentally based on social connections between individuals, and hence, they consist of sets of people connected to other people by interpersonal ties of some kind (e.g., kinship, friendship, work relationships, advice seeking). The structure of social networks has a dynamic effect on innovation performance and on innovation outcomes.

An ego network example will suffice to illustrate the different connectivity of individuals within a network (see Figure 3.1.) The illustration is of a small sample taken from the Copenhagen network data (work and strategic information networks). It shows the connectivity amongst our respondents, which may be categorized as three types: type A (the central black nodes), type B (the central white nodes) and one that is playing the role of broker (the grey node) between the two. Both the A's and the B's have many outgoing ties, but how they are connected in the larger network (with incoming ties) is different. The type A's are more likely to gather and share

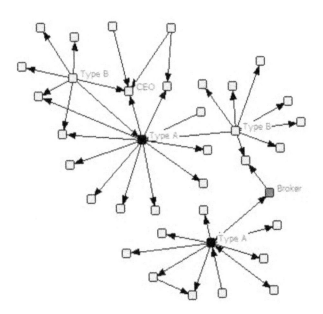

Figure 3.1 Different Patterns of Connectivity Around Egos

information faster and more efficiently than the B's because of these incoming ties. It cannot be claimed that type A is necessarily more of an innovator than type B, but the network position of the A's means that the diffusion of any innovative ideas and practices would occur more quickly if A's were involved (Rogers 2003).

The broker is the only person connecting the sub-network at the bottom of the figure to the rest of the network. This gives him/her a strong position in network terms, as s/he is bridging a structural hole in the network. This also points to the different positions of the otherwise similar A's—the A towards the top of the network has more ties that can be reached directly and is close to the CEO. The A towards the bottom can only reach the CEO and many other actors in this network through the broker.

In addition to ego network considerations, the transfer of knowledge among professionals in general is a key issue that has important organizational outcomes, e.g., for the diffusion of best practices, routines, experience and innovation (Carlile 2002; Tortoriello and Krackhardt 2010; Tasselli 2015). According to Barney (2001), these activities may affect our understanding of a resource-based view of the organization, enabling us to link the organizational capabilities of the organization to its competitive environment.

Other empirical network studies on high performers inside organizations show that these people are highly connected or central in the networks (many incoming and outgoing ties) and that the high performers have many connections to one another, while the low performers are less connected in general (see Hatala (2006) for a literature review). Previous studies have also shown that high performers tend to occupy network positions that bridge otherwise disconnected groups or clusters (Brass 1984; Podolny and Baron 1997; Mehra, Kilduff and Brass 2001)—in line with what Burt (1992) called structural holes. These are interesting results in relation to the findings of an Australian study on municipalities (Considine and Lewis 2007), as the same pattern that was found for being seen as an innovator is similar to that of high performers inside organizations.

Network studies are rapidly developing by being applied in new contexts or to explore new empirical phenomenon (Balkundi and Kilduf 2006) regarding high or low performers and applied to introduction programmes for new employees (Hatala 2006). The structures component of our framework (Chapter 2) is used to understand what broader elements either open up or close down pathways for innovation in public sector environments. The interpersonal network approach stands in contrast to this examination of governing structures and local contexts by introducing a more detailed examination of the relational networks that exist between individuals in organizations. How people are informally connected in a work environment is highly significant for understanding the transfer of information in general, and the creation and diffusion of innovation in particular.

Network Concepts and Innovation

Social network studies provide a large variety of concepts and measures that are useful for studying innovation. These include centrality, the strength of weak ties, openness and structural holes. Each of these are explained in the following sections, along with a discussion of trust and safety in relation to networks.

Centrality

Network centrality is a crucial network concept, and different types of centrality are relevant here. In-degree centrality is a measure of the importance or prestige of individuals within a network, as it rests on the number of direct nominations they have received from others (Wasserman and Faust 1994). This is relevant for our study, because it points to the 'go to' people who are likely to be crucial for dissemination of new ideas and thus innovation. Out-degree centrality is a measure of those who are active in sending out ties, and their role is related to the betweenness 'broker' measure. The measures of in-degree (receiving ties) and out-degree (sending ties) centrality, particularly in-degree, are used when there are asymmetric ties in a network to measure how many ties go through each node out of the maximum number of ties possible. It is an indicator that can help to locate those people who are regarded to be important.

Betweenness centrality is a measure of actors positioned between other actors who are not directly connected (Wasserman and Faust 1994) and is related to the idea of brokerage and structural holes discussed earlier. These actors are important in relation to innovation (which relies on openness and variety), and entrepreneurs are often regarded as being interested in seeking and benefiting from brokerage positions, which are associated with a high level of betweenness centrality (Burt 1992; Howells 2006; Boari and Riboldazzi 2014). According to Shi, Markoczy and Dess (2009), middle managers are likely to fill this position in strategic processes in organizations, and this was indeed found to be true in a study of city governments by Considine, Lewis and Alexander (2009). However, betweenness centrality can only be used on whole networks when network data is available for whole populations. It is a very sensitive centrality measure that can locate those who sit between important people (nodes). It can also be calculated for ego networks (associated with structural holes).

Previous studies of innovation networks in municipal governments have shown that in-degree centrality is related to hierarchical seniority and that innovators who are more adept at working through relationships outside formal structures are better able to get things done (Considine, Lewis and Alexander 2009; Lewis, Considine and Alexander 2011). Strategic information networks have been found to be important in locating innovators (Considine and Lewis 2007). Furthermore, innovator status seemed to depend more on being central in strategic information networks than on being central in advice networks (Considine and Lewis 2007).

The Strength of Weak Ties

Mutual dependency indicates something about the connectedness of the actors in a network: the positions that these actors take in the network and the 'ties' that connect them. This issue has been most famously addressed in terms of 'strong' and 'weak' ties (Granovetter 1973), or considerations of homophily and heterophily (McPherson and Smith-Lovin 1987). Heterophily is related to Granovetter's weak ties and to the idea of bridging social capital (Lewis 2010).

Strong and close ties imply that actors are similar in some way (homophily), which helps generate the trust that is necessary for the exchange and sharing of resources. Trust is often seen to be an asset of a network and a necessary condition for innovation (Powell 1991). But weak ties provide access to different resources (heterophily). Weak ties are often seen as important for innovation as they allow actors to break out of the 'groupthink' that can occur in situations where everyone is similar and tightly bound in closed networks (Burt 1992; Lewis 2010). Weak ties are therefore seen as bridges for connecting actors enmeshed in otherwise closed subgroups out of these. The link to innovation capacity is that social systems lacking in weak ties create an environment where new ideas will spread slowly, and where distinct subgroups will find it difficult to reach a compromise with the whole group (Granovetter 1983).

DiMaggio (1988) and Powell (1991) took the perspective a step further, suggesting that researchers look for isomorphism, which is found in social network terms where conformity rules, so that people take on the generally accepted norms, practice and routines. The social phenomenon that might follow this is that similar people clustering into a group become more alike over time, and that innovation decreases. This is often the case in organizations with a long history or strong traditions, or for people who remain in the same organization or same division for a long time (as sometimes happens for senior administrators). Mediators or moderators therefore play key roles in innovation capacity. These network roles are important to such organizations for sharing knowledge and information across divisions— because as Powell (1991) stressed, between the clusters (or divisions), there is heterogeneous knowledge and information, so when one mediates between organizations, divisions or groups, innovation tends to increase.

Empirical work on the role of mediators by Brass and Burkhardt (1993), Brass, Butterfield and Skaggs (1998), and Rodan (2010) examines the concept of social capital and the investigation of the underlying factors with regard to which people create network ties. More recently, scholars like Melamed and Simpson (2016) have empirically tested how values of ties affect their strength (strong ties) and the emergence of cooperation in dynamic relations (for example work relations). This result stands in contrast to the idea of strong ties being mostly present in stable relationships—instead, it points to the idea of tie strength being related to the presumed payoffs of cooperation.

In network studies, concepts of centrality are widely adopted, whereas the concept of heterophily is applied less often. Heterophily is related to the ability to gain different kinds of information (diversity), but also brokerage and closure measures, with regard to the ego networks around important individuals (Rogers 2003; Mulgan 2009). Such concepts are still under-utilized in organizational network studies and management applications. Recently, however, some scholars (e.g., Hollenbeck and Jamieson 2015) have begun advocating for their application to strategic human resource management in order to understand why some individuals are more integrated (better connected) in the organization than others, in order to strengthen their ability to create better value.

Openness

Innovation systems are often referred to as open systems (Chesborough 2003; Lundvall 2007). In both innovation systems and network theory, openness refers to the free flow of ideas, knowledge and experiences in an informal space with few restrictions on developing new and creative ideas (Foldy 2004). It is linked to the availability of multiple perspectives, related to the degree of heterophily amongst the people involved. Innovation is therefore alleged to emerge in environments where there is high openness and variety. Openness and diversity are hard to manage, and diversity (heterophily) might be hard to achieve within an organization or an organizational network that is rather homogeneous (similar with regard to certain attributes). Openness at both the individual and organizational levels is stressed as a predisposition for innovation to occur.

Both Granovetter (1973) and Burt (1992) made the point that innovation relies on the presence of groups with diverse perspectives, skills and resources, which stimulates creativity. People who have more diverse ties in their networks are more likely to have the capability to grasp or understand other people's ideas, even when these are very different from their own. Open-mindedness relies on individuals having social relations with people who do not necessarily share their ideas or beliefs but provide them with diversity, and hence a capacity to grasp and understand perspectives that are new to them. As mentioned above, both Powell (1990) and Burt (1992) emphasized that people who are alike tend to cluster, and that over time these clusters tend to share beliefs and perceptions and become even more alike, e.g., by building certain routines and habits. Mediators between clusters become important, because, between the clusters, the individuals are heterogeneous, and when somebody mediates between them, innovation seems to increase (Ricard 2015).

Structural Holes

As noted earlier, Burt (1992) labelled specific network configurations, where people have opportunities to act as brokers between unconnected others by dint of their network position, 'structural holes'. This gives an actor the role of *tertius gaudens*—a third party who benefits—and to use this position to play one competitor off against the other as long as the two others are not directly connected. Structural holes represent the absence of ties between an ego's alters. This is shown in the position of the broker in Figure 3.1. It relates to the empirical work on successful leaders, which has shown that leaders who have a higher proportion of structural holes are generally seen as higher performers (bringing more value to the organization) than those whose contacts (alters) are densely interconnected (Burt 2000).

Redundancy is a network measure of the diversity of network ties. If an actor has many ties that provide the same information, they have a high level of redundancy in their network. This is regarded as inefficient, because the same information could have been gained from a smaller number of contacts (Burt 2005). Effective size of ego networks is a second measure related to the brokerage potential held by certain individuals in networks: It is the number of alters that an ego has, minus the average number of ties that each alter has to other alters. In other words, it is ego's network size, reduced by its redundancy (Burt 1992).

Even though high performers in the organization have been linked to innovativeness to explain the underlying driving factors of network structure (why they create ties), it is not clear what the combination of strong and weak ties, structural holes and brokerage capacity offers the greatest opportunities for innovation at the organizational level (Powell and Grodall 2005). In addition, the factors that may provide individuals with an advantage regarding innovativeness may or may not be effective at the organizational level (Rodan 2010). However, Ahuja (2000) argues that the relationship between innovation capacity and network structure is contingent on personal relationships, and that what constitutes an enabling social structure for one specific type of action may well be disabling for others. Clearly, the form of action taken is likely to be contingent on what actors seek to gain by accessing the embedded resources available to them through networks. This brings us to the topic of social capital.

Social capital is an embedded resource that is created through ties between people within networks. While individuals can hold financial capital and human capital, social capital is only generated through connections with other people. The notion of trust is often related to social capital, and they are both often mentioned as factors that influence innovation (Walker 2008; Lewis 2010). However, it is important to separate distinct network configurations from the assumed values, emotions and actions arising from these.

Network structures provide the potential for individuals to exploit the opportunities associated with their own positions within these structures.

However, as we noted earlier in this chapter, two important authors on social capital have advanced very different views on how these opportunities might best be exploited. Burt's (2005) focus is on the competitive advantage to be gained by an individual who links otherwise unconnected actors or groups (structural holes). In contrast, Coleman (1988) emphasizes closure and density in networks in providing support and resources. This reflects their different orientations to the subject—Burt is interested in bridging and loose networks as providing opportunities for entrepreneurs (as the sources of innovation), while Coleman is interested in the cohesion of family support and its link to educational attainment (Lewis 2010). Burt's structural holes view sees ego as the broker who is able to achieve goals by accessing diverse information that others do not have. In contrast, Coleman's cohesive model, where almost everyone is directly connected to everyone else and not just to ego, has high redundancy.

Structurally, Burt's view situates ego at the centre of a star. Coleman's view envisages that many of an ego's alters will be directly connected not just to ego, but also to each other. Success in organizations (faster promotion, higher pay, perceived to be high performers) is related to structural holes theory by Burt (2000). The explanatory factors or mechanisms which he argues provide managers with performance benefits are:

- autonomy, being less constrained by their alters;
- entrepreneurial opportunities, as they broker between important connections;
- competition, as it is a structural position in which the leader's connections cannot conspire against him/her (ego) because they are disconnected;
- information arbitrage, where ego is a broker of heterogeneous information between alters and can gain access to different types of information; and
- innovativeness, where the interaction or the underlying driving factor behind why ego creates ties to support his/her abilities is the striving for creativity, which is stimulated by heterogeneous information and knowledge bases.

These five mechanisms have been the focus for many scholars in refining Burt's theory of structural holes (see, for example, Rodan 2010; Robins, Lewis and Wang 2012; Burt, Kilduff and Tasselli 2013) by linking knowledge heterogeneity, network structure and performance. Here, innovativeness arises because of the heterogeneity in the knowledge base (see also former empirical studies of this: Galunic and Rodan 1998; Rodan and Galunic 2004; Burt 2005) and contributes to creating an advantage that allows ego to ensure high innovativeness and thus high performance in an organization. An alternative explanation is the classical notion that 'knowledge is power' and that the heterogeneous information is a valuable asset to trade with in exchange for superior knowledge or new information, and not necessarily or intentionally, a desire to be involved in innovation. However, playing a social network role as mediator in sharing information or communication is as important to innovation as having heterogeneity in the knowledge base (Brass 1984; Brass and Burkhardt 1993; Brass, Butterfield and Skaggs 1998).

Before moving on to a consideration of trust and safety, it should be remembered that we talk about innovation capacity in relation to potentials of the network structure, not in relation to the actual implementation of innovations. There are, of course, many other factors involved in why new ideas are or are not created and implemented.

Trust and Safety

Many scholars have argued that trust has a beneficial effect on collaboration or cooperation in forming alliances (Lundvall 1992; Huxham and Vangen 2005). Trust is often related to the expectation that other actors will not behave in an opportunistic or self-seeking way if the opportunity should arise (Deakin and Michie 1997; Deakin and Wilkinson 1998; Nooteboom 2002). Trust therefore becomes especially important in situations where there is a high level of uncertainty, vulnerability or risk—and hence, it is related to innovation and the notion of creative destruction. In the business literature, developing new products is characterized by exactly these conditions in the formation of innovation networks (Parker and Vaidya 2001).

However, not many studies have explicitly examined levels of trust in specific social network ties (Lewis 2010). In fact, trust is often regarded as arising naturally from network ties between individuals. The notion of trust is also often related to social capital, which, as was discussed earlier, is a resource that can be accessed through ties within networks (Lewis 2010). But again, this is confusing the potential for network ties to create trust, with the mere existence of ties.

The explanation for the relation between trust and performance in the literature is usually that the exchange of information and especially innovative ideas is facilitated if actors trust each other. And networks in which ideas are exchanged more intensively are generally thought to have more innovative capacity. As noted above, both weak and strong ties can be functional here. Weak ties can facilitate innovation by linking loosely coupled actors, thus creating opportunities to bring in new perspectives, new ideas and alternative resources. Strong ties between actors can provide a platform on which high levels of trust can be built. This trust is important for the creation of an environment in which people feel safe.

In work situations with a high level of uncertainty, the need to learn is translated to individuals' need to make sense of what is happening around them and the need to take action. At the group level in the organization, a study by Edmondson (1999) showed that shared beliefs, values and perceptions provide individuals with psychological safety that enables them to learn in situations with the high levels of uncertainty that are associated with change and innovation. It enables them to share ideas, take action and fail without embarrassment in front of their colleagues. Edmondson (1999) carried out her research by examining 51 manufacturing teams. She examined the perceptions amongst colleagues about whether the team they work with would provide a safe environment for their individual risk taking at work in situations of uncertainty. Results showed a positive relationship between feelings of safety (that the team would be supportive in case of failures or when learning on the job) and team performance.

The idea of psychological safety at work relates to the concept of a safe haven and particular network structures—either with dense interconnections or strong ties among team members (related to Coleman's theory). Such network structures are seen to provide individuals with psychological safety when they *"need to ask questions, seek help, and tolerate mistakes in the face of uncertainty—while team members and other colleagues watch"* (Edmondson 1999, 380). This notion is very much related to the learning-by-doing concept and is crucial to the idea that innovation requires risk taking and an organizational willingness to tolerate failure. It is also clearly related to the level of trust between individuals: Without trust, it is unlikely that people will feel safe in relation to being able to fail.

Competition is generally seen as something good for innovation in the New Public Management literature, but previous social network studies found that when competition is reduced, firms, organizations and people are more likely to activate their relevant capabilities for complex problem solving (Katila, Rosenberger and Eisenhardt 2008). In addition, Uzzi (1997) found when studying garment firms that when people have trust in one another, they are more likely to share information and engage in complex problem solving where they activate their dissimilar capabilities (Davis and Eisenhardt 2011). Trust and safety are particularly important concepts for public sector innovation, because risk taking in public sector organizations is often frowned upon because of the importance of public accountability and the wise use of scarce public funds.

Conclusions

It is often said that diversity and innovation go hand in hand, while cohesion or groupthink stifle innovation. The idea of openness in social networks refers to the free flow of ideas, knowledge and experiences in an informal space with few restrictions on developing new and creative ideas (Foldy 2004). Managing innovation then seems especially related to the creation of organizational slack—safe havens and informal spaces. However, it seems important to include the right mix of diversity and cohesion in order to ensure both innovation and the accountability and legality that public bureaucracy must provide.

This chapter provides us with the concepts and measures we need for an examination of networks and innovation capacity. The preceding discussion indicates that while there are several theoretical and observed associations between network concepts and innovation capacity, the relationship is not a straightforward one. Indeed, it seems that it is likely some mixture of centrality, homophilous and heterophilous ties, brokerage, and trust and safety that provides the necessary network capacity for innovation. It is also apparent that certain types of networks might be important for specific innovation processes, but it is unlikely to be the case that there is a 'one size fits all' ideal type that supports innovation of all types and in all circumstances.

However, managing innovation seems especially related to the creation of organizational slack, openness and diversity in information, safe havens, locating the innovators and, finally, informal spaces that allow people to meet and discuss freely without the constraint of a strict formal political culture or hierarchy. It is linked to the availability of a variety of perspectives related to the degree of heterophily amongst the people involved and to the embedded resources that can be accessed through networks. So, while there is a link between network concepts and innovation, it is not straightforward. For public sector innovation to be supported, we would expect that it is a matter of the appropriate blend of formal and informal structures, diversity and redundancy, and safety, that provide the necessary conditions for innovation.

In Chapter 7, we explain how we gathered networking and ego network data from politicians and administrators in local governments and how we performed the empirical analysis, and we also present the results. To answer questions about the links between innovation capacity and network structures and sub-structures, we constructed network maps and analysed their structures for the three city governments. The link between networks and innovation capacity are examined in the concluding chapters of the book, where we test the importance of networks to innovation capacity (Chapter 9) and, finally, make some claims about the kinds of social network structures that appear to support public sector innovation (Chapter 10).

References

Ahuja, Gautam. 2000. "Collaboration networks, structural holes and innovation: A longitudinal study." *Administrative Science Quarterly* 45: 425–55.

Balkundi, Prasad, and Martin Kilduff. 2006. "The ties that lead: A social network approach to leadership." *The Leadership Quarterly* 17(4): 419–39.

Barney, Jay B. 2001. "Resource-based theories of competitive advantage: A ten-year retrospective on the resource based view." *Journal of Management* 27(6): 643–50.

Boari, Cristina, and Federico Riboldazzi. 2014. "How knowledge brokers emerge and evolve: The role of actors' behaviour." *Research Policy* 43(4): 683–95.

Borgatti, Stephen P., Martin G. Everett, and Linton C. Freeman. 2002. *Ucinet for Windows: Software for social networks analysis.* Harvard, MA: Analytic Technologies.
Brass, Daniel J. 1984. "Being in the right place: A structural analysis of individual influence in an organization." *Administrative Science Quarterly* 29(4): 518–39.
Brass, Daniel J., and Marlene E. Burkhardt. 1993. "Potential power and power use: An investigation of structure and behavior." *The Academy of Management Journal* 36(3): 441–70.
Brass, Daniel J., Kenneth D. Butterfield, and Bruce C. Skaggs. 1998. "Relationships and unethical behavior: A social network perspective." *Academy of Management Review* 23(1): 14–32.
Brass, Daniel J., Joseph Galaskiewicz, Henrich R. Greve, and Wenpin Tsai. 2004. "Taking stock of networks and organizations: A multilevel perspective." *Academy of Management Journal* 47(5): 795–817.
Burt, Ronald S. 1992. *Structural holes: The social structure of competition.* Cambridge, MA: Harvard University Press.
Burt, Ronald S. 2000. "The network structure of social capital." In *Research in organizational behaviour*, edited by Robert I. Sutton and Barry M. Staw, 345–423. Greenwich CT: JAI Press.
Burt, Ronald S. 2005. *Brokerage and closure: An introduction to social capital.* Oxford: Oxford University Press.
Burt, Ronald S., Marti Kilduff, and Stefano Tasselli. 2013. "Social network analysis: Foundations and frontiers of advantage." *Annual Review of Psychology* 64: 527–47.
Carlile, Paul R. 2002. "A pragmatic view of knowledge and boundaries: Boundary objects in new product development." *Organization Science* 13(4): 442–55.
Chesborough, Henry. 2003. Open Innovation: The new imperative for creating and profiting from technology. Boston, MA: Harvard Business School Press.
Coleman, James S. 1988. "Social capital in the creation of human capital." *American Journal of Sociology* 94 (supplement): 95–120.
Considine, Mark, and Jenny M. Lewis. 2007. "Innovation and innovators inside government: From institutions to networks." *Governance* 20(4): 581–607.
Considine, Mark, Jenny M. Lewis, and Damon Alexander. 2009. *Networks, innovation and public policy: Politicians, bureaucrats and the pathways to change inside government.* Basingstoke: Palgrave Macmillan.
Conway, Steve. 1995. "Informal boundary-spanning communication in the innovation process." *Technology Analysis and Strategic Management* 7(3): 327–42.
Davis, Jason P., and Kathleen M. Eisenhardt. 2011. "Rotating leadership and collaborative innovation: Recombination processes in symbiotic relationships." *Administrative Science Quarterly* 56(2): 159–201.
Deakin, Simon, and Jonathan Michie. 1997. "Contracts and competition: An introduction." *Cambridge Journal of Economics* 21(2): 121–5.
Deakin, Simon, and Frank Wilkinson. 1998. "Contract law and the economics of interorganizational trust." In *Trust within and between organization*, edited by Chistel Lane and Reihnhard Bachman, 146–72. New York: Oxford University Press.

DiMaggio, Paul. 1988. "Interest and agency in institutional theory." In *Institutional patterns and culture*, edited by Lynne G. Zucker, 3–22. Cambridge, MA: Ballinger Publishing Company.

Edmondson, Amy. 1999. "Psychological safety and learning behaviour in work teams." *Administrative Science Quarterly* 44(2): 350–83.

Foldy, Erica Gabriell. 2004. "Learning from diversity." *Public Administration Review* 64(5): 529–38.

Galunic, D. Charles, and Simon A. Rodan. 1998. "Resource recombinations in the firm: Knowledge structures and the potential for Schumpeterian innovation." *Strategic Management Journal* 19(12): 1193–1201.

Grandori, Anna, and Giuseppe Soda. 1995. "Inter-firm networks: Antecedents, mechanisms and forms." *Organizational Studies* 16(2): 183–214.

Granovetter, Mark. 1973. "The strength of weak ties." *American Journal of Sociology* 78(6): 1360–80.

Granovetter, Mark. 1983. "The strength of weak ties: A network theory revisited." *Sociological Theory* 1: 201–233.

Granovetter, Mark. 1985. "Economic action and social structure: The problem of embeddedness." *American Journal of Sociology* 91(3): 481–510.

Hatala, John-Paul. 2006. "Social network analysis in human resource development: A new methodology." *Human Resource Development Review* 5(1): 45–71.

Hollenbeck, John R., and Bradley B. Jamieson. 2015. "Human capital, social capital, and social network analysis: Implications for strategic human resource management." *The Academy of Management Perspectives* 29(3): 370–85.

Howells, Jeremy. 2006. "Intermediation and the role of intermediaries in innovation." *Research Policy* 35(5): 715–28.

Huxham, Chris., and Sev Vangen. 2005. *Managing to collaborate: The theory and practice of collaborative advantage*. London: Routledge.

Jones, Oswarld, and Martin Beckinsale. 1999. *Analysing the innovation process: Networks, micropolitics and structural change*. Research Paper 9919. Birmingham: Aston Business School. Accessed 7 July 2016. http://citeseerx.ist.psu.edu/viewdoc/download?doi=10.1.1.200.2735&rep=rep1&type=pdf.

Jones, Oswald, Steve Conway, and Fred Steward. 1998. "Introduction: Social interaction and innovation networks." *International Journal of Innovation Management* 2(2 Special issue): 123–36.

Katila, Riitta, Jeff D. Rosenberger, and Kathleen M. Eisenhardt. 2008. "Swimming with sharks: Technology ventures, defense mechanisms, and corporate relationships." *Administrative Science Quarterly* 53(2): 295–332.

Kilduff, Martin, Wenpin Tsai, and Ralph Hanke. 2006. "A paradigm too far? A dynamic stability reconsideration of the social network research program." *Academy of Management Review* 31(4): 1031–48.

Klijn, Erik Hans, and Joop F.M. Koppenjan. 2016. *Governance networks in the public sector*. Oxon: Routledge.

Lewis, Jenny M. 2010. *Connecting and cooperating: Social capital and public policy*. Sydney: UNSW Press.

Lewis, Jenny M. 2011. "The future of network governance research: Strength in diversity and synthesis." *Public Administration* 89(4): 1221–34.

Lewis, Jenny M., Damon Alexander, and Mark Considine. 2013. "Policy networks and innovation." In *Handbook of innovation in public services*, edited by Stephen Osborne and Louise Brown, 360–74. Cheltenham: Edward Elgar.

Lewis, Jenny M., Mark Considine, and Damon Alexander. 2011. "Innovation inside government: The importance of networks." In *Innovation in the public sector: Linking capacity and leadership*, edited by Victor Bekkers, Jurian Edelenbos, and Bram Steijn, 107–33. Houndsmills: Palgrave McMillan.

Love, James H. 1999. *Patterns of networking in the innovation process: A comparative study of the UK, Germany and Ireland*. Research Paper 9913. Birmingham: Aston Business School. Accessed 7 Jul 2016. http://citeseerx.ist.psu.edu/viewdoc/download?rep=rep1&type=pdf&doi=10.1.1.195.4317.

Lundvall, Bent-Åke. 1992. *National systems of innovation: Towards a theory of innovation and interactive learning*. London: Pinter Press.

Lundvall, Bengt-Åke. 2007. "National innovation systems—Analytical concept and development tool." *Industry and Innovation* 14(1): 95–119.

McPherson, J. Miller, and Lynn Smith-Lovin. 1987. "Homophily in voluntary organizations: Status distance and the composition of face-to-face groups." *American Sociological Review* 52(3): 370–79.

Mehra, Ajay, Martin Kilduff, and Daniel J. Brass. 2001. "The social networks of high and low self-monitors: Implications for workplace performance." *Administrative Science Quarterly* 46(1): 121–46.

Melamed, David, and Brent Simpson. 2016. "Strong ties promote the evolution of cooperation in dynamic networks." *Social Networks* 45(2016): 32–44.

Merluzzia, Jennifer, and Ronald S. Burt. (2013). "How many names are enough? Identifying network effects with the least set of listed contacts". *Social Networks* 35(3): 331–7.

Moritati, Marzia. 2013. *Systemic aspect of innovation and design: The perspective of collaborative networks*. London: Springer.

Mulgan, Geoff. 2009. *The art of public strategy: Mobilizing power and knowledge for the common good*. Oxford: Oxford University Press.

Nelson, Richard R. 1993. *National systems of innovation*. Oxford: Blackwell.

Newman, Janet, John Raine, and Chris Skelcher. 2001. "Transforming local government: Innovation and modernization." *Public Money & Management* 21(2): 61–8.

Nooteboom, Bart. 2002. *Trust: Forms, foundations, functions, failures and figures*. Cheltenham: Edward Elgar.

Parker, David, and Kirit Vaidya. 2001. "An economic perspective on innovation networks." In *Social interaction and organisational change: Aston perspectives on innovation network*, edited by Oswald Jones, Steve Conway, and Fred Steward, 125–63. London: Imperial College Press.

Pittaway, Luke, Maxine Robertson, Kamal Munir, David Denyer, and Andy Neely. 2004. "Networking and innovation: A systematic review of the evidence." *International Journal of Management Reviews* 5/6(3&4): 137–68.

Podolny, Joel M., and James N. Baron. 1997. "Resources and relationships: Social networks and mobility in the workplace." *American Sociological Review* 62(5): 673–93.

Polanyi, Karl. 1944. *The great transformation: The political and economic origins of our time*. Boston, MA: Beacon Press.

Powell, Walter W. 1990. "Neither market nor hierarchy: Network forms of organization." *Research in Organizational Behavior* 12(1990): 295–336.

Powell, Walter W. 1991. "Expanding the scope of institutional analysis." In *The new institutionalism in organizational analysis*, edited by Walter W. Powell and Paul J. DiMaggio, 183–203. Chicago: University of Chicago Press.

Powell, Walter W., and Stine Grodal. 2005. "Networks of innovators." In *The oxford handbook of innovation*, edited by Jan Fagerberg, David C. Mowery, and Richard R. Nelson, 56–85. Oxford: Oxford University Press.

Ricard, Lykke Margot. 2015. "Coping with system failure: Why connectivity matters to innovation policy." In *The evolution of economic and innovation systems (part of the series Economic Complexity and Evolution)*, edited by Adreas Pyka and John Foster, 251–76. Switzerland: Springer International Publishing.

Robins, Garry, Jenny M. Lewis, and Peng Wang. 2012. "Statistical network analysis for analysing policy networks." *Policy Studies Journal* 40(3): 357–401.

Rodan, Simon. 2010. "Structural holes and managerial performance: Identifying the underlying mechanisms." *Social Networks* 32(3): 168–79.

Rodan, Simon, and Charles Galunic. 2004. "More than network structure: How knowledge heterogeneity influences managerial performance and innovativeness." *Strategic Management Journal* 25(6): 541–62.

Rogers, Everett M. 2003. *Diffusion of innovations* (5th edition). New York: Free Press.

Shi, Weilei, Livia Markoczy, and Gregory G. Dess. 2009. "The role of middle management in the strategy process: Group affiliation, structural holes, and tertius lungens." *Journal of Management* 35(6): 1453–80.

Spiro, Emma S., Ryan M. Acton, and Carter T. Butts. 2013. "Extended structures of mediation: Re-examining brokerage in dynamic networks." *Social Networks* 35(1): 130–43.

Tasselli, Stefano. 2015. "Social networks and inter-professional knowledge transfer: The case of healthcare professionals." *Organization Studies* 36(7): 841–72.

Teske, Paul, and Mark Schneider. 1994. "The bureaucratic entreprenueur: The case of city managers." *Public Administration Review* 54(4): 331–40.

Tortoriello, Marco, and David Krackhardt. 2010. "Activating cross-boundary knowledge: The role of Simmelian ties in the generation of innovations." *Academy of Management Journal* 53(1): 167–81.

Uzzi, Brian. 1997. "Social structure and competition in inter-firm networks: The paradox of embeddedness." *Administrative Science Quarterly* 42(1): 35–67.

van Buuren, Arwin, and Derk Loorbach. 2009. "Policy innovation in isolation?" *Public Management Review* 11(3): 375–92.

Walker, Richard M. 2008. "An empirical evaluation of innovation types and organizational and environmental characteristics: Towards a configuration framework." *Journal of Public Administration Research and Theory* 18(4): 591–615.

Wasserman, Stanley, and Katherine Faust. 1994. *Social network analysis: Methodsand applications*. Cambridge: Cambridge University Press.

4 Leadership and Innovation

Public innovation does not happen by itself: It has to be initiated, created through interactions between various actors and types of knowledge, then fostered and, most importantly, implemented and adopted by the users. Creating new ways of 'doing' implies more complex ways of learning (Lundvall 2007). It follows that leadership is thought to be crucial for innovation. However, the questions of which leadership qualities are most likely to foster public innovation have seldom been addressed. There is a vast literature on charismatic or transformational leadership, as we will see in this chapter, and this is linked to innovation. However, most of this research has been conducted on private firms, and it generally has very little to do with what we know about linking innovation capacity to leadership activities and conceptual styles in the public sector (Bekkers, Edelenbos and Steijn 2011).

Leadership is the third component of our analytical framework of innovation capacity. As we have argued in earlier chapters, governance structures and informal networks are important in shaping any organizations' innovation capacity. But leadership is also crucial. Hence, in this chapter we move from the more (formal and informal) structural considerations to a consideration of the agency of leaders in these organizations and the kinds of leadership qualities that are seen as important for supporting innovation. If leadership is essential for innovation, then the question of which leadership qualities are necessary to stimulate and implement innovation is an important question in practice and for research (see Howell and Avolio 1993; van Wart 2012; Tummers and Knies 2013).

The leadership literature contains a staggering variety of theoretical perspectives on leadership (both public and private). A vast number of leadership qualities, activities and styles are mentioned. Some authors stress the initiating and visionary roles of leaders. Leaders are people who take the initiative, use their authority to foster change and implement those changes. This is related to transformational leadership, which dates back to Bass (1985, 1997) who conceptualized this style as a combination of components: inspirational, motivational, intellectual stimulation, individualized consideration and idealized influence (charisma) (Leong and Fischer 2011). The transformational leadership activities that belong to this style are a combination of creating a sense of urgency, deciding on the vision (and strategy) and making it happen. This leadership concept is very much based on a top-down image of the organization, as has been argued by van Wart (2012). Other authors place more emphasis on the facilitating role and activities of leaders. Leaders are people who encourage and motivate others to participate in the innovation process. In this perspective, aims and processes are not determined by the leader but developed in collaboration with others (Moss Kanter 1983).

Much of the leadership literature is internally focused (within organizations) and has a strong organizational and psychological flavour. There is little relationship between this and the fast growing literature on governance, networks and collaboration that has dominated public administration research in the past 20 years. In that literature, as we saw in Chapter 2, there is an emphasis on the wicked character of policy problems and the resource dependencies between (public and private and semi-private) organizations (Mandell 1990; Kickert, Klijn and Koppenjan 1997; Pierre and Peters 2000). It also stresses that collaboration is needed to achieve good policy solutions and outcomes, and has a different perspective on leadership than the more traditional, and mainly intra-organizational, leadership perspectives. In this chapter we provide an overview of leadership perspectives and place the network governance literature within this. We also examine how these different types might support public sector innovation.

Leadership Perspectives and Innovation: A Theoretical Overview

Different perspectives tend to emphasize different activities that are essential to leadership and also have different perspectives on innovation. In his overview on public leadership, van Wart identifies eleven different leadership styles with different leadership activities (van Wart 2012). He distinguishes styles like a directive style, a participative style, a supportive style, a charismatic style, a strategic style and a collaborative style. Other authors, however, distinguish quite different leadership styles or perspectives, and we consider a number of these in the following discussion.

A Conceptualization of Leadership Perspectives

In general, a distinction is made between more rational or transactional leadership perspective on the one hand, and transformational leadership perspective on the other. Transactional and rational leaderships perspectives tend to stress the exchange between leaders and followers (and the self-interests that are connected to these relationships) but also the monitoring and planning processes that have to be defined (van Wart 2012, 89). While transformational leadership perspectives share an emphasis on goals and performance, the rational/transactional perspective pays more attention to the charismatic characteristics of leaders and the symbolic processes needed to create change and transform organizations (Bass 1985, 1997; van Wart 2012).

Besides these two dominant perspectives, many authors also distinguish a more relational leadership perspective, sometimes called authentic leadership (Zehndorfer 2014), that emphasizes personal relations with followers and subordinates, where leaders support and help subordinates (van Dierendonck 2010; van Wart 2012; Tummers and Knies 2013).

Recently, a number of authors have added a new leadership style that places greater emphasis on how public organizations change in response to turbulent environments. This perspective tends to focus more on the path dependency of (public) organizations on the one hand, and their operational capacity building to promote change on the other (Piening 2013). We may call this a more entrepreneurial perspective on leadership. It relates to the transformational leadership perspective but is somewhat different: We argue that it most strongly resembles a neo-Schumpeterian entrepreneurial leadership style that is willing to take risks and to learn from mistakes in the search for new knowledge.

But underneath these very broad agreements about leadership theories and leadership styles, there are many significant differences in the literature. Thus, where one author includes a certain theory, for example, the leaders-member exchange theory (LMX theory) in the transactional style of leadership (van Wart 2012, 67), other authors categorize this under the relational style, which they contrast with the transactional and transformational leadership styles (Tummers and Knies 2013). This shows not only the variety in leadership theories but also the contrasting views about the demarcations and identities of various leadership theories.

Leadership and Governance

The mainstream leadership literature seems to largely ignore the leadership qualities and perspective that are emphasized in the literature on collaboration and network governance in the public sector. Much leadership literature pays very little attention to the fast growing inter-organizational collaboration and network governance perspectives that are now widespread in public administration research (Kickert, Klijn and Koppenjan 1997; Rhodes 1997; Pierre 2000). In his overview, van Wart spends about three of the 334 pages of his book on leadership discussing collaborative or network leadership. In another overview by Zehndorfer (2014), there is no mention at all of collaborative or network leadership. As we argued in Chapter 3, network governance is widespread and is likely to be particularly important for innovation.

Network governance is not really captured by the distinction between transactional and transformational leadership styles, nor by the relational/interpersonal leadership or entrepreneurial perspectives. The network governance perspective recognizes that actors have different values when framing problems and that none of the actors owns/possesses all the resources to tackle the problem by themselves. It follows that if actors have different perceptions about the nature of problems and preferences of the desirable solutions to them, then problem solving processes involve complicated negotiations in networks of (interdependent) actors. Networks require very specific leadership qualities and actions (Gage and Mandell 1990; Kickert, Klijn and Koppenjan 1997). Network theories of management and leadership tend to downplay the role of strong leaders and instead focus on collaborative leaders who are able to unite actors and explore content that is acceptable to all the involved stakeholders (Koppenjan and Klijn 2004; McGuire and Agranoff 2011). Hence, governance and network theories add another perspective of leadership that relates new ideas to more open processes of interaction.

Five Leadership Perspectives and Their Similarities and Differences

While the transactional and transformational perspectives are, in principle, general theories that have been *applied* to the public sector, the network governance perspective has been specifically *developed* to study the public sector. There is a clear contrast between transactional and transformational perspectives on leadership where (public) innovations are seen as being achieved by visionary leaders who initiate change, compared to network governance. Entrepreneurial perspectives focus more on the contingencies and strategic actions of leaders. In network governance, innovations are seen as produced by leaders who engage the necessary stakeholders in the search for new solutions. Interpersonal leadership lies somewhere in between these and tends to see innovation as resting on empowering people.

These considerations led us to identify five perspectives on public leadership that have special relevance for the topic of innovation: a transactional style, a transformational style, an interpersonal style, a network governance style and an entrepreneurial style. We argue that each of these perspectives will have different views on the following:

- The leadership picture: What is the role of leaders, and from where do they gain their legitimacy?
- Main activities: What kinds of activities are the most important for leaders to perform?
- Strategic direction: How is direction achieved in leadership—e.g., by setting goals, or by creating joint learning activities?
- Relationships with stakeholders: How are leaders' relationships with other actors (followers, other stakeholders etc.) viewed? Are these relationships seen as predominantly instrumental or as more cooperative?
- How is innovation viewed?

There are some striking differences between the five leadership perspectives, but there are also overlaps between the conceptual styles. In summary,
when it comes to the top-down character of leadership, the transactional,
transformational and entrepreneurial perspectives all appear to be quite
similar. The network governance and interpersonal perspectives are alike in
the sense that they both emphasize a more supportive style. However, the
network governance perspective has a strong focus on inter-organizational
collaboration, while the interpersonal perspective has a more intra-organizational focus and links to human relations management. In the following
sections, we further elaborate on these five leadership perspectives, based
around their different views on the five dimensions outlined above.

Transactional and Transformational Leadership

Leadership theories began with trait theories and skills theories (van Wart
2012; Zehndorfer 2014). Both of these strongly focus on a leader's personal-
ity (see: van Wart (2012, 59). In these rational theories, leaders are directive,
and it is their personal qualities that make the difference in their effectiveness. These qualities are regarded as more or less universal, meaning they
are thought to work in every situation. The leaders work in organizations
where their task or deliverables are well defined. It is a purely transactional
approach, which fits the rationality of the mainstream and more classical
management theories (Burrell and Morgan 1979).

Transactional Leadership

Traditional theories of leadership have a strong top-down character, assum-
ing that there is one best way to lead which is more directive in style (van
Wart 2012). Transactional theories therefore build on strong rational approaches but pay more attention to the relationship between leaders and followers. Although in transactional approaches, the leader is still presented as
a supervisor who should be leading people in the organization, more attention is paid to the reward structure and legitimacy of the leader. The reward
structure is mostly presented as a more or less rational process in which
calculative motivations are very important (Tummers and Knies 2013).

Thus, leaders motivate people in the organization to achieve good performance through payment or other reward systems. And it is important for
leaders to install stable systems of rewards and monitoring to facilitate good
performance. It is the leader who initiates the goals and the direction. The
transactional leadership perspective tends to look at different conditions for
a certain style (directive, supporting) in terms of task clarity, subordinate
training and so on. Attuned to these conditions, leaders are meant to align
their incentives to guide subordinates towards organizational goals.

In the transactional perspective, therefore, leaders rely mostly on rational incentives and strategies to obtain the desired performance, and the

relationship between leaders and other actors is characterized by a more or less clear hierarchy. Leaders try to steer by clarifying goals, monitoring the behaviour of subordinates and emphasizing task-oriented domains (van Wart 2012). In general, transaction theories are less focused on innovation and more on 'normal performance', which is a criticism aimed at them by transformational scholars (see: Avolio, Waldman and Yammarino (1991)). It is clear that innovation in a transactional perspective stems from leaders with the ability to steer and motivate employees towards the desired goals.

Transformational Leadership

The transformational perspective on leadership, first described by Bass (1985), builds on earlier transaction perspectives that emphasize the relationship between leaders and followers but adds a supportive style to complement the directive style and is more focused on excellent performance and change (van Wart 2012). Tichy and Devanna begin their book on transformational leadership by saying: "Transformational leadership is about change, innovation, and entrepreneurship" (Tichy and Devanna 1990, xii). Howell and Avolio claim: "A central thesis of Bass's (1985) theory is that transformational leadership goes beyond exchanging inducements for desired performance by developing, intellectually stimulating, and inspiring followers to transcend their own self-interests for a higher collective purpose, mission, or vision" (Howell and Avolio 1993, 891). Many scholars of the transformational style also emphasize that transformational leadership is not so much replacing transactional leadership but is performed in addition to it, so transformational leaders will also display transactional leadership behaviour (Howell and Avolio 1993).

Transformational leadership finds its inspiration in the fact that organizations function in a dynamic and rapidly changing world and need constant change and excellence to cope with that environment. Avolio, Waldman and Yammarino write, "The race to develop new technology has underscored the importance for organizations to develop a workforce that not only is responsive to change, but also promotes change to remain competitive" (Avolio, Waldman and Yammarino 1991, 9). This requires something particular of a leader: "To be successful, leaders will have to operate as change agents, fulfilling the role that has been labelled the transformational leader".

This style strongly emphasizes that the leader must change the organization, and the people in it, in order to achieve the necessary goals. This means that leaders should identify the key challenges and needs for change (and recognize opportunities), formulate a vision, change the institutional design of the organization (to make change happen by creating the conditions for it) and put the right incentives in place to overcome employee self-interest (see: Bass (1985, 1997); Leong and Fischer (2011); van Wart (2012)). Regarding the last activity, a supportive style is needed in which people in organizations are encouraged to cooperate with the innovation process (van

Wart 2012). Leaders must inspire people, motivate them to look beyond their individual interests and engage them in furthering the groups' and the organization's goals (see Box 4.1).

Box 4.1: The Four I's of Transformational Leadership

Transformational leadership literature sees transformational leaders as people that display four characteristics (the four I's; see Avolio, Waldman and Yammarino 1991; Zehndorfer 2014):

1 Individualized considerations; transformational leaders pay special attention to individual employees and their needs is being emphasized in the transformational leadership literature. This includes things like addressing individual concerns, stimulating individual confidence and acting as mentor. This does still have a slightly instrumental character as the formulation of Avolio et al shows where they say: "Transformational; leaders attempt to remove unnecessary "roadblocks" in the system that inhibit both the development of followers and their achieving optimal performance"(Avolio, Waldman and Yammarino 1991: 13).

2 Intellectual stimulation; leaders should change the way people think about problems and encourage people to look at problems in a new way but also stimulate them so that new ideas are actually considered.

3 Inspirational motivation; this involves specifying a mission and visons that inspire people and leads them away from self-interest and towards the needs and goals of the collective (Zehndorfer 2014). This can be done, for instance, by specifying and promoting professional development of employees, or by presenting challenging views and images of the future.

4 Idealised influence; this characteristic emphasizes that leaders should show followers that they can accomplish objectives. This characteristic very much focuses on the charisma of the leader to create a belief in the collective goals and objectives.

The four I's together form the ideal picture of the transformational leader. A person who with his charismatic performance inspires people, shows them the collective interest, creates fresh thinking and pays attention to individual people to make this all happen.

As this discussion shows, the transformational style places the leader in the centre—the charismatic person around whom changes and performance take place. Although there is a supportive element in the theories about transformational leadership, the leader is still seen as central and leadership is still regarded as a top-down activity. "Generally, transformational leadership is exhibited to a greater degree at the top end of organizations" (Avolio, Waldman and Yammarino 1991, 10).

Innovation is a core initiative of transformational leaders. Innovation is a necessary condition for survival in a competitive world, and by looking at new ways to do things and stimulate creative thinking, leaders must transformation organizations. As a consequence, innovation is seen as dependent upon strong charismatic leaders who initiate change and thereby make a difference to the structure and operation of the organization.

Interpersonal and Entrepreneurial Leadership

The transactional and transformational leadership perspectives elaborated above are clearly connected to each other, with transformational leadership building upon transactional perspectives. This is less the case in regard to the interpersonal and entrepreneurial perspectives. While the first has a strong human relations flavour and emphasizes the empowerment of employees, the second has a more strategic orientation and focuses on how leaders can shape the organization and their performance within the given (institutional) context.

Interpersonal Leadership

In contrast to transformational leadership theories, interpersonal or relationship-based theories of leadership emphasize how leaders interact with their employees and how they manage these relationships to get the best out of them (Tummers and Knies 2013). There is a wide variety of theories that could be labelled as interpersonal or relational. Leader-member exchange theory (LMX) and followership theory (Kellerman 2007) are related to earlier transactional theories and emphasize the exchange relations between leaders and followers/personnel. More recent interpersonal theories, like servant leadership (van Dierendonck 2010), tend to stress the facilitating role of leaders in empowering and supporting people in organizations in order to get things done, while more recently, there has been interest in authentic and ethical leadership (van Wart 2013b; Zehndorfer 2014).

Interpersonal leadership theories focus on developing employees and providing an example (authenticity) for them. This should lead to high quality in terms of follower-leader relationships (respect, affection and loyalty) and a psychologically stimulating climate (trust and fairness). These characteristics are meant to result in higher job satisfaction, more engagement, greater team effectiveness and better sustainability of the organization (van Dierendonck 2010; van Wart 2013b; Zehndorfer 2014).

Leadership characteristics that are considered important in this style are qualities like humbleness, authenticity and stewardship. In that sense, this perspectives clearly distinguishes itself from more transactional and transformational approaches to leadership which portray leaders as top-down and target-oriented, rather than people-oriented (van Dierendonck 2010; van Wart 2012; Tummers and Knies 2013). Humbleness refers to the ability to put one's own accomplishments in perspective. Authenticity refers to expressing oneself in ways that are consistent with one's own thoughts and feelings, and stewardships refers to the willingness to take responsibility for the larger institution and prioritize service over control and self-interest (van Dierendonck 2010). In the interpersonal perspective, especially servant leadership theory, leaders are pictured as more altruistic and determined to help other people in the organization. What this has in common with the transformational perspective is that leaders act as role models for employees. But this is not so much as a driver for changing the organization and setting targets, but as a person of integrity who helps develop employees (Zehndorfer 2014).

Ethical leadership is fundamentally a 'moral reformulation' of the transformational perspective or a combination of the transformational perspective with the interpersonal perspective. It arose partly in response to major scandals where private sector leaders have failed (such as Enron, or the banking crisis). In common with the transformational perspective, it valorises leadership by example and the display of drive and urgency. In common with the interpersonal perspective, it focuses on supporting employees and has less emphasis on targets and performance and more on team cooperation.

Ethical-based leadership theories tend to emphasize three major concerns according to van Wart (2013b): the intent of individuals, the proper means for doing well and selecting the proper ends. In this leadership perspective, leaders:

- Demonstrate integrity; this refers to honesty and telling the truth, but also to trustworthiness. Thus, leaders know and express their principles (public sector examples include principles like dedication to the public good and laws of the land and civic virtues) and abide by them;
- Emphasize the positive (also often called authentic, according to van Wart 2013b). Leaders are self-aware and are transparent and open to their employees. This is related to integrity, as discussed above; and
- Leaders know how to lead through service, spirit and sacrifice; leaders show a considerable amount of altruism and encourage employees to live by good public principles and also put the need of their employees first (van Wart 2013a, 2013b).

Overall, a different picture of leadership and innovation emerges for the interpersonal style, compared to the transformational theories mentioned earlier. The interpersonal leader is a facilitator who builds relationships *vis-à-vis* the people in the organization, provides a moral example and is willing to take responsibility for the whole organization and its members (stewardship). Thus, innovation is jointly produced by the leader and the employees (van Dierendonck 2010). The interpersonal or relational style of leadership emphasizes that it is about building and nurturing employees. Innovation results from the creativity of the individuals working in the organization, who have been empowered by the leader and the trusting atmosphere fostered by him/her.

Entrepreneurial Leadership

Public sector environments change rapidly due to frequent changes in policy or in the societal environment in which public organizations must operate (Pablo et al. 2007; Piening 2013). This points to the usefulness of a resource based view in understanding how (public) organizations adapt to such changing environments. The entrepreneurial perspective on leadership is one that is strongly present in recent theories of dynamic capabilities, for instance. It is also present in work on strategic styles of leadership (van Wart 2012), which emphasizes the strategic capacity to act, but also points to the path dependency of (public) organizations, which may find themselves caught up in past routines and organizational behaviour (Piening 2013) that inhibit innovation.

Dynamic capabilities may be defined as the "ability to integrate, build and reconfigure internal and external competences to address rapidly changing environments" (Teece, Pisano and Shuen 1997, 516). Such capabilities within an organization are meant to be an add-on to the resource-based view. Dynamic capabilities are distinctive processes that facilitate not only the ability to recognize changes in the strategic environment (information gathering), but also the processes of changing and shaping the company's asset positions in its adaptation to its environment (Teece 2007). Dynamic capabilities are therefore closely related to a firm's 'performance', which, according to Teece (1996), involves creating, deploying and protecting the intangible assets that support the business in the long run. In public organizations, these assets include the political environment but also the ability to obtain sufficient resources.

The recent entrepreneurial perspectives are inspired by earlier literature on the *entrepreneur*—a word borrowed from the French that today implies qualities of leadership that are considered important to innovation. There are many historical types of entrepreneurial leaders, but here we discuss the five types that have impacted on theoretical directions the most: one with roots in Kirzner's entrepreneurship, another with roots in the Schumpeterian tradition and a much earlier third with roots in the Irish-French scholar Cantillon (1755). Later scholars like Drucker (1985) and Knight (2005) take their departure in the risk-taking character of the entrepreneur from Cantillon. A fourth type comes from the American scholar Penrose, who introduced a more collective nature of the entrepreneur, and a fifth was introduced by Pinchot (1985) with the term intrapreneurship—meaning those leaders responsible for innovation inside large organizations (see Box 4.2). The Penrose entrepreneur type combines interpersonal skills with more network-like activities, whereas the others are more like the transactional leaders who are willing to take risks, exercises initiative and employ the resources needed.

Box 4.2: Entrepreneurial Leadership

Five scholars with original concepts of entrepreneurial qualities:

Cantillon (1755) first defined the entrepreneur as a risk taker. He described this type as one who buys a product at a certain price and then later sells it at an uncertain price. The entrepreneurial qualities lie in the acceptance of the risk of leading an enterprise, and in the success of adapting to changing environments.

Kirzner (1997) argued against the mainstream neoclassic economist's assumption of perfect competition, which neglects the role of the entrepreneur. He introduced the entrepreneur as someone with skills to discover new opportunities.

Schumpeter (1934, 1942) pointed to entrepreneurs as the source of innovation in his early research. Later, he pointed to the role of the large companies that in the 1930s started having their own R&D departments. He introduced the idea of innovation as creative destruction and thereby questioned the mainstream economic assumption of perfect equilibrium theory. Moreover, he suggested that it is the nature of competition to seek new knowledge and that innovation breaks with exiting routines and practices. He argued that it is entrepreneurial activities (a restless search for new knowledge) that create diversity, which competition then builds upon, and concludes that innovation is endogenous to economic growth (Schumpeter 1934).

Penrose (1959) argued for a more collective concept of entrepreneurship, claiming that modern organizations need to combine human resources to explore entrepreneurial opportunities. It then follows that a more relational approach and collective action is needed to create successful innovation. DiMaggio (1988) later applied this concept in relating it to the rise of new institutions based on the interest of organized actors with sufficient resources.

Pinchot (1985) introduced the term intrapreneur, referring to the act of behaving like an entrepreneur, while working within a large organization. This person takes responsibility for turning ideas into profitable products by assessing risk-taking and innovations.

In an entrepreneurial leadership view, innovation is likely to be strongly related to a leader's entrepreneurial ability to see a new business opportunity and subsequently decide to exploit it. In the later Drucker (1985) entrepreneurial leadership style, the entrepreneur is seen as a risk-taker. But in Schumpeter's view, it is not the entrepreneur who take risks, but the capitalist who takes risks by investing in the entrepreneur's idea (Schumpeter 1934). In both perspectives, the entrepreneur is a maverick who do not always go by the book.

Building Dynamic Capabilities as a Public Leadership Activity

In the resource-based view that comes from the strategic management research tradition, entrepreneurial leadership relates to Schumpeter's (1934) idea of creative destruction, where new knowledge can create new opportunities. But Teece (2007) also relates leadership to the notion of entrepreneurial skills needed in order to seize new business opportunities by taking advantage of existing knowledge. The last builds innovation incrementally rather than through some radical change.

Relating the concept of building dynamic capabilities in public organizations (Piening 2013) to entrepreneurial leadership, the focus is then on the leader's ability to sense and seize opportunities, while (re)directing resources quickly (Teece 2007). Here it is the leader's task to ensure the organization's survival or sustainability of its core activities by proactively adapting to a changing environment (Teece 1996). Activities then lie in the efforts of creating organizational conditions that are conducive to sense change and to seize new opportunities.

Seen from the entrepreneurial perspective, leaders initiate change through strategic actions, reshaping organizational routines and mobilizing resources. Leaders are clearly the core actors in the entrepreneurial perspective. The leader is strategizing in relation to risk and innovation approaches that include rewards and motivational techniques. Dynamic capabilities capture the essence of entrepreneurial leadership and of intrapreneurship (Pinchot 1985) within a large organization. Hence, innovation in this view calls for strong entrepreneurial leadership skills in adapting the organization to a changing environment.

Network Governance Leadership

The current wide variety of literature on governance, collaborative management and networks stresses that modern policy is made and implemented not by governments alone but in networks of interdependent actors (Kickert, Klijn and Koppenjan 1997; Rhodes 1997; Mandell 2001; Meier and O'Toole 2007; O'Leary and Bingham 2009). This literature stresses that to be successful in these networks, political leaders and administrators must engage in interactions with various stakeholders to be effective and actively manage their network (Koppenjan and Klijn 2004; Huxham and Vangen 2005; O'Leary and Bingham 2009).

Solving Wicked Problems in Complex Networks

Many authors have pointed to the difficulty of achieving solutions to policy problems in modern (network) society (Hanf and Scharpf 1978; Kickert, Klijn and Koppenjan 1997; Rhodes 1997; Agranoff and McGuire 2001). Many problems have become more complex because of changes in the nature of society (more plurality in values, more active citizens that foster their interest and organize themselves to influence policy-making processes and more dispersed information). There is, however, also a need for more integration in many policy-making and service delivery processes, and this makes the task more complex (Osborne 2010). Collaborative efforts are needed to bring knowledge together to solve problems (Bryson and Crosby 1992; Ansell and Gash 2008).

Consequently, many problems have a "wicked" character (Rittel and Webber 1973): There is little agreement among the involved actors on the nature of the problem, many different actors are involved and these actors do not always agree on the standards by which possible solutions should be judged. Politicians and public administrators find themselves in networks of interdependent actors (Hanf and Scharpf 1978; Kaufmann, Majone and Ostrom 1986; Marsh and Rhodes 1992; Kickert, Klijn and Koppenjan 1997; Rhodes 1997). Dependency relations between actors are crucial to the emergence and existence of networks (Hanf and Scharpf 1978). The resource dependencies around policy problems, service delivery or policy programs require actors to interact with one another and create more intensive and enduring interactions (Laumann and Knoke 1987). Networks are, on the one hand, consciously planned in the sense that actors deliberately interact and attempt to structure these interactions with organizations and rules, but, on the other hand, are also unplanned as a result of coincidental interactions and strategies, and previously created rules.

Network governance and leadership

As described in Chapter 2, network governance has now become a widespread reality for the public sector. There is a broad consensus that (network) management or leadership is essential and that the type of leadership and/or management required in networks and collaborative settings differs significantly from the classical image of organizational leadership (see Gage and Mandell 1990; Kickert, Klijn and Koppenjan 1997; Pierre 2000). Ansell and Gash (2008) talk about facilitating leadership: By this they mean that the task of a leader is to mediate between actors and empower the collaboration process. Huxham and Vangen (2005, 203) state: "This line of argument [about leadership] steers the theory in sharp departure from classical notions of leadership. . . . Not surprisingly, those researchers who have focused on leadership in collaboration have tended to emphasize relational leadership, processes for inspiring, nurturing, supporting and communicating". Kickert, Klijn and Koppenjan (1997, 11) argue that "managing networks, however, should not be confused with the "classical management approach". . . . Network management is, in essence, an inter-organizational activity". Thus, the leadership and management style appropriate in networks and collaborative processes is one of facilitating, activating actors and enhancing their collaboration (see also Gage and Mandell 1990; Agranoff and McGuire 2001).

Collaborative or network leadership, in comparison to the transformational perspective, is:

- Inter-organizational rather than intra-organizational;
- Collaborative and facilitating rather than charismatic and top-down; and

• Strongly focused on connecting actors and exploring interesting content rather than formulating challenging goals and visions.

The network governance leader is not a charismatic person who directs his/her troops in new directions, but someone who carefully examines the network of actors at his/her disposal, connects them to each other and facilitates the exploration of solutions to address problems that satisfy the involved actors so that they will deploy the resources needed to implement those solutions (Klijn, Steijn and Edelenbos 2010). Such leaders are also extremely aware that in order to solve societal problems they depend on the (resources of) other actors and therefore have to build trust and cooperation among actors with different perceptions of those problems, different ideas about desirable solutions to them and different interests (Koppenjan and Klijn 2004; McGuire and Agranoff 2011). Thus, the leader's activities are more aimed at facilitating interaction and search processes among actors and building solid coalitions of actors who can agree on packages of goals to solve societal problems (Koppenjan and Klijn 2004; Ansell and Gash 2008).

Network management strategies

The literature mentions many different network management strategies to guide interaction processes, so an exhaustive list is not provided here—see Gage and Mandell (1990), O'Toole (1988) and Agranoff and McGuire (2003) for some examples. Instead, four types of network management strategies are briefly outlined (adapted from Klijn, Steijn and Edelenbos (2010), in the following paragraphs.

> *Process agreements*—Rules for entrance into or exit from the process, conflict regulating rules, rules that specify the interests of actors or veto possibilities, rules that inform actors about the availability of information about decision-making moments etc.
> *Exploring content*—Searching for goal congruency, creating variation in solutions, influencing (and explicating) perceptions, managing and collecting information and research, creating variation through creative competition
> *Arranging*—Creating new ad hoc organizational arrangements (boards, project organizations etc.)
> *Connecting*—Selective (de)activation of actors, resource mobilizing, initiating new series of interactions, coalition building, mediation, appointment of process managers, removing obstacles to cooperation, creating incentives for cooperation.

Connecting strategies like the activation of actors or resources are required in order to begin. The network management literature stresses that the network manager has to identify the actors required for an initiative and actually create a situation in which they become interested in investing their resources (Hanf and Scharpf 1978). The interactions within the game itself also have to be managed. This can be done by appointing a process manager, who invests time and energy in connecting the actions and strategies of actors to one another during the interactions.

Once the game has begun, strategies for exploring content are necessary to clarify the goals and perceptions of actors (Fischer 2003) and to try to invest time and money in developing solutions that create opportunities for actors' participation. However, the process is sometimes short of creative solutions to satisfy the various actors involved. In such cases, more variation is required, for instance, by using different teams of experts who compete against one another to create solutions.

Arranging means setting (temporary) structures for consultation, interaction and deliberation, like project organization, communication lines etc. (Rogers and Whetten 1982). The transaction costs of these arrangements must be kept as low as possible (Williamson 1996), but at the same time, the arrangements have to be acceptable to the actors involved. Process agreements are another important strategy mentioned in the literature. These are temporary sets of rules for interaction that structure the interactions and protect each actor's core values (Koppenjan and Klijn 2004). The rules can be seen as ground rules for behaviour and interaction in the network that the actors in the network (explicitly) agreed on.

In summary, innovation in the network governance perspective on leadership is achieved by collaborative leaders who connect actors and are able to share their success with others, because they depend on the efforts and resources of the other actors around them (Ysa et al. 2014). It is therefore important to ensure that these actors are committed to the solutions that have been agreed upon and developed, but also that leaders intensively interact with other actors to develop innovative solutions that will deal with the problem at hand.

Leadership Qualities for the Five Perspectives

On the basis of these five perspectives, we created a list of leadership qualities, which are shown in Table 4.1 (and adapted from Ricard et al. 2016). The rationale behind these is grounded in the preceding discussion and related directly to the five 'ideal' theoretical types. Some leadership qualities fit with more than one leadership perspective. Being visionary, for instance, fits both in the transformational and the entrepreneurial leadership perspective. Further, some attributes (such as being authoritative) are expected to be positively associated with innovation in one perspective, but negatively associated with innovation in another. The overlap in this table neatly illustrates the overlapping theoretical perspectives on leadership in the literature.

Table 4.1 Leadership Qualities Aligned with the Five Theoretical Concepts

	Transactional	Transformational	Interpersonal	Network governance	Entrepreneurial
A Good communication skills			X	X	
B Visionary		X			X
C Takes initiative	X	X			X
D Authoritative	X				
E Visible leadership		X			
F Displays a long-term perspective		X		X	X
G Displays a short-term perspective	X				
H Good at gathering information				X	X
I Problem-oriented	X	X		X	X
J Results-oriented		X			X
K Inspirational					
L Provides intellectual stimulation			X		
M Committed to colleagues and organization		X	X	X	
N Willing to sacrifice self-interest			X		
O Good at mobilizing the resources needed		X		X	X
P Works collaboratively			X	X	
Q Knowledgeable			X		X
R Good at learning from mistakes			X		
S Willing to risk mistakes from employees					
T Open towards new ideas		X		X	X
U Takes all decisions alone	X	X			
V Involves others in key decisions			X	X	
W Always follows procedures	X				

Conclusions

Leadership theories and perspectives abound, and there are almost as many demarcations within the literature as there are authors. Finding a path through the leadership literature to apply these ideas to our empirical research required us to first distinguish the most important leadership perspectives and explicitly connect them to innovation, before creating items to measure them. In this chapter, we identified five styles of leadership: transactional, transformational, interpersonal, entrepreneurial and network governance leadership. We showed that these perspectives differ considerably in how they picture leadership roles, leadership activities and the requirements of leaders. We systematically elaborated the five perspectives and compared them with each other, identifying distinctions and overlaps.

This allows us to see the strengths and weaknesses of each of the leadership perspectives. While the transformational leadership is strong on charismatic leaders and shows the importance of motivation and leading the way, it may overestimate the possibilities of top-down leadership and ignore the fact that inspiring views may be useful to start a process, but might not achieve results in an interdependent world. This may also be the weak spot of the entrepreneurial perspective, which emphasizes strategy and the dominant role of the leader. Dependency and negotiation are very much present in the network governance perspective on leadership, but they are not attentive to the need for charisma, vision and motivation for the actors involved. The interpersonal perspective's strength is its focus on the relationship of leaders with employees and creating conditions to empower employees. But this may underestimate the role of context in achieving good outcomes.

Each of the styles distinguished in this chapter is connected to certain leadership qualities, which are shown as a list in Table 4.1. These items were used to gather data from senior administrators on which leadership qualities are important for supporting innovation. The empirical findings from this are presented in Chapter 9.

References

Agranoff, Robert, and Michael McGuire. 2001. "Big questions in public network management research." *Journal of Public Administration Research and Theory* 11(3): 295–326.

Agranoff, Robert, and Michael McGuire. 2003. *Collaborative public management: New strategies for local governments.* Washington, DC: Georgetown University Press.

Ansell, Chris, and Alison Gash. 2008. "Collaborative governance in theory and practice." *Journal of Public Administration Research and Theory* 18(4): 543–71.

Avolio, Bruce J., David A. Waldman, and Francis J. Yammarino 1991. "Leading in the 1990s: The Four I's of transformational leadership." *Journal of European Industrial Training* 15(4): 9–16.

Bass, Bernard M. 1997. "Does the transactional and transformational leadership paradigm transcend organizational and national boundaries?" *American Psychologist* 52: 130–39.

Bass, Bernard M. 1985. *Leadership and performance beyond expectations.* New York: Free Press.

Bekkers, Victor J.J.M., Jurian Edelenbos, and Bram Steijn, editors. 2011. *Innovation in the public sector: Linking capacity and leadership.* Basingstoke: Palgrave Macmillan.

Bryson, John M., and Barbara Crosby. 1992. *Leadership for the common good: Tackling public problems in a shared-power world.* San Francisco, CA: Jossey-Bass.

Burrell, Gibson, and Gareth Morgan. 1979. *Sociological paradigms and organizational analysis: Elements of the sociology of corporate life.* London: Heinemann.

Cantillon, Richard. 1755. *Essai sur la nature du commerce en général.* London: MacMillan.

DiMaggio, Paul. 1988. "Interest and agency in institutional theory." In *Institutional patterns and culture,* edited by Lynne G. Zucker, 3–22. Cambridge, MA: Ballinger Publishing Company.

Drucker, Peter. 1985. *Innovation and entrepreneurship.* London: Heinemann.

Fischer, Frank. 2003. *Reframing public policy: Discursive politics and deliberative practices.* Oxford: Oxford University Press.

Gage, Robert W., and Myrna P. Mandell, editors. 1990. *Strategies for managing intergovernmental policies and networks.* New York/London: Preager.

Hanf, Kenneth, and Fritz W. Scharpf, editors. 1978. *Inter-organisational policy making: Limits to coordination and central control.* London: Sage.

Howell, Jane M., and Bruce J. Avolio. 1993. "Transformational leadership, transactional leadership, locus of control, and support for innovation: Key predictors of consolidated-business-unit-performance." *Journal of Applied Psychology* 78(6): 891–902.

Huxham, Chris., and Sev Vangen. 2005. *Managing to collaborate: The theory and practice of collaborative advantage.* London: Routledge.

Kaufmann, Franz-Xaver, Giandomenico Majone, and Vincent Ostrom, editors. 1986. *Guidance, control and evaluation in the public sector: The Bielefeld interdisciplinary project.* Berlin: Walter de Gruyter.

Kellerman, Barbara. 2007. "What every leader needs to know about followers". *Harvard Business Review* 85(12): 84–91.

Kickert, Walter J.M., Erik-Hans Klijn, and Joop F.M. Koppenjan, editors. 1997. *Managing complex networks: Strategies for the public sector.* London: Sage.

Kirzner, Israel M. 1997. "Entrepreneurial discovery and the competitive market process: An Austrian approach." *Journal of Economic Literature* 35(1): 60–85.

Klijn, Erik-Hans, Bram Steijn, and Jurian Edelenbos. 2010. "The impact of network management strategies on the outcomes in governance networks." *Public Administration* 88(4): 1063–82.

Knight, Frank Hyneman. 2005. *Risk, uncertainty and profit.* New York: Cosimo, Inc.

Koppenjan, Joop F.M., and Erik-Hans Klijn. 2004. *Managing uncertainties in networks.* London: Routledge.

Laumann, Edward O., and David Knoke. 1987. *The organizational state: Social choice in national policy domains.* Madison, WI: University of Wisconsin Press.

Leong, Lai Yin Carmen, and Ronald Fischer. 2011. "Is transformational leadership universal? A meta-analytical investigation of multifactor leadership questionnaire means across cultures." *Journal of Leadership & Organizational Studies* 18(2): 164–74.

Lundvall, Bengt-Åke. 2007. "National innovation systems—Analytical concept and development tool." *Industry and Innovation* 14(1): 95–119.

Mandell, Myrna P. 1990. "Network management: Strategic behavior in the public sector." In: *Strategies for managing intergovernmental policies and networks*, edited by Robert W. Gage and Myrna P. Mandell, 20–53. New York: Praeger.

Mandell, Myrna P., editor. 2001. *Getting results through collaboration: Networks and network structures for public policy and management.* Westport, CT: Quorum Books.

Marsh, David, and Roderick A.W. Rhodes, editors. 1992. *Policy networks in British government.* Oxford: Clarendon Press.

McGuire, Michael, and Robert Agranoff. 2011. "The limitations of public management networks." *Public Administration* 89(2): 265–84.

Meier, Kenneth, and Lawrence J. O'Toole. 2007. "Modelling public management: Empirical analysis of the management-performance nexus." *Public Administration Review* 9(4): 503–27.

Moss Kanter, Rosabeth. 1983. *The change masters.* New York: Simon & Schuster.

O'Leary, Rosemary, and Lisa Blomgren Bingham, editors. 2009. *The collaborative public manager.* Washington, DC: Georgetown University Press.

O'Toole, Lawrence J. 1988. "Strategies for intergovernmental management: Implementing programs in interorganizational networks." *Journal of Public Administration Research and Theory* 11(4): 417–41.

Osborne, Stephen P., editor. 2010. *The new public governance?* London: Routledge.

Pablo, Amy L., Trish Reay, James R. Dewald, and Ann L. Casebeer. 2007. "Identifying, enabling and managing dynamic capabilities in the public Sector." *Journal of Management Studies* 44(5): 687–708.

Penrose, Edith T. 1959. *The theory of the growth of the firm.* New York: John Wiley.

Piening, Erk P. 2013. "Dynamic capabilities in public organizations." *Public Management Review* 15(2): 209–45.

Pierre, Jon, editor. 2000. *Debating governance: Authority steering and democracy.* Oxford: Oxford University Press.

Pierre, Jon, and B. Guy Peters. 2000. *Governance, politics and the state.* Basingstoke: Macmillan.

Pinchot, Gifford. 1985. "Who is the intrapreneur?" In *Intrapreneuring: Why you don't have to leave the corporation to become an entrepreneur*, edited by Gifford Pinchot, 28–48. New York: Harper & Row.

Rhodes, Rod A.W. 1997. *Understanding governance: Policy networks, governance, reflexivity, and accountability.* Buckingham: Open University Press.

Ricard, Lykke Margot, Erik Hans Klijn, Jenny M. Lewis, and Tamyko Ysa. 2016. "Assessing public leadership styles for innovation: A comparison of Copenhagen, Rotterdam and Barcelona." *Public Management Review*, DOI: 10.1080/14719037.2016.1148192.

Rittel, Horst, and Melvin Webber. 1973. "Dilemmas in a general theory of planning." *Policy Sciences* 4(2): 155–69.

Rogers, David L., and David A. Whetten, editors. 1982. *Interorganizational coordination: Theory, research, and implementation.* Ames, IA: Iowa State University Press.

Schumpeter, Joseph A. 1934. *The theory of economic development.* Cambridge, MA: Harvard University.

Schumpeter, Joseph A. 1942. *Capitalism, socialism and democracy* (5th edition 1976). London: George Allen and Unwin.

Teece, David J. 1996. "Firm organization, industrial structure, and technological innovation." *Journal of Economic Behavior in Organizations* 31(2): 193–224.

Teece, David J. 2007. "Explicating dynamic capabilities: The nature and microfoundations of (sustainable) enterprise performance." *Strategic Management Journal* 28(13): 1319–50.

Teece, David J., Gary Pisano, and Amy Shuen. 1997. "Dynamic capabilities and strategic management." *Strategic Management Journal* 18(7): 509–33.

Tichy, Noel M., and Mary Anne Devanna. 1990. *The transformational leader*. New York: Wiley.

Tummers, Lars, and Eva Knies. 2013. "Leadership and meaningful work in the public sector." *Public Administration Review* 73(6): 859–68.

van Dierendonck, Dirk. 2010. "Servant leadership: A review and synthesis." *Journal of Management* 37(4): 1228–61.

van Wart, Montgomery. 2012. *Leadership in public organizations: An introduction*. New York: M.E. Sharpe.

van Wart, Montgomery. 2013a. "Lessons from leadership theory and the contemporary challenges of leaders." *Public Administration Review* 73(4): 553–65.

van Wart, Montgomery. 2013b. "Administrative leadership theory: A reassessment after 10 years." *Public Administration* 91(3): 521–43.

Williamson, Oliver E. 1996. *The mechanisms of governance*. Oxford: Oxford University Press.

Ysa, Tamyko, Vicenta Sierra and Marc Esteve. 2014. "Determinants of network outcomes: The impact of managerial strategies." *Public Administration* 92(3): 636–655.

Zehndorfer, Elesa. 2014. *Leadership: A critical introduction*. London: Routledge.

Part II

A Comparison of Three Cities

Barcelona, Copenhagen and Rotterdam

5 The Innovation Environment

Governance Structures and Economic Challenges

This chapter examines the innovation environment of each of the three cities in the study. It includes a description of the governance structures in each nation and the rating of each nation and municipality on international innovation scales. It also provides contextual information on each city and outlines the formal structure of each municipal government. The strategy used to sample politicians and senior administrators from each municipality is then described. We then present results from the survey on the most important current and future socioeconomic challenges nominated by people inside and outside each municipality. The chapter concludes with a comparison of the innovation environments of the three cities.

Governance Structures and Innovativeness

The innovation capacity of any public sector organization is related to the environment within which it is located. Therefore, an important first set of considerations is the formal structures within which each municipality is located. What kind of governance structures are important for innovation? Based on an analysis of the literature, Voorberg, Bekkers and Tummers (2015) found several aspects of the environment could function as important for innovation. The first of these is the social and political complexity of the environment in which public organizations operate which leads to specific demands that function as an external 'trigger' for innovation. The second is the characteristics and degree of the legal culture in a country or policy sector, which shapes the level of formalization and standardization and the degree of rule-driven behaviour. They also reported that the type of governance and state tradition in a country or policy sector, which affects the amount of discretion that public sector organizations have to explore and implement new ideas, has an impact on innovation. Finally, they noted that the allocation of resources, resource dependency and the quality of relationships between different (public and private) organizations at different levels also have an impact on how well innovation practices are supported.

More specifically, the formal structures that have been previously identified as being positively related to innovation capacity (Voorberg, Bekkers and Tummers 2015) are political and administrative triggers such as crises and competition, a decentralized state, corporatist governance traditions and strong civil society. Factors that are regarded as having a negative effect on innovation capacity include a strong formalized, centralized, rule-bound and silo-bound legal culture.

Using this as a starting point, we investigated the innovation environments in each city. This was based on a combination of a documentary analysis of material available, mostly on the relevant national and municipal websites and in the local media. We also examined some international indicators of national and city innovativeness. Finally, as part of the study, we use the information gathered from our survey respondents on the most important socioeconomic challenges they are facing and the most significant innovations that the city has introduced in the last year. This is supplemented with the view on socioeconomic challenges and significant innovations from people outside the municipality.

The three cities in this study reflect different geographical areas and varying state and society traditions. A comparison of the strength of local government and the innovativeness score for the three cities and nations included in this study is shown in Table 5.1. The strength of local government is based on assessments made by Loughlin and Peters (1997) and Pollitt and Bouckaert (2011). The national innovation score is based on 25 indicators of human resources, research systems, R&D expenditure, investment, entrepreneurship and intellectual assets, innovators and economic effects. It is essentially a knowledge economy measure, created by the European Commission, and provides a very general indication. It appears to reflect the relative strength of each nation's economy. An innovation city index is also shown in Table 5.1. This index compares 445 cities around the world, and the analysis is based on the potential for creation, implementation and communication of ideas in urban economies. It is calculated using 162 indicators across 31 segments and the three factors of cultural assets, human infrastructure and networked markets. Hence, it has a much broader scope than the European Commission measure. Most of the things included

Table 5.1 Local Government Strength and Innovation Scores for Cities in the Study

City	Strength of local government in the nation	Innovation union scoreboard index 2013 (national)[1]	Innovation city score[2]
Barcelona, Spain	Strong local governments	.414	48
Copenhagen, Denmark	Moderately strong local government	.728	56
Rotterdam, the Netherlands	Moderately strong local government	.629	47

within it are not directly related to government at any level, although some of them might result from different policies.

Based on this comparison, Spain has the strongest local governments of these three nations. In comparison, central governments in the UK, for example, are stronger than in these three nations. Denmark is the 'most innovative' based on the European Commission's Innovation Index, while the Netherlands is lower than Denmark and Spain is substantially lower than the other two nations. Copenhagen is higher than the other two cities on the Innovation city score. It is classified as a NEXUS city—a critical nexus for multiple economic and social innovation segments. Barcelona and Rotterdam are much more similarly ranked and scored and are both categorized as HUB cities, with dominance or influence on key economic and social innovation segments.

These assessments of strength of local government and innovativeness are very simplified and aggregated. They are provided simply as background on the three cities included in the study to provide some of the local context that helps frame the innovation capacity of municipalities. Both the information on governance structures within nations and the strength of local government, as well as national and city-level indicators of 'innovativeness' are very imperfect measures. In general, they suggest that Copenhagen might be 'more innovative'. But Copenhagen is the capital city of Denmark, which neither of the other two cities is, which gives it a different place in the national context. These, and many other factors, have an impact on the innovation capacity of cities.

The Three Cities in the Study

Having provided some general background on the nations and cities, this section takes a more detailed look at some contextual information for each of the three cities and the city governments, at the time the empirical data for this book was collected.

Barcelona

Barcelona is the capital city of Catalonia, an autonomous community of Spain. Among the 8,119 municipalities of Spain, Barcelona is the second largest (after Madrid). More specifically, it has a population of 1,611,822 (2013 figure). From the restoration of the Spanish democracy (in 1979) until 2011, the city council was governed by the *Socialist Party of Catalonia* (social democratic party). From 2011 to 2014, the mayor of the city council was from the Catalan nationalist coalition of liberal and Christian democratic parties (*Convergència i Unió*). Since 2015, a new "citizens' movement" backed by several left wing parties is governing the city.

The city council of Barcelona has a long history in the field of innovation. One example is the successful hosting of the 1992 Olympic Games. More recently, Barcelona has been awarded the European Capital of Innovation (iCapital) prize by the European Commission "for introducing the use of new technologies to bring the city closer to citizens" (European Commission 2014).

Since September 2011, Barcelona's city council has been developing the "Barcelona as a people city" project. This is based on introducing the use of new technologies to foster economic growth and the welfare of its citizens through:

- Open data initiatives, offering valuable information to individuals and private companies;
- Sustainable city growth initiatives on smart lighting, mobility (e-vehicle) and residual energy (heating and cooling networks);
- Social innovation;
- Promotion of alliances between research centres, universities, private and public partners within the scope of the project; and
- Providing better 'smart services' in a flexible, continuous and agile way through ICT—used as a means to launch innovation in different areas of the city.

As noted by the Mayor of Barcelona at that time, the innovative ecosystem of Barcelona is based on three pillars: Open Government, the Smart Cities project and the improvement of mobility. Moreover, the Mayor stated that innovation was a cross-cutting theme within the city which was expected to reactivate the economy and to help create jobs. These two elements (i.e. reactivate the economy and reduce unemployment) and the recovery from the economic crisis were regarded by the Mayor as the main challenges for the city of Barcelona.[3]

The Municipal Council is the highest level of political representation of the citizens in the government of the city. It has 41 councillors and is chaired by the Mayor. Of the 41 councillors, 15 of them are in the government, and the rest are the opposition. The main tasks of the Municipal Council are to establish the direction of municipal action and resolve the matters of the city with advisory, planning, regulatory and fiscal executive functions. The Municipal Council operates in Plenary Assemblies and in commissions. The Assembly has the representation of five political parties.

The six Municipal Council's commissions (City Council Commissions) are:

- Commission for Presidency and Internal Affairs;
- Commission for the Economy, Business and Employment;
- Commission for the Environment and Urban Habitat;
- Commission for Culture, Knowledge, Creativity and Innovation;
- Commission for Quality of Life, Equality, Youth and Sports; and
- Commission for Safety and Mobility.

The 'Comission de Govern' (Government Commission) is the executive branch. It is formed by 24 councillors, who are led by the Mayor, with five deputy-mayors (lieutenant-mayors) and 17 city councillors, each in charge of an area of government, and five non-elected councillors (appointed by the Mayor). The areas of government of the executive branch are:

• Area of the Mayor's Office, Interior, Safety and Mobility;
• Area of Economic, Business and Employment;
• Area of Urban Planning, Infrastructures, Housing, Environment and ICT;
• Area of Quality of Life, Equality and Sports; and
• Area of Culture, Knowledge, Creativity and Innovation.

Within the municipal administration, the chief executive office is responsible for the services that the city council provides to the citizens. More specifically, it has to ensure that the services are efficient and appropriately responsive to citizens' demands. One of the main bodies of the municipal administration is the deputy manager's office for territorial coordination. The municipality of Barcelona is divided into 10 districts, but since 2009, Barcelona has been divided into 73 neighbourhoods in order to improve the service from the City Council. An overview of the structure can be seen in Figure 5.1.

The chief executive's office has the following sub-units:
• Deputy Manager's office for the coordination of the municipal business entities;
• Manager's office for culture, knowledge and innovation;
• Manager's office for economy and economic promotion;
• Manager's office for quality of life, equality and sports;
• Manager's office for urban housing;

   • Manager's office for environment and urban services

• Manager's office for prevention, safety and mobility;

Figure 5.1 Barcelona Municipality Structure 2014

- Manager's office for resources; and
- Manager's office for human resources and organization.

Finally, the city council has 12 public companies that relate to the following fields and issues: culture, education, finance, markets, sports, social services, people with disabilities, urban planning, urban landscape and quality of life, housing, parks and gardens and the Mies van de Röhe Foundation.

Barcelona is governed by a City Council, formed by 41 councillors and a Mayor, who are elected for a four-year term. Barcelona is subjected to a special municipality law (Municipal Charter of Barcelona), and following this, it is organized in two levels: a political level with elected council members, and an executive level, which administers the programs and executes the decisions made on the political level. The law gives the Mayor wide prerogatives regarding the executive commissions, but also gives the council a veto regarding matters decided by central government.

The commissions of Municipal Council assume powers of decision-making and oversight, in addition to those which are strictly informative. They make decisions on the issues that are to be submitted to the Municipal Council, although their resolutions are not binding. They advance, control and oversee the activities of the organs of municipal executive administration and monitor periodically the execution of the program of action, in relation to their areas of competence. Each commission is composed of a number of councillors, proportional to the number of councillors each political party has in the plenary. The plenary is formed by 41 city councillors having advisory, planning, regulatory and fiscal executive functions. Among their decision-making functions are the authorization and awarding of certain administrative and private contracts, as well as the initial approval of ordinances and regulations relative to their respective sphere of action.

Copenhagen

Copenhagen is the capital city of Denmark and is home to around 0.6 million people. By the year 2025, it is estimated that the population in the city of Copenhagen will have increased by more than 100,000 citizens, to almost 0.7 million (Statistics Denmark 2014).

Frank Jensen was in his second term as Lord Mayor, after winning a second election in November 2013, just as the survey for this study was concluding. His first four years as Lord Mayor coincided with the economic crisis and the priority was on 'kick starting Copenhagen':[4] investing in new green city areas, the regeneration of old city areas and new infrastructure to create both new jobs in the city and address many of the socioeconomic challenges it was facing.

In early 2013 he remarked: *"The city we want to create is an open, tolerant and secure city. A diverse metropolis that is the most important gateway for foreign business investments and international events. And a natural centre for the Sound and Baltic Sea regions. Copenhagen is a city worth visiting, living in and investing in. Furthermore, Copenhagen must be the City of the citizens now and in the future".[5]*

In a newspaper interview in mid-2013,[6] he said that the biggest socioeconomic challenge facing Copenhagen was unemployment, especially amongst young people. This is a social challenge that requires job creation, but also better integration and inclusion in the city, as other problems include increasing ghettos, and the challenges of creating affordable apartments for average income people. The fight against crime and creating a safe city is also high on this agenda, with a focus on preventing the isolation of minority populations. Copenhagen also has an impressive reputation for sustainability, which comes from successes like the district heating system and its bicycle culture (World Wildlife Fund 2016).

The city of Copenhagen is the largest municipality within Denmark with a population of 569,557 people (2014 figures from Statistics Denmark). The city is governed by Copenhagen's municipal council (the 'Borgerrepræsentationen') and a substantial administration. Council elections are held in November, every four years. Every Lord Mayor of Copenhagen since 1903 has come from the Social Democratic party. The most recent election was 2013 and was held just as the survey for this study was concluding.

The City Council is the supreme political authority in the City of Copenhagen. Its 55 members outline the framework for the responsibilities and duties of the committees. The Lord Mayor is the Chairman of the City Council, convening the meetings and setting the agenda. The City Council is then divided into seven committees: the Finance Committee and six standing committees with specialized fields of responsibility. The responsibility of the administration is therefore divided between seven Mayors, with seven administrations and seven committees, and the Lord Mayor is the Mayor of Finance.

The seven mayors are all elected politicians and the only politicians working full time in the municipality. The remaining politicians (48) in the City Council are not receiving any salary from the municipality. They are regarded as part-time politicians and usually they have a daytime job as a schoolteacher, student or consultant. Politicians do, however, receive fees from the standing committees, as board members or from their seats in the external companies owned (or partly owned) by the municipality like the metro (train), harbour, water, central heating and renovation companies. Some of these seats are quite prestigious and lucrative. They are divided among the political parties after each local election.

The seven committees and seven administrations are: Finance, Healthcare, Employment and Integration, Culture and Leisure, Social Services, Technical and Environmental, and Children and Youth. In addition to a mayor, each administration has one executive director and two executives (similar to individual CEOs in other municipalities), then various levels of staff beneath these. Figure 5.2 shows the formal structure of the municipality; the

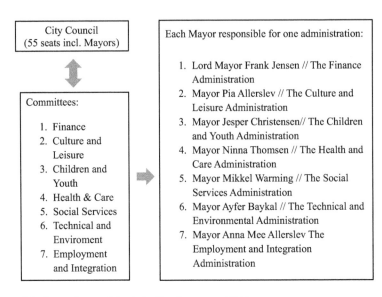

Figure 5.2 Copenhagen Municipality Structure 2013

seven committees, the seven mayors and the seven departments, including the incumbents in 2013 prior to the election in November.

Because the city government is divided into seven administrations, the task of integration formally occurs through the interaction of the civic duties of the 55 representatives (politicians) in the City Council. The City Council is the formal government decision-making body and the council meetings are overseen by the Lord Mayor, who chairs the meetings. Council meetings are held every Tuesday. This constitutes the government body of the city of Copenhagen. Its functionally divided administrative structure seems likely to have some negative consequences for innovation, because there is little formal requirement for each administrative division to work with the other six. As we noted in the first part of this book, innovation is thought to rely on gaining different sources of information and being able to work across boundaries. However, it may be that there are other informal ways that people within these administrations communicate with their colleagues elsewhere, which is not part of the formal structure.

Rotterdam

Rotterdam is the second-largest city of the Netherlands. The city contains one of the largest ports in the world, located near the mouth of the Rhine-Meuse-Scheldt delta, giving access to the European hinterland. This strategic location gives Rotterdam the label 'gateway to Europe'. It is a city that is famous for its modern architecture, among other things. The city centre was almost completely destroyed by German bombings in the Second World War, and new, eye-catching architecture is still constructed regularly.

Rotterdam has nearly 620,000 inhabitants, living within 325.79 km². The population is relatively young, not highly educated and highly diverse in terms of ethnic background, culture and religion. There are more than 170 nationalities present in the city.[7] A large proportion of the inhabitants were not born in the Netherlands (48.9%), which makes it the most diverse city in the Netherlands. Rotterdam is also the first large Dutch city to have a mayor of immigrant descent. Mayor Ahmed Aboutaleb was born in Morocco and is a Muslim.

At the time of the survey, the city was governed by a coalition of PvdA (Labour Party), VVD (Liberal Party), D66 (Progressive Left) and CDA (Christian Democrats). Shortly after we finished the survey, local elections were held. The Labour Party lost almost half of its seats. The populist 'Leefbaar Rotterdam' ('Liveable Rotterdam') gained the most votes. The party formed a coalition with D66 and CDA.

In their coalition agreement 'Full Speed Ahead', the following ambitions were central:

- Rotterdam's citizens take responsibility and have 'more to say';
- The municipality innovates and gives others the opportunity to do so;
- Safety in Rotterdam's neighbourhoods increases, they become greener and cosier;
- The city and port become more connected, the economy grows;
- There are more chances for Rotterdam's citizens, and they will take them; and
- In our own environment, we look after each other.

The Aldermen state that they want to make Rotterdam the 'laboratory of the Netherlands', with a lot of room for experimentation. Citizens will get 'the right to challenge' and take over from the municipal administration if they think they can do better. The Aldermen use the hashtag #Kendoe— which has a similar meaning to President Obama's 'yes, we can' campaign message.

As in all other Dutch municipalities, the main legislative body in Rotterdam is the City Council (a political body comparable to a parliament). Chairman of the council, (Lord) Mayor Aboutaleb is a member of the Labour Party and has been the mayor since 2009. In the City Council, 45 elected politicians have seats, and elections are held every four years. The position of member of the council is not a full-time job. Council members get some financial compensation for their political work, but most of them hold a job besides their council membership. After every election the political party with the most seats forms a majority coalition with other parties. They select representatives who together make up the municipal government, called Municipal Executive Committee. The Executive Committee is composed of the mayor and (currently) six aldermen or (vice) mayors. They are comparable to national ministers with policy portfolios, and the different policy sectors are divided between them.

The municipality was previously divided into fourteen 'sub-municipalities' with their own elections, councils and administrations. Since the beginning of 2014, the administration is integrated and the district councils are replaced by non-political 'district advisory committees'. This change in structure was often mentioned by our respondents both as an innovation and a challenge for the municipal organization. The municipal administration is now divided into seven divisions, all headed by a CEO and subdivided into departments and teams. The structure is shown in Figure 5.3.

Rotterdam has a unified formal structure, especially after abolishing the sub-municipalities. Formal decisions are made in the City Council but practically the city Aldermen have a very prominent position because this is where integration occurs and decision lines come together. The municipal council approves (or does not) the decisions being presented to them by the Aldermen. In practice, many decisions are taken by the city Aldermen and prepared beforehand by civil servants, and the City Council only discusses a small number of the issues, and only the most salient parts of the issues. This seems a good condition for innovation because it allows information to be brought together, but it is also a very centralized structure. Traditionally, Rotterdam is a city with a long history of citizen involvement and external stakeholder influence, especially in the field of environmental planning. In the 1970s Rotterdam's city renewal approach became famous because citizens where part of the project groups that had possibilities of making environmental decisions about their neighbourhoods. In the 1990s, however, this approach was abandoned.

A final consideration is the socioeconomic context of these cities. A number of indicators are provided in Table 5.2. Barcelona is by far the largest of the three cities (1.6 million people), while Copenhagen and Rotterdam

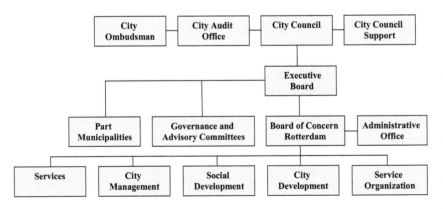

Figure 5.3 Rotterdam Municipality Structure 2014

Table 5.2 Characteristics of the Three Cities

Name of city	Barcelona	Copenhagen	Rotterdam
City information	Capital city of Catalonia (autonomous region), 2nd largest city in Spain	Capital city of Denmark	Industrial port city, 2nd largest city in the Netherlands
Population (million)	1.6	0.6	0.6
Percentage born in other countries and ethnicity	24% of the inhabitants in Barcelona are from other areas of Spain, and 17% are from other countries, mostly Pakistan, Italy, China, Ecuador, Bolivia and Morocco.[8]	23.3 % of the inhabitants in Copenhagen municipality were born in another country (2012 figure). 14.6 % are from non-Western countries and 8.7 % from Western countries	48.9% of the inhabitants in Rotterdam municipality were born in another country. 37.5% from non-Western countries, mainly Thailand (8%), Turkey (7.8%) and Morocco 6.7%)[9]
Unemployment rate (for the city)	18.2 (2015)[10] 22.1% (2015) for Spain as a whole[11]	5.2% (2016, first quarter) 4.3% for Denmark as a whole[12]	12% (2015) 6.7% for the Netherlands as a whole[13]

are of a similar size (around 0.6 million people). Copenhagen is the capital of Denmark and its largest city, while neither of the others are national capitals. Rotterdam is by far the most diverse in regard to the percentage of its inhabitants born in other countries. It also has the highest level of non-Western-born inhabitants. Finally, unemployment is by far the lowest in Copenhagen and Denmark more generally, while Barcelona (and Spain) has the highest unemployment rate. Rotterdam's unemployment rate is in between the other two cities but is relatively high compared to the overall rate in the Netherlands, signalling that it has a high level of socioeconomic disadvantage within the national context.

Sampling and Summary of the Respondents from Each City

Barcelona

The survey was sent to every manager of the Barcelona City Council (that is, to all people at the top three levels of the administration). All the districts of the City Council were included in the study, and all of the eight areas (see Table 5.3). The survey was conducted during March 2014.

Table 5.3 Barcelona Sample and Response Rates

Division	Number of staff at senior levels	Number of responses	Response rate (%)
Politicians (in government)	15	7	47
Managers	233	66	28
General management	11	7	9.6
Districts coordination	46	12	16.4
Resources	47	11	15
Economy, business and employment	21	6	8.2
Life quality and sports	20	5	6.8
Prevention, security and mobility	27	4	5.4
Culture, knowledge, creativity and innovation	21	9	12.3
Urban habitat	40	19	26
Total	248	73	29

From a selected list of the whole population of 248 senior managers (the top-three levels) and politicians, we managed to collect answers to the online questionnaire from 66 administrators and seven politicians (73 responses in total). Hence, the responses do not necessarily represent the whole population of senior managers and politicians in the city of Barcelona.

Copenhagen

For the survey, all the Mayors were invited, but the Mayor of Health and Care was the only one to give us permission to approach the politicians/ council members of the health committee. We were unsuccessful in getting many politicians due to the timing, as the election was only a few weeks after we began to gather the data. However, we were given permission to approach the senior managers as potential participants in the following six divisions: Health and Care, Employment and Integration, Culture and Leisure, Social Services, Technical and Environmental, and Children and Youth Departments.

From November 2013 to February 2014, 175 responses were gathered through invitations to the online questionnaire. From a selected list of the whole population of 464 senior managers (the top-three levels) and mayors, we collected answers from 173 senior managers and one politician, and one mayor was interviewed face to face (Table 5.4). Hence, the responses do not represent the whole population of senior managers in the city of

Table 5.4 Copenhagen Sample and Response Rates[a]

Division	Politicians/senior administrators invited	Responses[b]	Response rate (%)
Mayors	6	1	16.6
Politicians (not mayors)	16	1	6.3
Total politicians	**22**	**2**	**9.1**
Health and care	118	52	44.1
Children and youth	21	7	33.3
Employment and integration*	29	3	10.3
Culture and leisure	88	53	60.2
Technical and environmental*	106	17	16.0
Social services	102	41	40.1
Total administrators	**442**	**173**	**39.1**
Total	**464**	**175**	

[a]These are 'worst case' estimates—there were significant numbers of email bounce-backs, and people who did not complete the survey but indicated they were in relatively junior positions and should not have been in our sampling frame (particularly for divisions marked*). When these are excluded, the actual response rate is around 50 per cent.
[b]Number of responses is calculated as those who answered questions beyond the initial two.

Copenhagen, and the small number of politicians included means that we are unable to make any claims in regard to them.

Rotterdam

Together with our contact person at the municipality, we composed a committee with four relevant staff members and met to discuss how to approach the politicians and administrators. We gained access to the contact details of the top administrators and had contact with the secretaries of the mayors and council members. From January to March 2014, we sent out invitations to complete the online questionnaire. Table 5.5 shows the numbers and response rates for mayors, council members and administrators. We obtained responses for a total of 171 people—nine politicians and 162 administrators. Hence, for Rotterdam, as for the other two cities, we have a sample that is not necessarily representative of the administration in general and has a small number of politicians.

Before moving on to a consideration of the socioeconomic challenges and significant innovations in each of these municipalities, a summary of the characteristics of the respondents from each city is provided (Table 5.6). As noted above, we have a small number of politicians in Barcelona and Rotterdam, but very few from Copenhagen. The information on levels is

Table 5.5 Rotterdam Sample and Response Rates

	Invited	Responses[a]	Response rate %
Mayors (Aldermen)	8	5	62.5
Council members	45	4	8.8
Administrators	330	162	49.1
Administration		16	
Public Services		7	
City Management		30	
Social Development		28	
Work and Income		9	
City Development		33	
Service Organization		34	
Other / missing		5	
Total	383	171	44.6

[a]Number of responses is calculated as those who answered questions beyond the initial two.

Table 5.6 Characteristics of Respondents from Each City

	Barcelona (n=71)	Copenhagen (n=175)	Rotterdam (n=171)
% Politicians	9.9	1.1	7.5
% Level 1 (CEOs and Directors)	14.1	0.6	13.2
% Level 2 (Line Managers)	66.2	25.7	41.4
% Level 3 (Centre and Programme Managers)	9.9	72.6	37.9
% Female	36.1	57.0	43.8
% Postgraduate degree (Master's or PhD)	52.8	61.2	65.7
% Attended conference in the last 12 months	91.7	82.5	64.9
% Attended training in the last 12 months	43.1	77.6	48.9
% Attended excursion in the last 12 months	22.2	32.7	57.6
Years worked in municipality (mean)	16.9	12.8	14.8
Years worked in private firms (mean)	5.99	0.23	0.39
Years worked in non-government organizations (mean)	1.94	0.16	0.07
Years worked in other public sector organizations (mean)	5.48	0.34	0.29

not directly comparable: For Copenhagen, information on the levels was provided by the Human Resource Department of Copenhagen municipality and was coded as background information in the personal link to the survey. Rotterdam's respondent levels were added afterwards on the basis of the organizational structure, but some were difficult to place because their hierarchical position (for example for programme managers) was unclear. The criterion used for the levels was the number of staff placed directly under them. We have very few responses from administrators at level 1 from for Copenhagen and many more at level 3.

Females comprised more than half of the respondents in Copenhagen, while they were outnumbered in the other two municipalities. Respondents in Rotterdam had the highest levels of qualifications, followed by Copenhagen, then Barcelona. Conference attendance was lower for Rotterdam staff than for the other two cities, but they were much more likely than their counterparts elsewhere to have been on an excursion in the last year. Training in the last year was much higher for Copenhagen than the other two cities. The mean number of years worked in the municipality varied from almost 17 years for Barcelona staff, to 14.8 for Rotterdam and 12.8 for Copenhagen. Experience of working in other sectors was very minimal in Copenhagen and Rotterdam but quite substantial for Barcelona in both private firms and other public sector organizations. These differences are important in some of the analyses that follow and are referred to when this is the case.

The View from Outside the Cities

While most of this study was directed at gaining a view of innovation capacity from those inside the three city governments (elected politicians and administrators), we were also interested in considering the perspective of people who were outside but had some involvement with these cities. This provides an 'outside view' of the important socioeconomic challenges facing each municipality and what innovations people outside the municipality recognized as significant, which could be expected to differ from the 'inside view'.

To identify these people, during the survey, respondents were asked to nominate up to five people regarded as important in the local community (but outside the municipal government) in regard to innovations to address socioeconomic development challenges. Our respondents were also asked to provide information on the position and the organization for each person they nominated. In most cases the names of people were provided, while in others, organizations were nominated but no specific individual was named. A list of people was then constructed with the aim of interviewing about 25 of them in each location to gain their views on the socioeconomic challenges in the municipality, significant innovations and the innovativeness of the municipality (this last aspect is examined in Chapter 6).

For Barcelona, 25 people nominated as innovators in the community were interviewed. Some 20 people identified in the local community in Copenhagen were interviewed, and a total of 35 interviews were conducted in Rotterdam with people nominated by respondents to the survey. Information on the organizations they belong to and the numbers interviewed in all three cities are shown in Appendix A.

Socioeconomic Challenges in the Cities

As part of the survey, our respondents were asked to nominate up to five current and future socioeconomic challenges facing their city. A list of challenges was created based on these nominations, and these are shown in tables for each city. Respondents used their own words to describe socioeconomic challenges and significant innovations, so the terms in Tables 5.7 to 5.9 represent composite categories which have been interpreted by the local researchers. The outside people were asked to nominate up to five current and future socioeconomic challenges, using the same question.

For Barcelona, the most important current and future socioeconomic challenges are shown in Table 5.7. The challenges that were nominated the most by those within the municipality were assistance to vulnerable people and unemployment. Following these two most nominated challenges, were good management, economic revitalization and Barcelona's image.

For Barcelona, there is a reasonable level of correspondence between the most nominated by people inside and outside the municipality, relating to assistance to vulnerable people and unemployment. However, people outside the municipality did not nominate exemplary management, consolidation of

Table 5.7 Socioeconomic Challenges Nominated for Barcelona

Position in municipality's list	Challenge	Number of nominations (n=315)	Number of outsider nominations (and rank) (n=93)
1	Assistance to vulnerable people	51	18 (1)
2	Unemployment	40	6 (2)
3	Exemplary management of public administration	26	Not mentioned
4	Economic revitalization	22	5 (3)
5	Consolidation of Barcelona brand	22	Not mentioned
6	Facilitate efficient mobility of people and goods	20	Not mentioned
7	Education	20	Not mentioned
8	Framework to develop (balanced) tourism	16	5 (3)
9	Sustainable development of the city (environment and pollution)	16	2 (5)
10	Assume that we are in the information society	15	Not mentioned

the Barcelona brand or the efficient mobility of people and goods as major challenges, as did those inside.

For Copenhagen, the municipality's most nominated challenges related to financial cuts, demographic changes, environmental problems, political inclusion and social integration. All of these received 40 or more nominations (see Table 5.8). These were followed by organizational integration issues between the municipality's seven administrations, unemployment and unnecessary bureaucracy.

The socioeconomic challenges nominated in Copenhagen by the outsiders are quite aligned with the nominations from people within the municipality. They tend to be richer in details on how the socioeconomic challenges relate to one another and more focused on creating a balance between financial concerns and social problems. By far the most nominated by outsiders were

Table 5.8 Socioeconomic Challenges Nominated for Copenhagen

Position in municipality's list	Category	Examples	Number of nominations (n=394)	Number of outsider nominations (and rank) (n=65)
1	Financial	Financial cuts in the public sector, increased competition for resources, wanting higher quality for less (includes the economic crisis and its effects on the city's business life)	46	3(7)
2	Demography (Scale & Scope) A growing population & changes in demography	A rapid growth in the size of population challenges the resources of the current welfare system—needs adaptation e.g., an ageing population—a growing and more diverse need for eldercare— challenges the current scope and resources	45	6(2)

(*Continued*)

Table 5.8 Continued

Position in municipality's list	Category	Examples	Number of nominations (n=394)	Number of outsider nominations (and rank) (n=65)
3	Environmental (urbanization)	Infrastructure: pollution and traffic jams—securing green areas in the city (despite a growing population) CO_2 reductions/climate change adaptation (heavy rain) e.g., getting rid of the rainwater.	44	18(1)
4	Political inclusion	Inclusion of business life, local members, citizens, users and community leaders in development of the city	40	3(7)
5	Social equity (integration)	Avoid poverty and social isolation (centred on specific locations) through better inclusion—also related to equity in health profiles	40	6(2)
6	Organizational	Getting the big picture of a big municipality—the seven central administrations working together (includes decentralization of responsibility)	27	4(6)
7	Unemployment and training	Unemployment (motivation, youth education and trainee jobs) includes the creation of jobs on special terms	23	5(5)
8	Political/ Organizational	De-bureaucracy: getting rid of political rules that makes no sense	20	2(10)

Position in municipality's list	Category	Examples	Number of nominations (n=394)	Number of outsider nominations (and rank) (n=65)
9	Social housing and diversity	Affordable apartments (for low and average income people) with shorter waiting lists	13	6(2)
10	Social care jobs	Securing qualified staff in the city for social care jobs (in kindergartens, schools, eldercare)	10	3(7)

environmental issues (third in the municipalities list). Demographic challenges, social housing and health inequality were all nominated frequently, and all of these were fairly highly nominated by the municipality, too.

The five most important socioeconomic challenges nominated by insiders for Rotterdam are shown in Table 5.9. The challenges that were mentioned the most relate to unemployment and welfare dependence, the mismatch between education levels and the labour market and the diverse composition of Rotterdam's population, which is related to social segregation and inequality. These were followed by physical infrastructure problems, health care service reforms, a lack of economic activity and unemployment.

The most highly nominated socioeconomic challenges nominated in Rotterdam by outsiders were the physical environment and economic/business activity, followed by unemployment and segregation. Again, there is a high level of correspondence between the number of nominations by those outside and those inside the municipality.

Some of the most frequently nominated socioeconomic challenges were common across the three cities: unemployment and education, pressure on welfare systems and a range of financial difficulties (cuts, lack of economic activity, economic revitalization). Environmental problems, including housing and transport issues of various kinds, were also raised in each city. Inclusion and integration were nominated in Copenhagen and Rotterdam, particularly in relation to the diversity of the city's population in Rotterdam's case, but this was not raised in Barcelona.

A number of more inward looking challenges were mentioned by the cities too: Copenhagen raised the issue of organizational integration between the municipality's seven administrations, and unnecessary bureaucracy. For Barcelona, good management consolidation of the city's branding and being part of the information society were seen as challenges. Interestingly, none

Table 5.9 Socioeconomic Challenges Nominated by Rotterdam Municipality

Position in municipality's list	Category	Examples	Number of nominations (n=451)	Number of outsider nominations (and rank) (n=117)
1	Unemployment/ Poverty	• unemployment • poverty • social benefit dependence	76	14(3)
2	Education attainment / Youth	• mismatch education— labour market • school dropout • inactive youth	61	13(5)
3	Diversity/ Segregation	• multiculturalism • individualization • social segregation, lack of participation • inequality	54	14(3)
4	Physical environment /City development	• housing market • pollution, unsustainability • immobility, inaccessibility • unattractive city	49	17(1)
5	Organization of public health care	• decentralization of health care • budget cuts in public service • inequality in health (care)	48	8(8)
6	Economic/ Business activity	• lack of business activity • unfavourable business climate	48	17(1)
7	Labour market	• lack of jobs • especially for lower educated	44	10(7)
8	Demography/ Educational level	• unfavourable population composition • lack of highly educated people	31	11(6)
9	Safety/Crime	• crime • (benefit) fraud	19	1(10)
10	Multi-problem neighbourhoods	• disadvantaged multi-problem neighbourhoods especially 'Zuid'	13	6(9)

of the most highly nominated challenges in Rotterdam were about internal municipality structures or reforms.

Comparing the socioeconomic challenges nominated by the insiders and outsiders for each city indicates that there is a very strong overlap in Copenhagen and Rotterdam in regard to what are seen as the major challenges. The ten most nominated challenges by those inside the city were all nominated by those outside. Three of the top five challenges were the same for Copenhagen, and four of the five were the same for Rotterdam. In Barcelona, while three of the municipality's top five were also in the top five for outsiders, there is much less overall agreement in the top ten in this case. Only five of the ten most nominated by city insiders were nominated by outsiders.

Conclusions

As we argued in the first part of this book, the innovation capacity of a city is linked to the environment within which it is located. We have examined a range of characteristics which are seen to be related to this, including national and municipal governance structures, the formal organizational structures of city governments, the local socioeconomic context and perceived challenges and recent innovations enacted by the cities. This chapter provides a solid contextual background for the next chapter, which is focused on innovation drivers, supports and innovation capacity.

The analysis provided in this chapter indicates that Spain has stronger local governments with more autonomy than either Denmark or the Netherlands. Denmark rates the highest of these three nations on the European Commission's innovation scoreboard, and Copenhagen is the highest on the Innovation Cities index. However, these are broad and highly aggregated measures—the first largely related to national socioeconomic indicators, and the second largely related to the private sector and a raft of other contextual factors. Hence, little can be established in regard to direct connections between these overall indicators and the innovativeness of the city governments.

In regard to the formal structures of the city governments, it is the City Council that has the ultimate decision-making power in each case, despite the very different structures and processes that precede any such decisions being considered. Copenhagen has seven administrative divisions, which operate quite independently. It is only at the political level (through the City Council) that the city operates as a single entity. The organizational structures for Barcelona and Rotterdam are more integrated than for Copenhagen. Barcelona is the largest of the three cities with the highest unemployment rate; Copenhagen has the lowest unemployment rate, and Rotterdam is the most ethnically diverse and has an unemployment rate that is relatively high in national terms.

A number of socioeconomic challenges were frequently nominated by all three cities, including unemployment and education, pressure on welfare systems, a range of financial difficulties and environmental problems. Inclusion and integration were nominated in Copenhagen and Rotterdam, particularly in relation to the diversity of the city's population in Rotterdam's case, but not in Barcelona. Some more internal challenges were also mentioned in Copenhagen and Barcelona, but these were not amongst the most highly nominated challenges in Rotterdam. Comparing the views of insiders and outsiders, the main findings were that the nominations of socioeconomic challenges in each of the cities by the outsiders were quite similar to the nominations from people within the municipality, although the order differs. For Barcelona, there was a lower level of correspondence between the challenges nominated by people inside and outside the municipality.

Notes

1 European Commission Innovation Union Scoreboard website <http://ec.europa.eu/enterprise/policies/innovation/facts-figures-analysis/innovation-scoreboard/index_en.htm>, accessed 15 August 2014.
2 Innovation Cities 2014 Index website <http://www.innovation-cities.com/indexes>, accessed 15 August 2014.
3 See: http://premsa.bcn.cat/2014/07/04/xavier-trias-volem-compartir-amb-donostia-lestrategia-de-barcelona-dimpulsar-la-innovacio-transversalment-a-tota-la-ciutat-per-generar-confianca-i-llocs-de-treball
4 *Politikken* (newspaper)København vil bygge sig ud af Finanskrisen, 24 March 2010
5 Københavns Kommune (Copenhagen Municipality) website <www.kk.dk>, accessed 10 June 2013.
6 *Information* (newspaper) København har brug for en ny Planlov, 18 June 2013.
7 See: http://rotterdam.nl/onderzoek
8 Data (2016) from the worldpopulationreview.com, accessed 19 June, 2016.
9 From: Publiekszaken Rotterdam, bewerking COS, Centrum voor Onderzoek en Statistiek, 29–04–11 (website:http://www.rotterdam.nl/COS/standaardtabellen/demografie/D05%20Bevolking%20Rotterdam%20naar%20land%20van%20nationaliteit,%20op%201–1–2000–2011.pdf
10 From the Statistical Yearbook of Catalonia, www.idescat.cat, accessed 19 June, 2016.
11 From the National Statistics Institute (INE). Spain has the second highest unemployment rate among the countries in the European Union after Greece.
12 From: Danmarks Statistik. http://www.statistikbanken.dk/10316, accessed 18 June 2016.
13 From: Gemeente Rotterdam, Economische Verkenningen Rotterdam 2016 (website:http://evr2016.publizines.nl/)

References

European Commission. 2014. "Barcelona Is 'iCaptical' of Europe." Accessed 8 Jul 2016. http://europa.eu/rapid/press-release_IP-14–239_en.htm.
Loughlin, John, and B. Guy Peters. 1997. "State traditions, administrative reform and regionalization." In *The political economy of regionalism*, edited by Michael Keating and John Loughlin, 41–62. London: Frank Cass.

Pollitt, Christopher, and Geert Bouckaert. 2011. *Public management reform: A comparative analysis—New Public Management, governance, and the neo-Weberian state* (3rd edition). Oxford: Oxford University Press.

Statistics Denmark. 2014. "FRKM114: Population Projections 2014 by Municipality, Sex and Age (DISCONTINUED)." Accessed 8 Jul 2016. http://www.statistik-banken.dk/FRKM114.

Voorberg, William H., Victor J.J.M. Bekkers, and Lars G. Tummers. 2015. "A systematic review of co-creation and co-production: Embarking on the social innovation journey." *Public Management Review* 17(9): 1333–57.

World Wildlife Fund. 2016. "We Love Cities website." Accessed 8 Jul 2016. http://www.welovecities.org/.

6 Innovation Capacity
Drivers and Supports

In the previous chapter, we compared the formal organizational structures, socioeconomic contexts and challenges, and significant innovations for each city. These are all important factors in establishing environments that are more and less supportive of innovation. In this chapter, we turn our attention to innovation drivers and supports and significant innovations in each city. We also examine the innovation capacity of these cities, as rated by those both inside and outside their municipal governments.

Innovation Drivers and Barriers

To examine the innovation drivers and barriers in each city, we asked people about a range of internal and external factors that have an impact on their capacity to innovate. We provided them with a list of 18 procedures, structures and contextual factors that might either help or hinder innovation in their municipality and asked them to indicate which of these help/hinder. The results for this are shown in Tables 6.1 to 6.3.

For Barcelona, the procedures most likely to help innovation were the pay and promotion system, the values and culture of administrators, municipal elections and the quality of proposals from local politicians (see Table 6.1). The factors most likely to hinder innovation were the city's business elite, national government pressure on municipalities, the quality of proposals from administrators, the annual budget process, statutory and advisory committee meetings and the structure of the municipal government. Factors seen as neither helping nor hindering innovation were public meetings and the media. Opinion was divided on the impact on innovation of the municipal corporate plan, the current financial crisis, the values and culture of local politicians and directives from the EU.

The procedures that were most likely to be seen as helping innovation in Copenhagen were municipal elections, followed by the municipality's meetings (statutory committee, advisory committee and public), the pay and promotion system and the business elite of the city. The items that were most likely to be seen as hindering innovation were national government pressure, the municipality's organizational structure and the annual budget process.

Table 6.1 Innovation Drivers/Barriers in Barcelona

(n=71)	Percentage				
	Mostly hinders	*Hinders more than helps*	*Neither helps nor hinders*	*Helps more than hinders*	*Mostly helps*
1 The annual budget process	9.9	39.4	19.7	23.9	7.0
2 The municipality's corporate plan	1.4	23.9	35.2	26.8	12.7
3 The municipality's statutory committee meetings	12.7	35.2	45.1	7.0	0
4 The municipality's advisory committee meetings	4.3	14.5	50.70	29.0	1.4
5 The municipality's public meetings	15.7	32.9	41.4	10.0	0
6 Pay and promotion system	23.6	36.1	33.3	2.8	4.2
7 Values and culture of executive management (not politicians)	5.6	11.1	25.0	36.1	22.2
8 Organizational structure of the municipal government	6.9	29.2	34.7	20.8	8.3
9 Quality of proposals coming from officers/administrators (not politicians)	2.8	8.5	31.0	45.1	15.5
10 Municipal election campaigns	21.4	30.0	35.7	12.9	0
11 Values and culture of elected politicians (including Mayors)	12.7	21.1	38.0	18.3	9.9
12 Quality of policy proposals coming from local politicians (including Mayors)	5.7	24.3	37.1	27.1	5.7
13 National government pressure on municipalities	31.0	33.8	31.0	2.8	1.4
14 Directives from the EU	2.9	20.0	52.9	21.4	2.9
15 The current economic crisis	14.1	16.9	28.2	32.4	8.5
16 The business elite of the city	8.6	7.1	51.4	31.4	1.4

(*Continued*)

Table 6.1   Continued

(n=71)	Percentage				
	Mostly hinders	Hinders more than helps	Neither helps nor hinders	Helps more than hinders	Mostly helps
17 Media attention	1.4	28.6	48.6	21.4	0
18 Contact with and involvement of citizens and community groups	2.8	11.1	20.8	48.6	16.7

Things that were mostly seen as neither helping nor hindering were the corporate plan, citizens and community group involvement and the quality of proposals from both administrators and local politicians. Opinion was quite split on directives from the EU and the current economic crisis (see Table 6.2).

In Rotterdam, it was the involvement of citizens and community groups, the economic crisis and the city's business elite and media attention that were regarded as most helpful to innovation (see Table 6.3). Procedures regarded as hindering rather than helping were the annual budget process, the organizational structure of the municipal government, the municipality's corporate plan, municipal elections and directives from the EU. Factors seen as neither helping nor hindering included the municipality's advisory committee meetings, the quality of proposals coming from administrators and from local politicians. Opinion was split on whether the values and culture of administrators and of local politicians either helped or hindered, and likewise in regard to pressure from national government.

No clear picture arises from this, with different procedures, structures and contextual factors seen as barriers and drivers of innovation in each case. For example, the economic crisis was seen as helpful in Rotterdam, while opinion on this was quite divided in Barcelona and Copenhagen. Similarly, municipal elections were seen as helpful in Barcelona and Copenhagen, but as a hindrance in Rotterdam. National government pressure on municipalities was seen as a hindrance in Barcelona and Copenhagen, but in Rotterdam opinion was divided. Finally, directives from the EU were regarded as a hindrance to innovation in Rotterdam, but opinion on this was split in Barcelona and Copenhagen.

An overall score for innovation drivers was created by summing the responses for each of these 18 items. This provides a general indication of how helpful a municipality's procedures, structures and context are seen to be in regard to innovation. This has a maximum score of 90, in the case where an individual rated each of the 18 items at the maximum of five. Copenhagen scored the highest on this, with a mean score of 68.4. Rotterdam and Barcelona were significantly lower, at 58.6 and 53.0, respectively.

Table 6.2 Innovation Drivers/Barriers in Copenhagen

(n=140)	Percentage				
	Mostly hinders	Hinders more than helps	Neither helps nor hinders	Helps more than hinders	Mostly helps
1 The annual budget process	5.0	33.6	38.6	5.7	17.1
2 The municipality's corporate plan	0.7	18.6	62.1	5.7	12.9
3 The municipality's statutory committee meetings	2.9	18.8	23.2	2.9	52.2
4 The municipality's advisory committee meetings	1.4	10.1	37.7	3.6	47.1
5 The municipality's public meetings	2.9	8.6	41.7	2.9	43.9
6 Pay and promotion system	5.1	20.3	26.1	2.2	46.4
7 Values and culture of executive management (not politicians)	1.4	10.1	52.5	23.7	12.2
8 Organizational structure of the municipal government	10.9	23.2	26.1	1.4	38.4
9 Quality of proposals coming from officers/ administrators (not politicians)	0.7	2.9	56.5	20.3	19.6
10 Municipal election campaigns	6.5	21.0	8.7	0.7	63.0
11 Values and culture of elected politicians (including Mayors)	2.9	19.7	50.4	5.1	21.9
12 Quality of policy proposals coming from local politicians (including Mayors)	5.8	24.1	33.6	2.2	34.3
13 National government pressure on municipalities	12.4	40.9	16.1	2.2	28.5
14 Directives from the EU	13.9	35.0	8.8	1.5	40.9
15 The current economic crisis	13.1	21.2	29.9	3.6	32.1
16 The business elite of the city	1.5	2.9	43.1	7.3	45.3
17 Media attention	8.0	26.8	32.6	6.5	26.1
18 Contact with and involvement of citizens and community groups	0	2.9	57.2	25.4	14.5

Table 6.3 Innovation Drivers/Barriers in Rotterdam

(n=150)	Percentage				
	Mostly hinders	*Hinders more than helps*	*Neither helps nor hinders*	*Helps more than hinders*	*Mostly helps*
1 The annual budget process	12.0	49.3	31.3	6.0	1.3
2 The municipality's corporate plan	10.7	35.3	48.0	4.7	1.3
3 The municipality's statutory committee meetings	7.5	29.9	52.4	8.8	1.4
4 The municipality's advisory committee meetings	3.4	15.8	58.2	20.5	2.1
5 The municipality's public meetings	0.7	11.8	52.8	32.6	2.1
6 Pay and promotion system	10.0	35.3	50.0	4.7	0
7 Values and culture of executive management (not politicians)	6.7	21.5	38.9	28.9	4.0
8 Organizational structure of the municipal government	16.1	43.0	32.2	8.7	0
9 Quality of proposals coming from officers/ administrators (not politicians)	4.7	18.8	59.1	16.1	1.3
10 Municipal election campaigns	11.6	31.3	44.9	10.9	1.4
11 Values and culture of elected politicians (including Mayors)	3.4	24.3	45.3	26.4	0.7

(n=150)	Percentage				
	Mostly hinders	*Hinders more than helps*	*Neither helps nor hinders*	*Helps more than hinders*	*Mostly helps*
12 Quality of policy proposals coming from local politicians (including Mayors)	2.7	20.9	57.4	18.2	0.7
13 National government pressure on municipalities	7.4	31.5	25.5	32.9	2.7
14 Directives from the EU	10.1	34.9	38.9	15.4	0.7
15 The current economic crisis	8.7	18.8	9.4	51.7	11.4
16 The business elite of the city	0	2.1	38.4	51.4	8.2
17 Media attention	5.4	17.6	28.4	43.9	4.7
18 Contact with and involvement of citizens and community groups	0	5.4	18.4	59.9	16.3

Innovation Supports: Networking and Boundary Spanning

While there are a series of structures, processes and other factors that are likely to either support or inhibit innovation, as examined in the previous section, there are also a number of aspects of interconnectedness that are widely regarded as supporting innovation. As was discussed in Chapter 3, one of these is the ability to reach outside an organization to access different information from a range of sources. The other is the ability to span boundaries both within and outside an organization to develop relationships and mobilize resources. We examined both of these in our survey.

To gain information on the level of external networking for each city, we asked a question that included frequency in communication with 13 types of external organizations. The results can be seen in Table 6.4. The aim was to gauge the amount and frequency of external contact that our respondents had with a range of organizations about municipality-related matters. This included communication by phone, email or in person, but excluded bulk email circulars.

Table 6.4 Frequency of Communication About a Municipality-Related Matter

Barcelona (n=52)	Percentage				
	Never	Less than monthly	Monthly	Weekly	Daily
An officer in another municipality	9.6	7.7	51.9	30.8	0
A politician from another municipality	1.9	30.8	51.9	15.4	0
An officer in the region	3.8	11.5	19.2	48.1	17.3
An officer in the national department that regulates municipalities	57.7	21.2	13.5	7.7	1.4
An officer from another national government department	21.2	38.5	30.8	9.6	0
An officer from the EU	5.8	34.6	26.9	26.9	5.8
A representative from a business association	65.4	34.6	0	0	0
A leader of a medium or large private firm	65.4	28.8	3.8	1.9	0
A representative of citizen's group	63.5	25.0	9.6	1.9	0
A representative of a union	17.3	30.8	25.0	23.1	3.8
A representative of a community sector peak organization	3.8	34.6	26.9	28.8	5.8
A representative of the media	9.6	21.2	17.3	28.8	23.1
An officer from the national association of municipalities	13.5	38.5	26.9	17.3	3.8

Copenhagen (n=136)	Percentage				
	Never	Less than Monthly	Monthly	Weekly	Daily
An officer in another municipality	15.4	34.6	23.5	22.1	4.4
A politician from another municipality	80.9	14.7	4.4	0	0
An officer in the region	66.9	22.2	8.8	2.2	0
An officer in the national department that regulates municipalities	78.7	20.6	0.7	0	0
An officer from another national government department	53.7	32.4	12.5	1.5	0
An officer from the EU	89.7	7.4	2.9	0	0
A representative from a business association	38.2	39.0	16.9	5.9	0
A leader of a medium or large private firm	35.3	35.3	22.1	6.6	0.7

Copenhagen (n=136)	Percentage				
	Never	*Less than Monthly*	*Monthly*	*Weekly*	*Daily*
A representative of a union	5.9	39.7	34.6	16.2	3.7
A representative of a community sector peak organization	19.9	53.7	19.1	6.6	0.7
A representative of the media	19.3	54.8	18.5	6.7	0.7
An officer from the national association of municipalities	60.3	27.9	10.3	1.5	0

Rotterdam (n=132)	Percentage				
	Never	*Less than Monthly*	*Monthly*	*Weekly*	*Daily*
An officer in another municipality	3.0	38.6	34.1	20.5	3.8
A politician from another municipality	47.7	37.1	10.6	3.8	0.8
An officer in the region	53.0	34.1	12.1	0.8	0
An officer in the national department that regulates municipalities	59.8	30.3	8.3	1.5	0
An officer from another national government department	37.1	42.4	17.4	2.3	0.8
An officer from the EU	83.3	15.9	0.8	0	0
A representative from a business association	28.8	37.9	22.7	9.8	0.8
A leader of a medium or large private firm	22.7	37.1	27.3	12.1	0.8
A representative of citizen's group	24.2	44.7	17.4	11.4	2.3
A representative of a union	58.3	31.1	9.8	0.8	0
A representative of a community sector peak organization	27.3	43.2	20.5	6.8	2.3
A representative of the media	33.3	43.2	17.4	6.1	0
An officer from the national association of municipalities	49.2	37.9	10.6	2.3	0

The most frequent external contact reported in Barcelona municipality was with officers in the region and with the media, followed by contact with politicians and administrators in other municipalities, the EU, community sector organizations and unions and the national association of municipalities (see Table 6.4). The lowest levels of contact were with business associations, firms, citizen's groups and national government departments.

For Copenhagen, the most frequent external communication is with administrators in other municipalities, unions and citizen's groups and community sector organizations. There is remarkably little contact with the regions, the EU, national government departments and the national organization for municipalities. There is also very little contact with politicians in other municipalities, but this is not surprising, because almost all the participants in the survey are administrators rather than politicians.

In Rotterdam, the most frequent external contact was with administrators in other municipalities, business associations and firms. There was remarkably little contact with the regions, the EU, the national organization for municipalities and national government departments. There is also a low level of contact with unions, community sector organizations and citizen's groups. Contact with politicians in other municipalities was not high, probably because most of the participants in the survey are administrators rather than politicians.

The scores for each of these 13 items were summed to give an overall score for external communication, which was then pro-rated (against the maximum possible score of 52) to give a percentage score. The mean for this new variable was 25.8, indicating that most people surveyed were in contact with external organizations less than monthly. A comparison of these mean scores across the municipalities shows that Barcelona had much more external communication, with a mean of 32.1, than the other two with means of 24.4 for Copenhagen and 24.7 for Rotterdam.

We also asked our respondents a question about the presence of boundary spanners who link people together and mobilize resources through these connections. Boundary spanning both within and outside the municipality, including developing of relationships and understanding other organizations' priorities, was examined through six questions. The results of this can be seen in Table 6.5.

The presence of boundary spanners was reported as higher in Barcelona municipality than in the other two cities, particularly in regard to actively taking care of good information exchange with other organizations, mobilizing resources, developing and sustaining relationships with other organizations and knowing what other organizations find important.

Copenhagen participants in the survey were generally of the view that either a few or some people were involved in boundary spanning activities. The highest levels were associated with mobilizing resources in the divisions, taking care of connecting with the community and working across the silos within the municipality, followed by knowing what other organizations find important.

For Rotterdam, the presence of boundary spanners is generally higher than for Copenhagen, with more people seeing that quite a lot of their colleagues are doing all types of boundary spanning, but particularly knowing what other organizations find important, developing relationships outside of the municipality and actively take care of connecting developments in the community with the municipality.

Table 6.5 Presence of Boundary Spanners

People in this municipality (politicians and administrators)	None	A few	Some	Quite a lot	Many
Barcelona (n=53)	*Percentage*				
actively develop and sustain relationships with organizations outside the municipality	11.3	24.5	47.2	17.0	0
know what other organizations find important	15.1	24.5	45.3	15.1	0
actively take care of good information exchange with other organizations	1.9	13.2	43.4	28.3	13.2
actively take care of connecting developments in the community with the internal procedures of the municipality	13.2	41.5	37.7	7.5	0
can quickly mobilize the resources needed in the divisions/departments	3.8	28.3	41.5	20.8	5.7
can quickly mobilize the resources needed in the municipality	238	39.6	26.4	24.5	5.7
Copenhagen (n=121)	*Percentage*				
actively develop and sustain relationships with organizations outside the municipality	2.5	35.5	52.1	6.6	3.3
know what other organizations find important	4.1	35.0	48.8	10.7	0.8
actively take care of good information exchange with other organizations	3.3	47.1	38.0	8.3	3.3
actively take care of connecting developments in the community with the internal procedures of the municipality	2.5	36.4	44.6	14.9	1.7
can quickly mobilize the resources needed in the divisions/departments	1.7	30.6	47.9	15.7	4.1
can quickly mobilize the resources needed in the municipality	2.5	50.4	40.5	3.3	3.3
Rotterdam (n=116)					
actively develop and sustain relationships with organizations outside the municipality	9.5	45.7	39.7	5.2	0
know what other organizations find important	0.9	17.2	52.6	28.4	0.9

(*Continued*)

Table 6.5   Continued

People in this municipality (politicians and administrators)	None	A few	Some	Quite a lot	Many
actively take care of good information exchange with other organizations	0.9	21.6	62.1	14.7	0.9
actively take care of connecting developments in the community with the internal procedures of the municipality	0.9	36.2	43.1	18.1	1.7
can quickly mobilize the resources needed in the divisions/departments	2.6	42.2	42.2	12.1	0.9
can quickly mobilize the resources needed in the municipality	1.7	54.3	33.6	8.6	1.7

The scores for each of these items were summed to provide a measure of the presence of boundary spanning in each city. This can vary between zero and 24 (totalling up six items on a scale that varies from zero to four). The highest score was found for Barcelona at 19.9, followed by Rotterdam at 17.5 and Copenhagen at 16.2.

Significant Innovations in the Cities

Participants in the survey were asked to nominate up to five innovations of importance in the municipality. A top ten list of the most nominated innovations is shown for each city in the following tables. Outside interviewees were also asked to nominate up to five innovations of importance in the municipality, again using the same question as were used to ask those inside the municipality. The most significant innovations for each city, as nominated by insiders and outsiders, are shown in Tables 6.6 to 6.8.

The results for Barcelona are shown in Table 6.6. The innovation most frequently nominated by those inside the municipality was sustainable public procurement, followed by a new bus network and the Smart City initiative. Next was Open Government, aimed at improving the transparency of the City Council. The organization and the hosting of international events was often nominated, as were a number of urban development projects, recognition of Barcelona as a brand, a new means for engaging with citizens and some employment and housing service initiatives.

For Barcelona, many of the same innovations were nominated by insiders and outsiders. The sustainable public procurement initiative, which topped the list for the municipality, was not mentioned by the community, not surprisingly given that it is an internal (and so not highly visible) innovation. However, the community nominated projects to reduce (youth) unemployment, promotion of the Port of Barcelona and the nautical cluster as

Table 6.6 Innovations Nominated for Barcelona

Position in municipality's list	Category	Examples	Number of insider nominations (n=288)	Number of outsider nominations (and rank) (n=66)
1	New service	Sustainable public procurement (procure the best on offer, cut lifetime costs and lower CO_2 emissions) Payment within 30 days (improve the liquidity of suppliers)	20	Not mentioned
2	New service	New bus network—improves connectivity between the lines and accessibility for all users	14	7(1)
3	New service	Smart City—providing better services through more flexible use of ICT	12	2(6)
4	Organization	Open Government initiative (improving transparency)	11	Not mentioned
5	Recognition	Organization of international events (e.g., the Mobile World Congress)	10	5(2)
6	Urban development	"Les Glòries" square—replace a traffic junction with a green zone BUITS plan—promotes the involvement of citizens and non-profit associations in the regeneration of 'empty zones' Superblocks project—to make the city more pedestrian-friendly	10	5(2)

(*Continued*)

Table 6.6   Continued

Position in municipality's list	Category	Examples	Number of insider nominations (n=288)	Number of outsider nominations (and rank) (n=66)
7	Recognition	International brand recognition of the city of Barcelona—fostering quality tourism to the city	10	Not mentioned
8	Organization	Co-responsibility tables—establishing spaces to collaborate with individual citizens and groups to solve problems and encourage innovation	9	4(4)
9	Service	Barcelona growth initiative—fighting the economic crisis and high levels of unemployment	8	Not mentioned
10	Service	Housing—strategic plan for social inclusion (2012–2015): social housing access, stock, emergency allocations	7	3(5)

significant innovations that did not appear on the municipality's most nominated list (see Table 5.10).

The most highly nominated innovation by those in the municipality in Copenhagen (Table 6.7) related to an organizational development known as trust based management. The next most frequently nominated innovations were citizen outreach and IT developments, followed by after-hours self-service and virtual and active services, and organizational collaboration strategies.

There is a high degree of correspondence between the significant innovations nominated by those inside and outside the municipality in Copenhagen, although technical and environmental innovations topped the outsiders' list but were only ninth for the insiders, and organizational developments were higher priorities within the city.

For Rotterdam, the ten most important recent innovations nominated by municipality respondents are compiled in Table 6.8. The innovations most

Table 6.7 Innovations Nominated for Copenhagen Municipality

Position in municipality's list	Category	Examples	Number of insider nominations (n=397)	Number of outsider nominations (and rank) (n=41)
1	Organizational development	Trust-based management (new governance system)—a step towards where everybody can take responsibility towards easier solutions in the organization: trust better than control, e.g., eldercare service no more based on minutes but a so-called flexible visit	62	4(4)
2	Citizens outreach	Focus on social capital, empowerment and use of informal sector (the volunteers) decentralization via local centres, outreach via cafes, festival, mobile music school, vote bus and Fablab (where citizens test and shares ideas)	49	5(2)
3	IT and organizational developments	Digital Copenhagen. Digitalization and new IT solutions to improve public administration— e.g., shared service centre which works across the administrations	48	3(6)

(*Continued*)

Table 6.7 Continued

Position in municipality's list	Category	Examples	Number of insider nominations (n=397)	Number of outsider nominations (and rank) (n=41)
4	New service	After-hours via self-service: Open libraries, culture houses, gyms	35	4(4)
5	New service	From passive to active citizens in eldercare: virtual rehabilitation programs (exercise programs), telemedicine and medicine check by pharmacist (DÆMP project)	34	5(2)
6	Organizational development	Cross-sectoral collaboration and bottom-up collaboration	32	Not mentioned
7	Organizational development	New management tools	26	Not mentioned
8	New products	Developments and implementations of welfare technology: robots, virtual rehabilitation, medical box, apps etc.	20	3(6)
9	Technical and environment	Infrastructure, i.e., the climate plan, green roofs, green public private partnerships, integration of new public service products, such as electrical bikes and cars, and fuels cell cars. Sustainability focus: food waste café, sun-driven library on the beach	12	9(1)

Position in municipality's list	Category	Examples	Number of insider nominations (n=397)	Number of outsider nominations (and rank) (n=41)
10	New service	Incubators for staff's ideas for new products and services: The Idea Clinic, Living Lab, work smarter etc.	7	Not mentioned

Table 6.8 Innovations Nominated for Rotterdam

Position in municipality's list	Category	Examples	Number of insider nominations (n=517)	Number of outsider nominations (and rank) (n=109)
1	Digital public service	• digital public service • municipal use of social media and apps • open data	70	6(6)
2	Uniform, digital management (internal)	• 1 centralized administration • 1 centralized service organization • mobile working • digital process design	68	3(9)
3	Citizen engagement and consultation	• needs and wishes of citizen leading • 'Rotterdam people' focused working • investments after citizen consultation	66	15(3)
4	Collaborative governance	• think and work in networks • new role for government • 'taking care of' instead of 'taking care for' • less implementation, more 'in charge'	60	20(2)

(*Continued*)

Table 6.8   Continued

Position in municipality's list	Category	Examples	Number of insider nominations (n=517)	Number of outsider nominations (and rank) (n=109)
5	Organization of public health care	• decentralization of health care • neighbourhood teams • front line working, 'behind the front door' • social return for received benefit	57	15(3)
6	Organizational structure (internal)	• integration of organization • clusters instead of divisions • un-bridged, out of thematic silo's • efficient and effective working	55	5(8)
7	Physical environment /city development	• district development with private partners • social impact bonds • social return on investment • public-private partnerships	45	23(1)
8	Centralized, user-led public service	• 1 phone number/office for all questions • personal digital environment • tailor-made service • service by appointment • hospitality	33	2(10)
9	District focused working	• policy dependent on the district • tailor-made working • un-bridged, out of the policy silo's	29	7(5)

Position in municipality's list	Category	Examples	Number of insider nominations (n=517)	Number of outsider nominations (and rank) (n=109)
10	Governance/ Administrative structure (external)	• abolition of city districts • replaced by non-political district commissions	18	6(6)

mentioned relate to digitalization and centralization of public services and internal processes. Citizen engagement was also highly nominated as was collaborative governance, the organization of health care and internal organizational structures.

The insiders and outsiders lists were similar in Rotterdam, although the order of priorities again differed with the physical environment/city development and collaborative governance being the most highly nominated by the outsiders, while these were seventh and fourth on the municipality's list.

In summary, each city nominated a number of internal organizational developments as amongst their most important innovations over the last months, and each of them nominated collaborative governance of some kind (collaboration, networks, integration, co-responsibility). New IT developments also featured in each city's list of most nominated innovations, and so did the urban environment in different ways (transport and housing in Barcelona, green developments in Copenhagen and private investment in Rotterdam). They all described new service innovations in different areas. Both Copenhagen and Rotterdam nominated citizen engagement in their lists, but this was not mentioned in Barcelona. Instead, Barcelona nominated its efforts to gain recognition as important innovations.

As was the case for the socioeconomic challenges identified in Chapter 5, there was a high degree of correspondence between the nominations by insiders and outsiders in regard to the most frequently nominated innovations, particularly for Copenhagen and Rotterdam. In Copenhagen, the five innovations most nominated by those within the municipality were the same as those nominated by those outside, and seven of the top ten were the same. Rotterdam and Barcelona outsiders nominated only three and two of the ten most nominated by those inside the municipality, but for Rotterdam, all of the ten most frequently nominated appeared on both the inside/outside lists. The degree of agreement was lower for Barcelona with six of the ten nominations by the municipality also nominated by outsiders.

Innovative Capacity

In addition, we examined the innovative capacity of each of the three cities, as rated by the politicians and administrators themselves. This provides a self-assessment of how innovative those who work in these cities believe them to be, and it delivers some further contextual information about each city in regard to its overall outlook towards innovation.

The self-rated innovation capacity of each city was scored on a seven-point scale, with the highest score (seven) meaning extremely innovative and the lowest score (one) indicating not innovative at all. They were asked this in three parts:

- This municipality is innovative;
- My immediate colleagues are innovative; and
- The division/department I work in is innovative.

A measure of self-rated innovativeness was constructed by adding these three items together, to provide a summary measure of how innovative the staff in each city regarded their municipality to be. This measure can vary between a minimum of three and a maximum of 21 and was divided by three (the number of items) for this analysis, so that it falls between one and seven allowing for, comparison with the outsiders score (described in the next paragraph). The mean self-rated innovativeness scores for Copenhagen and Rotterdam were quite similar at 4.40 and 4.17 (respectively). Barcelona's was highest at 4.76.

The innovativeness of each municipality was also scored by those outside the municipality using a version of the same question but with a single item (the municipality is innovative). This provides a valuable counterpoint to the evaluations of those inside the municipality. The question was asked on the same seven-point scale as for those inside. Barcelona again scored highest at 4.96, but this was only slightly higher than the score of 4.85 for Copenhagen. Rotterdam was much lower, at 3.32. For both Barcelona and Copenhagen, those outside the municipality regard it as slightly more innovative than those inside. The opposite is true of Rotterdam, with those outside viewing the municipality as less innovative than it regards itself.

A summary of innovation supports and innovativeness ratings is shown in Figure 6.1. This shows that Barcelona scores the highest on boundary spanning, networking and innovativeness as rated by both insiders and outsiders. Copenhagen and Rotterdam are lower and more similar in their scores for the first two of these measures. The innovativeness scores are very similar, with the most interesting finding being that those outside the city in Rotterdam see it is substantially less innovative than it sees itself to be.

A final analysis undertaken for this chapter on the innovation environment was an examination of correlations between the scores for innovation drivers, innovation supports and self-rated innovativeness. Overall, there is a strong and positive correlation between seeing the municipality as having more innovation drivers, and regarding it as innovative (Spearman's rank correlation coefficient = 0.151, significant at $p<.01$). This relationship is

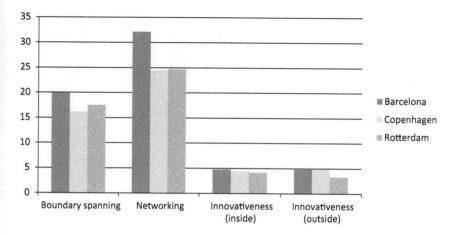

Figure 6.1 Innovation Supports and Innovativeness in Three Cities

also significant and positive for both Barcelona and Rotterdam, but not for Copenhagen.

There is a strong and positive correlation between the level of external contact (networking) and self-rated innovativeness (0.242, p<.01), indicating that people who have more contact with others outside the municipality also rate their municipality as more innovative. This relationship is positive and significant in Copenhagen but not in Rotterdam and Barcelona. There is also a very strong and positive correlation between the presence of boundary spanners and self-rated innovativeness (Spearman's rank, .362, p<.01), indicating that people who regard their municipality as engaging in more boundary spanning also rate their municipality as more innovative. This relationship is significant and positive in each of the three cities.

Conclusions

The impact of procedures, structures and contextual factors can be clearly seen in this chapter, with the innovation drivers being perceived to be quite different in each city. That the same factor can be regarded as helping in one city and hindering in another surely demonstrates the importance of local conditions on shaping the innovation environment. When looking for a set of innovation drivers in city governments, it is apparent that what works in one context will not necessarily transfer to another. Overall, Copenhagen had a much more positive view of innovation drivers in the municipality than did either Barcelona or Rotterdam.

Similarly, we see a different pattern of external networking for each of the three cities, with some contacts being seen as more important than others in each location. In terms of quantity of networking, it was Barcelona that scored the highest, pointing to a more outward looking focus of that city's administrators compared to their counterparts in Copenhagen and Rotterdam. Boundary spanning follows a similar pattern, with Barcelona leading on this measure.

The most significant innovations over the last 12 months included a number of internal organizational developments, collaborative governance arrangements, new IT developments and physical urban developments. New service innovations of different kinds were mentioned in each city too, as was citizen engagement. There is also a high degree of correspondence between the significant innovations nominated by those inside and outside the municipality in Copenhagen and also in Rotterdam, although the order of priorities differed. Again, there was a greater internal/external difference for Barcelona. In both Copenhagen and Barcelona, a number of organizational and largely internal innovations that were highly nominated by those inside were (unsurprisingly) not nominated by outsiders.

Barcelona also had the highest score on self-rated innovativeness, and the outsiders also rated their city highest on innovativeness. However, the differences between these scores were small and, for Barcelona and Copenhagen, quite strongly aligned for insiders and outsiders. The most interesting finding was that Rotterdam outsiders did not rate the city as highly as the administrators did on innovativeness.

Finally, there are positive relationships between innovation drivers, innovation supports (networking and boundary spanning), and innovativeness, although these do not hold in each of the individual cities. Given that these are all perceptual measures and reported behaviours, this suggests that there might be more and less positive overall orientations to innovation in different cities. That is, if administrators see their process and structures as supporting innovation, they are also more likely to report more networking and boundary spanning and to see their city as more innovative. The relationships between these factors will be returned to and analysed in more detail in Chapter 9.

7 Innovation Networks
Connections and Brokerage

Throughout this book, networks have been regarded as having a crucial contribution to innovation capacity. In this chapter, we present the empirical material from the survey that relates specifically to the social networks of the people we surveyed. As in the other chapters of Part II in this book, which examine the effects on innovation capacity of innovation environments, innovation drivers and supports, and leadership qualities, here we investigate social networks. Openness and diversity in whole network structures, as well as the presence of external contacts, are expected to have a positive effect on innovation capacity. So are the social networks that connect particular individuals into micro-level structures of brokerage and support, which are seen to be crucial to innovation. To make progress in understanding innovation capacity, we need to embed our analysis in *"the routine dynamics of actively self-reproducing social context, where constitutive elements and relations are generated and reinforced"* (Padgett and Mclean 2006, 1464).

Social Networks

In network studies, it is generally not possible to map entire networks, and it is often difficult to know where a particular network finishes. Sampling of individuals (egos) who nominate those they are connected to (alters) is a common method of obtaining a view of the network, and that was the approach taken here. In this study, the alter-attribute questions are reported by ego (not alter), which could produce inaccuracies. But our question relates to those whom people consider they work with most on projects, and those they go to when seeking strategic information. Therefore, the information provided about each alter's position and organization should be reasonably accurate. These data are based on our respondents' information—it is not necessarily those they actually go to. But we are interested in social influence and how it affects each ego's behaviour and social role in the transfer of information. Hence, for our purposes, it is important to know what ego thinks is true of a relationship (Borgatti, Everett and Johnson 2013).

We asked our respondents to provide information on two types of relationships: those they work with most on projects, and those they go to for strategic information. The first of these questions (people worked with most frequently on projects) captures information about networks of people working together and enables an exploration of their patterns of connectedness and centrality. Working together on projects is related to either competition (Burt 1992, 2005) or trust (Coleman 1988) and possible safe havens (Edmondson 1999). Work networks are seen as an important factor that influences the performance of individuals, groups and the organization as a whole. Hence, we are interested in examining work relationships between senior administrators in their daily work context. The level of choice of alters is lower for this type of network, because even though our respondents are relatively senior, they do not always get to choose who they work with on projects.

The second network type (based on strategic information seeking) has previously been found to be important in locating innovators in municipal governments (Considine and Lewis 2007). These are personal networks, where our respondents have a good deal of choice with regard to which people they go to in order to mobilize the embedded resources that come from ties with others (Granovetter 1985; Moritati 2013).

The networks examined here consist of exchanges of information with hidden economic values (Grandori and Soda 1995). The whole networks are first examined to understand the differences between the overall structure of work networks and strategic information networks. We are also interested in whether the information coming from external contacts matters in relation to network position. Hence, this analysis incorporates the external networking activity of our respondents as reported in Chapter 6.

We are also interested in brokers and in contrasting the Burt and Coleman types as described in Chapter 3. Both of these are likely to be important for innovation, based on different theories that privilege either low redundancy of ties and opportunities to benefit from this bridging position (Burt), or high redundancy of ties and hence a lot of support (Coleman). In short, we are interested in locating those individuals who connect people and play an important role in the transfer of strategic information. More specifically, we aim to locate the brokers who are active in sharing (in-coming ties), and in gathering (out-going ties) strategic information across the municipality. Hence, we also analyse particular egos and their set of direct ties, as a means of understanding these micro-structures.

The questions asked (known as name-generators) were as follows:

• Looking back over the last six months, who did you **work with the most on projects** in the municipality? (*List up to five people, either inside or outside the municipality, and indicate each person's position and organization or relationship to you.*); and

• Looking back over the last six months, who did you go to most when you wanted to get **strategic information** about something in the municipality (including background information not yet available in reports etc.)? (*List up to five people, either inside or outside the municipality, and indicate each person's position and organization or relationship to you.*)

Each of the surveyed senior administrators and politicians (egos) was asked to nominate five people (known as alters). This is the average number of nominations for the most frequent, important or memorable relations (Marsden 1990). This produces a reasonable number of relations for making network maps for analysis (Merluzzia and Burt 2013). The nominations provided by each person are aggregated and used to generate the matrices of social relationships that network maps are based upon. These networks are analysed using a range of measures on whole networks and ego networks, which are described in Chapter 3.

Network maps for each city government are presented in the following section, where they are analysed and compared. The ego networks are then analysed to detect the social roles played by important (in network terms) individuals. These are examined with a range of centrality measures as well as an analysis of structural holes and the social roles played by different types of brokers (see Chapter 3 for explanations of these terms). The network datasets were merged with the available 'individual attribute data' (e.g., formal levels in the hierarchy) and other data gathered from the city surveys. Of particular interest is the relationship between network position and networking (external contact) reported by these individuals.

The number of respondents for whom we have social network data is shown in Table 7.1. The distribution of respondents across levels differs by municipality, and this, along with the varying municipal formal structures, has an effect on the resulting networks, as we shall see.

Table 7.1 Number of Respondents in the Social Network Analyses

Formal level	Barcelona		Copenhagen		Rotterdam		Total
	Work	Strategic	Work	Strategic	Work	Strategic	
Level 1: Top executives	7	10	0	0	22	15	32
Level 2: Mid-level managers	47	47	21	19	51	42	119
Level 3: Centre or programme managers	7	7	58	54	41	37	106
Politicians	7	7	1	1	4	4	12
Total	71	71	80	74	118	98	269

Network Structures in Three City Governments

The network maps for the two types of networks and each city are shown in Figures 7.1 to 7.6. The network maps show each person as a dot; the lines represent the nominated relationships (ties) between people. The direction of the nomination from one person to another is shown by the arrowhead. This shows the direction of the relationship from the person who is the nominator (ego) to the person who has been nominated (alter). The maps in this chapter were produced using Netdraw (Borgatti 2002), and correlation coefficients were calculated using UCINET (Borgatti, Everett and Freeman 2002). The divisions and the formal positions at the administrative levels are indicated by the different shades and shapes of the nodes. The size of the nodes is based on the networking these individuals reported based on their levels of contact with 13 different external organizations (as described in Chapter 6). This networking behaviour is important, because it is predicted to have a positive effect on innovation capacity and stands in contrast to the more formal social position that comes from the hierarchical structure of bureaucracies.

Barcelona

The project work network for Barcelona is shown in Figure 7.1. Divisions are indicated by different shades and shapes (see key under the map), and

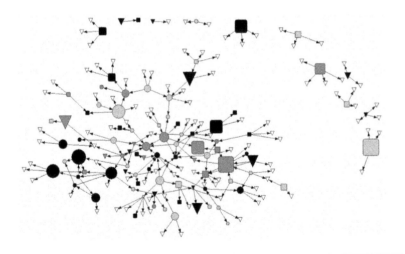

Barcelona's eight divisions: General Management = black square, Districts Coordination = black circle, Resources = black triangle, Economy, Business and Employment = grey square, Life Quality and Sports = grey circle, Prevention, Security and Mobility = grey triangle, Culture, Knowledge, Creativity and Innovation = silver square, Urban Habitat = silver circle, Not in the survey = white triangles

Figure 7.1 Barcelona Work Network

the white triangles are nominated alters who are not among our surveyed egos. There is one large component with almost everyone in it (89 per cent) and small components consisting of only one ego and his/her alters. The network is based on 71 egos and their nominated alters, consisting of 200 ties. There are many ties going to one division (black squares) in Barcelona, which is General Management. Barcelona's most central nodes (based on in-degree) are from two divisions: General Management (black squares) and Districts Coordination (black circles). The politicians are spread across the divisions, sitting in: General Management, Districts Coordination, Resources, Economy, Business and Employment, and Urban Habitat. This differs from Rotterdam, where politicians and aldermen sit together in the division 'Bench of Mayors & Aldermen'. There was no correlation between in-degree centrality and networking.

The strategic network for Barcelona is shown in Figure 7.2. This map is based on 71 egos and their nominated alters. It consists of 267 ties. In the strategic information network for Barcelona, there is one large component and again some small components consisting of single egos and their alters.

When examining the level of external networking, it seems to be those in a formal position in the hierarchy that are central. In both maps, we see that those who have a lot of incoming ties (in-degree centrality), shown by the arrowheads, are small in node size. For example, a few nodes in General Management (black squares) are high in in-degree centrality (shown by

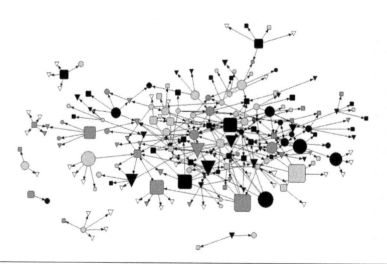

Barcelona's eight divisions: General Management = black square, Districts Coordination = black circle, Resources = black triangle, Economy, Business and Employment = grey square, Life Quality and Sports = grey circle, Prevention, Security and Mobility = grey triangle, Culture, Knowledge, Creativity and Innovation = silver square, Urban Habitat = silver circle, Not in the survey = white triangles

Figure 7.2 Barcelona Strategic Information Seeking Network

the direction of the arrowhead). In addition, we see one central node with external communication from Life Quality and Sports (grey circle), which is an executive director. In contrast, when looking at out-degree (out-going ties where arrowheads are shown moving away from ego), we see a large node from Culture, Knowledge, Creativity and Innovation (silver square) in the project work network on the right-hand side as a group of his/her own, while actively seeking its superior in the strategic information seeking network (entering the large component at the right-hand lower edge). We found no significant correlation between level of external communication and in-degree centrality.

Copenhagen

The work network for Copenhagen is shown in Figure 7.3. The map includes many star-like ego network structures and some working across the divisions, although the clustering of nodes with the same shapes into components (separate sub-graphs) is fairly clear. There are many alters with only one tie—and many of those are external people. The two largest divisions, in terms of the number of nodes in the map, are the divisions from which more people participated in the survey (Health and Care, Culture and Leisure, and Social Services). There is one quite large component (connected

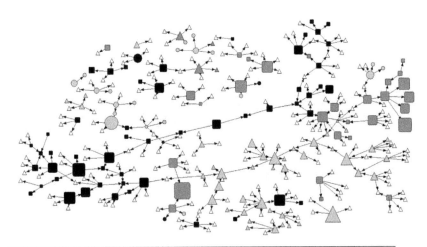

Copenhagen's seven divisions: Health and Care = black square, Children and Youth = black circle, Employment and Integration = grey triangle, Culture and Leisure = grey square, Finance = silver square, Technical and Environmental = silver circle, Social Services = silver triangle, Not in the survey = white triangles

Figure 7.3 Copenhagen Work Network

sub-graph) running through the middle and consisting mainly of people in Health and Care on the left-hand side (black squares) and Social Services (silver triangles) on the right-hand side, with the people from Culture & Leisure just above (grey squares).

There are three smaller components and a few single egos with their nominated alters. There is no single highly central actor. This map is based on 80 egos and their alters—a total of 314 ties. The pattern in Copenhagen is clear—ties mainly rest within the divisions, and the few nodes in this sample from the Lord Mayor's Division (Finance) are spread across the divisions. Those people who reported a high level of external networking sit on the edges of the work network. There was a strong and positive correlation between in-degree centrality and networking (Spearman's rank correlation coefficient =.354, p<.01).

Figure 7.4 shows the strategic information network for Copenhagen. This is based on 74 egos and their nominated alters (168 ties in total). This network is substantially smaller than the work network and directed more to people inside the municipality. In this network, there are more components of medium-sized groups, and the clustering of people into divisions is even more obvious than in the work network. Those who do more networking are more central in this network. This visual point is confirmed by a positive

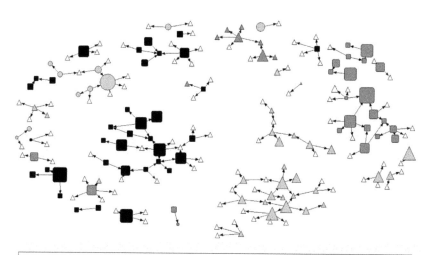

Copenhagen's seven divisions: Health and Care = black square, Children and Youth = black circle, Employment and Integration = grey triangle, Culture and Leisure = grey square, Finance = silver square, Technical and Environmental = silver circle, Social Services = silver triangle, Not in the survey = white triangles

Figure 7.4 Copenhagen Strategic Information Seeking Network

and significant correlation between in-degree centrality in the strategic network and external contact (Spearman's rank correlation coefficient =.264,
p<.05).

Rotterdam

The work network for Rotterdam (see Figure 7.5) is based on 118 egos and
their nominated alters, consisting of 409 ties in total. It has no single highly
central actor, but there is one large main component and then a number of
smaller components. There is some grouping of people into divisions but
also quite a lot of connections across the divisions. Many people whom they
work with on projects are outside our survey population. With many more
egos and alters in this map than the map for Copenhagen, and with a better
spread across divisions, this provides a more complete network map. There
was no correlation between in-degree centrality and networking.

Figure 7.6 shows the strategic information network for Rotterdam. This
is based on 98 egos and their nominated alters, consisting of 342 ties. The
strategic information network for Rotterdam consists of one large component containing many people from the City Management division (grey
squares), City Development (silver squares) and Social Development (grey
circles). We do see a pattern of people tending to cluster together in their

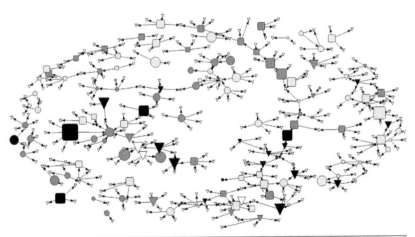

> **Rotterdam's nine divisions:** Bench of Mayors & Aldermen = black square, City Council = black
> circle, Administration = black triangle, City Management = grey square, Social Development = grey
> circle, Work and Income = grey triangle, City Development = silver square, Service Organization =
> silver circle, Public Services = silver square, Not in the survey and ~3 egos with missing information
> = white triangles

Figure 7.5 Rotterdam Work Network

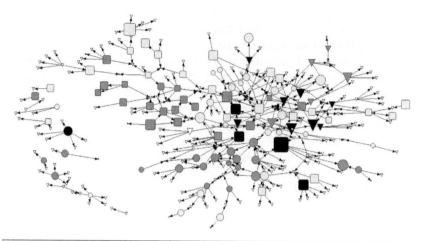

Rotterdam's nine divisions: Bench of Mayors & Aldermen = black square, City Council = black circle, Administration = black triangle, City Management = grey square, Social Development = grey circle, Work and Income = grey triangle, City Development = silver square, Service Organization = silver circle, Public Services = silver square, Not in the survey and ~3 egos with missing information = white triangles

Figure 7.6 Rotterdam Strategic Information Seeking Network

divisions. In Rotterdam, we found no significant correlation between frequency of external contact and in-degree centrality. There are a number of very central people in the large component. The arrowheads indicate the many in-going ties directed towards them in both networks. Centrality in the Rotterdam work network is linked to upward nominations to division directors—those in charge of staff and budget allocation—while centrality in the strategic network is higher for program directors—those in charge of strategic directions. We found no significant correlation between the strategic network in-degree centrality and the level of external networking.

The organizational structure is reflected in the strategic information seeking network behaviour. It could be expected that formal structure would have an impact on informal network structure. This is investigated through studying the network structure and comparing it to the data we have on formal structure, formal levels and organizational structure. The maps for each city indicate that the informal structure mirrors the organizational structure of each municipality. Rotterdam and Barcelona each have one large component functioning as the central administration. There are many ties going to one division in Barcelona and Rotterdam, but only a few ties between them and the large component. Barcelona's central nodes (in-degree) are from two departments. Copenhagen's work network reflects its formal structure of seven separate administrations (divisions). Both Rotterdam's and Barcelona's strategic information network ties are centred on one large component. Hence, in each of these three cases, informal networks seem to be shaped by the formal organizational structure.

An examination of the patterns of external networking in these networks shows that, overall, we find a significant and positive correlation between reported high levels of external networking and in-degree centrality in strategic information networks (Spearman's rank correlation coefficient =.202, p<.01). This means that those who have access to more external information are also the people that others go to for strategic information. Individually, we find this relationship holds for Copenhagen, but not for either Rotterdam or Barcelona. There are significant correlations between networking and in-degree centrality for both the work and strategic information networks in that city.

Network Centrality and the Hierarchy

The six network maps (Figures 7.1–7.6), based on these two sets of interpersonal network ties, demonstrate that the formal structure of city governments (organizational structure and hierarchy) are strongly reflected in the (informal) network structure. Now we move on to examine whether there is an emerging pattern in centrality across levels of the administrative hierarchy in the networks of the three municipalities. Is centrality more concentrated at different levels, based on actual measures? Centrality measures (in-degree and betweenness) are shown in Table 7.2 for the two different networks. As this is a directed network (from ego to alters), in-degree centrality measures can be used to discover who is the most popular, and betweenness (directed) reveals who sits between unconnected nodes.

The pattern in regard to in-degree centrality is broadly similar for both the work and strategic information networks. For all three municipalities, level 1 administrators (directors) have the highest mean score of incoming ties (they are the people that respondents 'go to' the most). In Rotterdam the politicians are also quite central as 'go-to' people for the work network. Centrality is more distributed across levels in Denmark and the Netherlands than in Spain, although it should be remembered that the respondents are not evenly spread across formal levels and are distributed differently in different cities. We suspect that the political culture in Spain is more formal and hierarchical and that this had an impact on why we had more higher-level administrators responding.

In contrast, the brokers in both networks (based on their betweenness directed centrality), appear at different levels in each city. They reside at level 2 in Copenhagen and levels 3 (work) and 2 (strategic information) for Barcelona, while they are level 1 administrators in Rotterdam, as well as politicians for the work network. This again is likely to be effected by

Table 7.2 Network Centrality Across the Hierarchy

Formal levels	Project work				Strategic information seeking			
	Degree		Betweenness		Degree		Betweenness	
	(In-degree*)		(Directed)		(In-degree*)		(Directed)	
	Mean	SD	Mean	SD	Mean	SD	Mean	SD
Barcelona								
Level 1	.013	.012	41.27	.001	.012	.015	.001	.013
Level 2	.005	.006	26.73	.001	.004	.006	.005	.001
Level 3	.009	.009	67.73	.002	.009	.009	.002	.002
Politicians	.006	.008	23.85	.008	.008	.008	.0006	.0008
Copenhagen								
Level 1	.0054	.0032	.00	.00	.0057	.0033	.00	.00
Level 2	.0037	.0032	1.48	4.37	.0039	.0032	1.66	4.53
Level 3	.0013	.0016	.095	.65	.0014	.0018	.28	1.47
Politician[1]	.00		00.		.00		.00	.00
Rotterdam								
Level 1	.0038	.0037	27.78	70.9	.0080	.0073	6.09	8.9
Level 2	.0014	.0016	8.09	25.3	.0027	.0032	.82	8.1
Level 3	.0010	.0017	5.94	30.1	.0016	.0033	1.02	5.9
Politicians	.0031	.0043	28.33	69.4	.00		.00	

Note: These scores are based on binary data (1 if there is a tie, 0 if none). Ties are directed.

*In-degree scores are normalized as they are dependent on the size of the network.

the different distribution across the levels for the respondents from different cities—particularly for Copenhagen where there were few respondents from level 1. However, it does suggest that it is the more senior people in Rotterdam who are playing the role of brokers, compared to the situation in the other two cities. Politicians only appear to be central in Rotterdam in the work networks. This might be related to the number of these in the sample; however, there were more politicians (proportionally) in the Barcelona case.

In all three cities, there is a significant level of overlap between being central in the work network and in the strategic network: The 'go-to people' (in-degree) are largely the same in the two networks (Spearman rank correlation coefficients of 0.66 for Rotterdam, 0.70 for Barcelona and 0.79 for Copenhagen), and correlations are also strong for the brokers (betweenness) in both networks (0.49 for Copenhagen and Rotterdam and 0.67 for Barcelona). For Barcelona and Rotterdam, there is some overlap in regard to who is playing both a central role in the work network and a brokerage role in the strategic information network (with correlation coefficients of 0.19

and 0.24, respectively). But there is very little overlap in betweenness in the work network and in-degree for strategic information for all three cities.

In summary, the network maps (Figures 7.1–7.6) illustrate two points: First, the results confirm that work networks are more outward-oriented than strategic information seeking networks, which are more inward-directed in all three cities. Second, adding the level of external networking for the three cities indicates that, although there is a significant and positive correlation overall between in-degree centrality and networking, this only appears to be significant for Copenhagen. Third, those people with high levels of external communication (networking) also tend to be the 'go to' people in the strategic information network. This suggests that people who cultivate external ties, which are important for openness and information diversity, are also the people that are sought out by their internal colleagues. This makes them doubly interesting in regard to innovation, as they are likely to be important for both gathering new information externally, and spreading it internally. Fourth, we can say that with regard to formal levels, the top level of administrators has many in-coming ties, while the brokers sit at different levels in different cities. In the next section, we drill down into ego networks to discover more about who the brokers are and how their immediate networks are structured.

Network Brokers: Structural Holes and Closure

In this section, the analysis is based on the network structures around particular individuals, rather than the whole networks examined so far in this chapter. This is based on the theories of Ron Burt and James Coleman (discussed in Chapter 3). Structural holes (Burt 2005) are important for innovation, because they provide opportunities to access different resources effectively. Cohesion (Coleman 1988) is an important measurement for innovation capacity, as it relates to the advantages that can be gained from closeness and support.

The following analysis is concerned with uncovering structural positions of brokerage that either support Burt's or Coleman's theory. In both cases, we are looking for the network sub-structures around individuals who connect otherwise disconnected alters. To locate the important egos for the next step in the analysis, ego-betweenness directed was calculated for the strategic information networks. This was done in order to zoom in on the important brokers and on the structural conditions facilitating the brokerage role in each of the cities. Betweenness was computed within the components (see the earlier maps), because not all egos are connected to each other. Betweenness directed was used, because the network ties are directed. The individuals with the highest betweenness centrality scored (the brokers) are considered here in isolation from the larger strategic information network. The individuals with the highest scores in each city are shown in Table 7.3, which provides some information on their level and the division they work in.

These individuals were extracted, along with their immediate ties, from the whole strategic information network for each city, and their ego networks are shown in Figures 7.7–7.9. In these maps, divisions are shown as different shapes and shades, and the white triangles indicate alters who are not included in our survey. The size of the label on each node (a unique ID) is proportional to the size of ego's betweenness (directed) centrality.

The most striking thing about the broker map for Barcelona (Figure 7.7) is that although a similar number of egos were extracted for analysis, this map is still connected, in contrast with the disconnected maps that emerge for Rotterdam and Copenhagen. For Barcelona, three people (egos 166, 5 and 69) have many in-coming ties. Ego 5 (silver square) and ego 69 (black circle)—both level 2 administrators—have a lot of variety and not much redundancy in their ties (Burt). A set of connections on the left-hand side are redundant as in-coming ties, and ego 166 (black square) has a lot of variety and slightly more redundancy in his/her in-coming ties. This person is a politician. Ego 28 (grey square) is a broker with little redundancy in his/her ties. This ego is a classic Burt type, and his/her ties go out to people in other divisions. This is a level 1 administrator (director) in Economy, Business and Employment, who connects with a politician (ego 166) and has in-coming

Table 7.3 Top Brokers in Strategic Information Networks

	Barcelona	Copenhagen	Rotterdam
1	Ego 5, mid-level manager in Culture, Knowledge, Creativity and Innovation	Ego 25, mid-level manager in Health and Care	Ego 211, executive director in Social Development
2	Ego 69, mid-level manager in Districts Coordination	Ego 73, mid-level manager in 'Health and Care'	Ego 66, executive director in Social Development
3	Ego 28 executive director in Economy, Business and Employment'	Ego 170, mid-level manager in Technical and Environmental	Ego 38, level-3 manager in Social Development
4	Ego 133, mid-level manager in Districts Coordination	Ego 360, mid-level manager in Social Service	Ego 75, executive director in Social Development
5	Ego 315, level-3 manager in Culture, Knowledge, Creativity and Innovation	Ego 318, mid-level manager in Social Service	Ego 150, executive director in City Development
6	Ego 201, level-3 manager in Economy, Business and Employment	Ego 51, mid-level manager in Health and Care	Ego 173, mid-level manager in City Management
7	Ego 166, politician		

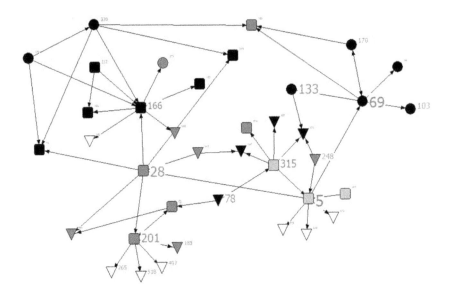

Figure 7.7 Barcelona Brokers

ties from other departments. Ego 315, a level 3 administrator in Culture, Knowledge, Creativity and Innovation, is linking across departments.

The broker map for Copenhagen (Figure 7.8) is dominated by level 2 administrators, as would be expected from the previous analysis (see Table 7.2). There are two Burt broker types, ego 360 and ego 318, who both belong to Social Services (silver triangles) and are both mid-level managers (level 2). One of them works as innovation manager and the other as leader of the citizen's centre for handicapped people. They are connected to each other through ego 339, who is a mid-level manager in Social Services. Egos 25 and 73 in Health and Care (black squares) are both mid-level managers with some closure in their ego networks due to redundant ties going from ego 73 to alter 476 (white triangle) and the in-coming tie from ego 22 to ego 25. Finally, ego 170 (silver circle) is another mid-level manager in the Technical and Environmental division. It is not shown in this map for the sake of simplicity, but ego 170 has many out-going ties to external people. She is a 'go to' person for strategic information, which is shown by the in-coming ties from her colleagues in the same division. There are no Coleman types amongst these brokers. Interestingly, all these brokers report high levels of external networking in their daily work, and they sit between people within their divisions, not across them.

In Rotterdam (Figure 7.9), all the actors with highest betweenness centrality are (not surprisingly) in the main component. The largest number are from Social Development (grey circles), followed by City Management

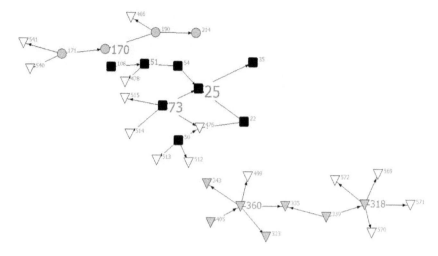

Figure 7.8 Copenhagen Brokers

(black squares). In Rotterdam these brokers are the directors (level 1), as could be expected based on the previous analysis (see Table 7.2) plus one level 3 leader in Social Development (grey circle)—ego 38. Ego 66 has a large ego network with little redundancy in out-going ties (Burt) but more in in-coming ties. It is clear that this ego has few constraints in his/her ego network. Ego number 75 responded to the survey but did not nominate the people he/she would go to. However, he/she seems to be a 'go-to' person. There is closure (Coleman) in the network between egos 38, 64, 75 and 71. They all belong to Social Development (grey circles). Ego 173 is a director in City Development who is brokering between the divisions of ego 169 in Service Organization (silver circle) and ego 75 in Social Development (grey circle). Another broker from a different department, ego 150, a director in City Development (silver square) plays an interesting broker role: Ego 67 from City Management (grey square) directs a tie to ego 150 and also to ego 80, which brings closure but also provides ego 150 with information from other departments and from people at different levels in the formal hierarchy.

This analysis of brokers shows that the ego network structures around them display characteristics of both Burt's entrepreneurial actor, who uses ties to gather diverse information from individuals who are not connected to each other, and Coleman's version, where an ego's alters are connected and there is more closure. This results in potentially greater support, but also more redundancy. A mixture of each of these appears in each municipality, suggesting that both types might be important in a public sector context, providing a different view of brokerage than is found in the private sector innovation literature. However, overall we found more Burt types in

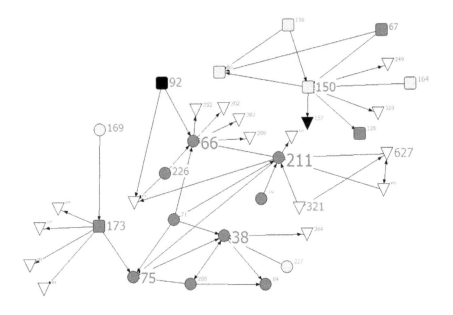

Figure 7.9 Rotterdam Brokers

Copenhagen, more Coleman types in Barcelona and the biggest mixture of types in Rotterdam. When brokerage acts either as a transfer, conducting resources from one party to another, or as coordinator, allowing third parties to act together without a direct relationship, closure through shared ties is said to be costly (Spiro, Acton and Butts 2013). Another explanation, which we see evidence for here, is that more closure might be related to spanning divisions: The brokers with closure in their ego networks also seem to be playing a bridging role across divisions in both Rotterdam and Barcelona—but not in Copenhagen (which is likely related to that city's formal organizational structure). A third explanation relates to the duration of relationships, as the tie that brings closure often appears over time, when the broker becomes the matchmaker (Spiro, Acton and Butts 2013). This might be the case in both Barcelona and Rotterdam, where our respondents have worked longer in the municipality compared to those in Copenhagen.

These ego networks structures are important, and reducing the mixture of diversity and closure in brokers' immediate ties to a single measure for each broker means losing important information. Hence, the best use that can be made of the social network information is at the level of overall and ego-level structures. In Chapter 9, where we model the impact of the different aspects of our framework on innovation capacity, we are not able to incorporate this complexity. Instead, we use the more straightforward single indicator of networking, based on the level of external contact that people reported. However, we return to some of the social network analysis findings in Chapter 10, to add more depth to understanding the important role that networks play in supporting innovation.

Linking these network findings to innovation suggests that in a public sector context, including the right mix of diversity and closure in the organizational structure is crucial to the shape of informal networks and hence to innovation and its operational efficiency. Informal network structures and in particular, the structures around brokers, provide varying levels of opportunities and constraints on action. For innovation to be possible, it is argued in the literature (as we have seen in Chapter 3) that both variety, through ties to actors who are different, and support, through ties to those who are similar in some way, are likely to be important. In line with Burt's optimal performance, both are required. The reason that ties to similar others (homophily) and the support that is assumed to arise from these are particularly important here is that innovation is a risky business. In a public sector context in particular, individuals need to feel safe to come up with ideas and test them out, without being looked down upon or dismissed by their colleagues. This brings us to the matter of trust.

Brokers and Trust

In addition to gathering information on ties, we asked our respondents to indicate the level of trust and importance that they attached to each of these ties. This was included in the surveys for Copenhagen and Rotterdam but not for Barcelona. Trust in each tie was rated on a five-point scale where five indicates the highest level of trust. The tie strengths were mostly scored as 4 or 5, with some scoring 3 and 2. The mean score for trust varied little, ranging between 4.19 and 4.49. The scores for strategic information were slightly higher for both cities (4.49 for Copenhagen and 4.29 for Rotterdam) than the scores for the work network (4.40 and 4.19).

These figures show that there is some variation between the cities and the two types of networks, but not much. They suggest three things. First, it seems that people are likely to be listing as their network alters only those that they trust. While there is some variation in the level of trust (not everyone was rated at the top of the scale), it is nevertheless clear that it is the people who are trusted that are being nominated in both of these networks. Second, people tend to have more trust in the people they seek strategic information from than those that they work with on projects. This is not surprising, as individuals have less choice in regard to who they work with on projects, whereas they are more likely to seek out people they trust when looking for strategic information. Third, slightly higher levels of trust were reported by people in Copenhagen than in Rotterdam. This could be related to the organizational structure of Copenhagen, with seven divisions that are functionally separated. As we have seen in this chapter, people's networks tend to follow this structure, and this likely leads to a greater sense of closeness (and trust) within the divisions.

The levels of trust in the ego networks of the brokers identified in Table 7.3 (and shown in Figures 7.8 and 7.9) were examined by using the trust-weighted betweenness of their immediate ties. This is a measure of betweenness that incorporates the individual tie information as a level of trust (which can vary from one to five), rather than the tie being either simply present or absent. Using this valued tie data, we find that in Copenhagen and Rotterdam, two of the most important brokers are in the top five in regard to their level of trust betweenness. This indicates that in situations of both closure and non-redundancy, the brokers have high trust.

Conclusions

This chapter analysed the interpersonal connections between individuals based on their work on projects and on seeking strategic information. We first examined whole networks in order to identify where the 'go to' people sit in the networks and in the formal hierarchy and the relationship between network position and the level of external contact (networking). We then focused on the brokers in the strategic information network.

In each of these three municipalities, informal networks seem to be shaped by the formal organizational structure. Copenhagen's seven separate divisions are reflected in these interpersonal networks, while both Rotterdam and Barcelona have more ties across departments, in line with their single organizational structures. There is a significant relationship between centrality and external networking overall, but this is only found for Copenhagen when examining individual cities. For both the work and the strategic information networks, level 1 administrators are the 'go to' people in each city. The brokers are located at different levels in the different cities, and they are more senior in the case of Rotterdam than in the other two municipalities.

The mixture of broker types also varies across the cities. The traditional entrepreneurial broker is the most frequent type in Copenhagen, Barcelona's brokers are more likely to have closure and in Rotterdam, there is a mixture of both types. The higher levels of closure in Barcelona and Rotterdam could be explained by the fact that our respondents from these cities have worked longer in the municipality, compared to Copenhagen, which tends to lead to more connections. While brokers' ego network structures vary across jurisdictions, so do the organizational structures, political culture and variations in training, education and seniority. Finally, the overall level of trust in these networks is high, particularly for the strategic information networks, and in Copenhagen. The level of trust in particular ties is also high for some but not all of the brokers, suggesting that trust is high in situations of both closure (as could be expected) but also non-redundancy. This is further discussed in Chapter 10.

Note

1 No standard deviation here, as there was only one politician respondent.

References

Borgatti, Stephen P. 2002. *NetDraw: Graph visualization software.* Cambridge, MA: Analytic Technologies.

Borgatti, Stephen P., Martin G. Everett, and Linton C. Freeman. 2002. *Ucinet for Windows: Software for social networks analysis.* Harvard, MA: Analytic Technologies.

Borgatti, Stephen P., Martin G. Everett, and Jeffrey C. Johnson. 2013. *Analyzing social networks.* London: Sage.

Burt, Ronald S. 1992. *Structural holes: The social structure of competition.* Cambridge, MA: Harvard University Press.

Burt, Ronald S. 2005. *Brokerage and closure: An introduction to social capital.* Oxford: Oxford University Press.

Coleman, James S. 1988. "Social capital in the creation of human capital." *American Journal of Sociology* 94 (supplement): 95–120.

Considine, Mark, and Jenny M. Lewis. 2007. "Innovation and innovators inside government: From institutions to networks." *Governance* 20(4): 581–607.

Edmondson, Amy. 1999. "Psychological safety and learning behaviour in work teams." *Administrative Science Quarterly* 44(2): 350–83.

Grandori, Anna, and Giuseppe Soda. 1995. "Inter-firm networks: Antecedents, mechanisms and forms." *Organizational Studies* 16(2): 183–214.

Granovetter, Mark. 1985. "Economic action and social structure: The problem of embeddedness." *American Journal of Sociology* 91(3): 481–510.

Marsden, Peter V. 1990. "Network data and measurement." *Annual Review of Sociology* 16: 435–63.

Merluzzia, Jennifer, and Ronald S. Burt. (2013). "How many names are enough? Identifying network effects with the least set of listed contacts." *Social Networks* 35(3): 331–7.

Moritati, Marzia. 2013. *Systemic aspect of innovation and design: The perspective of collaborative networks.* London: Springer.

Padgett, John F., and Paul D. McLean. 2006. "Organizational invention and elite transformation: The birth of partnership systems in Renaissance Florence." *American Journal of Sociology* 111(5): 1463–568.

Spiro, Emma S., Ryan M. Acton, and Carter T. Butts. 2013. "Extended structures of mediation: Re-examining brokerage in dynamic networks." *Social Networks* 35(1): 130–43.

8 Fostering Innovation
Leadership

Earlier in this book, we examined different perspectives on leadership and how these relate to innovation in the public sector (see Chapter 4). Five different perspectives on leadership were described, and a number of characteristics of each of these were identified. In this chapter, we use these five perspectives to empirically examine public managers' perceptions of what is important for public innovation. The analysis proceeds by first examining the five types using a theory-driven approach. Some of the leadership types (transactional, transformational, interpersonal, entrepreneurial and network governance) proved to be more robust than others. We then undertook a comparison across the three cities in our survey. This reveals both similarities and differences in terms of which types were seen to be effective in supporting innovation. It also reveals a nuanced set of leadership styles, which include a transformational style, and one that is more dedicated to motivating employees, risk taking and including others in decision making.

Measuring Perceptions of Leadership for Innovation

For this empirical examination of leadership, we used the survey responses from the 365 top-level managers in Barcelona, Copenhagen and Rotterdam municipalities. The survey included both politicians and administrators in all three municipalities. However, as we have noted earlier in this book, relatively few politicians work full time in the municipalities compared to the number of senior administrators—and we got few replies from them. For the purposes of this analysis, the few politicians in our sample were removed (seven in Barcelona, two in Copenhagen and nine in Rotterdam). The number of respondents is sufficient for scale development purposes, which requires at least 300 (Nunnally and Bernstein 1994).

The survey consisted of twenty-three leadership attributes derived from the five theoretical concepts and then translated into practical statements (shown in Chapter 4). A five-point Likert scale was used, with respondents asked to rate these statements in relation to the degree to which they perceived the attributes to be present, in relation to leadership and past innovations in the municipality. The overall question they were asked was:

> '*Thinking about your administration/municipality in relation to important innovations, to what degree do you think the leadership (both politicians and administrators) has displayed the following qualities and behaviours?*'

Based on the formulation of the question, respondents should be referring to leadership qualities that they think are present within their municipality, in regard to the innovations that they had familiarity with. Hence, the responses are senior managers' perceptions of the leadership qualities they think were present when important innovations were happening: This is not the same as responding in terms of what was, or was not, empirically carried out and evaluated as successful or unsuccessful in regards to innovation.

The order of the items was randomized in the online survey in Copenhagen and Barcelona, so that the items appeared in a different order for each respondent answering the statements, but this was not the case for Rotterdam. However, we found no systematic bias/peculiarities that might have made the responses to the fixed sequence different. To avoid 'acquiescence bias', we included a few items with antonyms to check for systematic peculiarities, for example, one item was 'displayed a long-term perspective' while another was 'displayed a short-term perspective'. Before carrying out this analysis, we checked for collinearity amongst the variables and factorability of the individual samples and overall sample (using the Kaiser-Meyer-Olkin measure of sampling adequacy and Bartlett's test of Sphericity) to check if the samples were suitable for exploratory factor analysis. The analysis in this chapter is based on responses from those with no missing values in the series of leadership questions (365 people).

Our empirical strategy was to first define the groups of leadership attributes reported by our respondents and then examine differences between the three cities. We used the five perspectives outlined in Chapter 4 (a 'top-down' approach) to test whether they could be observed empirically in the survey responses. This was done using an exploratory factor analysis using dimension reduction with principal axis factoring (promax rotation). In moving from 23 scale items (observed variables) to three factors, all analyses were performed using covariance matrices. Reliability analysis on each of the five types was then used to examine which factors were coherent and which were not.

The final step in this first phase of analysis was to construct a model to be tested using a confirmatory factor analysis (CFA), to see how well this hypothesized five factor model fitted the data and to examine the correlations between the five latent constructs testing the model fit. We did this on the whole sample with all three cities combined, because we had no *a priori* hypotheses about why the leadership qualities present should differ from place to place.

The second phase of the analysis used an exploratory factor analysis (EFA) for each city separately to examine leadership types (a 'bottom-up' approach). In this step, we wanted to test whether different combinations of items appeared in the different cities, on the basis of covariance, rather than related to the hypothesized five leadership types outlined earlier in this chapter. This second phase added a more nuanced view of perceptions of leadership types within each of our cities.

Testing Five Ideal Types of Leadership for Innovation

Exploratory Analysis

Measuring scales were adapted from the leadership literature and modified for our purposes. An exploratory factor analysis: Principal Axis Factoring extraction with promax rotation and Kaiser Normalization was performed to extract factors, as we expected some of the factors to be related. The scree plot suggested that a two factor solution was appropriate (based on where the elbow bend appears), while four factors had eigenvalues greater than 1. We experimented with three, four, and five factor solutions. The three factor solutions gave us too much overlap between the five theoretical concepts. For the four factor solution, the rotated pattern matrix indicated that the motivational factors from the interpersonal concept (dedicated to colleagues and willing to sacrifice self-interest) loaded together with two important items of the network governance styles (works collaboratively and includes others in key decisions).

In the literature, interpersonal leadership styles are very much about intra-organizational processes, whereas network governance is about inter-organizational relations. The fifth factor has an eigenvalue close to one (.948). Because we postulated five theoretical leadership types, we used the five factor model in the results that follow. Table 8.1 shows the factor loadings of the scales with the five factors extracted, and with factor loadings below 0.3 supressed to facilitate interpretation. These five factors explain 59 per cent of the variance.

Table 8.2 provides an analysis of how close the predicted location of the items on the leadership types (factors) turned out to be. The most notable divergence was the interpersonal type which, in theory, overlapped significantly with the other leadership types (see Chapter 4). The exploratory factor analysis showed that almost exclusively altruistic qualities loaded onto one factor (number 4)—so in the following, this factor is called the altruistic leadership type.

To examine how well the variables conform to the five types that we postulated, we also tested the reliability of these scales using Cronbach's alpha score (Tabachnick and Fidell 2014). In four out of the five scales, the degree of reliability was high—0.85 for transformational, 0.79 for entrepreneurial, 0.74 for interpersonal skills that almost reflected the altruistic motivational variable and 0.68 for network governance, which is just below the 0.7

Table 8.1 Leadership Pattern Matrix with Five Factor Solution

(n=365)	Factors				
	1	2	3	4	5
F Displays a long-term perspective	.82				
B Visionary	.82				
L Provides intellectual stimulation	.70				
E Visible leadership	.64				
K Inspirational	.63				
Q Knowledgeable	.42				.39
A Communication skills	.38				
W Always follows procedure		-.68			.42
T Open towards new ideas		.64			
C Takes initiatives		.62			
S Willing to risk mistakes by employees		.57			
O Good at mobilizing the resources needed		.44			
J Results-oriented		.34			
U Takes all decisions alone			-.842		
V Involves others in key decisions			.584		
D Authoritative			-.520		
P Works collaboratively			.371		
N Willing to sacrifice self-interest				1.0	
M Committed to colleagues				.48	
R Good at learning from mistakes				.32	
G Displays a short-term perspective		-.49			.64
I Problem-oriented					.45
H Good at gathering information					.39
Variance explained (percentage)	35.0	8.2	6.5	5.0	4.1

Table 8.2 Leadership Type Items and Scales (Theoretical and Empirical)

Item	Leadership type (from theory)	Leadership type (Exploratory factor analysis)	Leadership type (Confirmatory factor analysis)
A Communication skills	Interpersonal	Transformational (low)	Transformational (low- out)
B Visionary	Transformational, Entrepreneurial	Transformational	Transformational
C Takes initiative	Transactional, Transformational, Entrepreneurial	Entrepreneurial	Entrepreneurial
D Authoritative	Transactional	(-) network gov.	(out)
E Visible leadership	Transformational	Transformational	Transformational
F Displays a long-term perspective	Transformational, Network gov., Entrepreneurial	Transformational	Transformational

(Continued)

Table 8.2   Continued

Item	Leadership type (from theory)	Leadership type (Exploratory factor analysis)	Leadership type (Confirmatory factor analysis)
G Displays a short-term perspective	Transactional	Transactional	Transactional
H Good at gathering information	Transactional, Network gov., Entrepreneurial	Transactional (low)	Transactional (low-out)
I Problem-oriented	Transformational	Transactional	Transactional (low-out)
J Results-oriented	Transformational	Transactional	Entrepreneurial
K Inspirational	Transformational	Transformational	Transformational
L Provides intellectual stimulation	Interpersonal	Transformational	Transformational
M Committed to colleagues and organization	Transformational Interpersonal Network gov.	Altruistic	Altruistic
N Willing to sacrifice self-interest	Interpersonal	Altruistic	Altruistic
O Mobilizing the resources needed	Transformational, Network gov., Entrepreneurial	Entrepreneurial	Entrepreneurial
P Works collaboratively	Network gov.	Network gv. (low)	Network gov.
Q Knowledgeable	Interpersonal	Transformational	Transformational
R Good at learning from mistakes	Interpersonal	Altruistic (low)	Altruistic
S Willing to risk mistakes by employees	Interpersonal	Entrepreneurial	Entrepreneurial
T Open towards new ideas	Entrepreneurial	Entrepreneurial	Entrepreneurial
U Takes all decisions alone	Transactional	Transactional	Transactional
V Involves others in key decisions	Network gov.	Network gov.	Network gov.
W Always follows procedures	Transactional	Transactional, (-)Entrepreneurial	Transactional

desirability level for further analysis (Nunnally 1978). However, newly developed measures can be accepted with an alpha value of 0.60 in an exploratory study like this (Nunnally 1978), and in the case of large samples (defined as more than 200), even this guideline is frequently relaxed (Howell and Avolio 1993). The fifth scale (transactional) was not as coherent, producing an alpha of 0.44 when each of the five items expected to be related to this scale was included. The scales and their reliability scores are shown in Table 8.3.

Table 8.3 Leadership Types: Descriptive Statistics, Cronbach's Alpha Coefficients and Correlations

Factors	No. of items	Mean	S.D.	1	2	3	4	5
1 Transformational	7	22.65	4.8	.85				
2 Entrepreneurial	5	16.4	3.5	.67	.79			
3 Network gov.	2	6.6	1.5	.61	.56	.67		
4 Altruistic	3	9.2	2.7	.65	.67	.68	.74	
5 Transactional	5	16.5	2.5	.22	.41	.29	.56	.44

Note: All correlations are significant at p<0.01; Cronbach's alpha coefficients are shown on the diagonal (in bold) and correlation coefficients are below the diagonal.

Table 8.3 shows that the correlations between the five scales (below the diagonal) are in most cases reasonably high, with the exception being the transactional factor. The transformational and altruistic factors have the highest correlations with the other scales, with the network governance and entrepreneurial factors not far behind. The observation that various leadership scales correlate with each other is supported by others (e.g., van Knippenberg and Sitkin 2013).

Confirming the Leadership Types

To further test if our proposed model structure relating items to types had a good fit, a CFA was used. We used a structural equation model to specify our model, based on the exploratory and reliability analyses presented above, indicating which variables should load onto which factors and then testing for the level of fit of this structure. We also looked for which items and factors were correlated. In contrast to EFA, a CFA can estimate models where two or more latent variables are assumed to co-vary. CFA directly estimates factor co-variances, and control for these in the calculation of parameters for items, such as our factor loadings (Kline 2010). The fit indices of the model are used to assess the goodness of fit of the data in relation to this model.

The model initially used the same five ideal types of leadership, and the data gathered using the 23 scale items on leadership, as for the previous analysis (the EFA). The CFA model is used to calculate factor loadings and covariance and to test the model's goodness of fit. We then looked at possible modifications to optimize the goodness of fit based on the reliability analysis in Table 8.3. Taking a closer look at the correlations of variables which load on the transactional factor (pattern matrix in Table 8.2), there was room for improvement following the initial test results.

Next, only items with correlations above 0.4 were included in the model—except for item (P) 'works collaboratively' with 0.371, which was retained because it is theoretically important for the network governance construct (and it worked well in the model). We were more strict on the transactional type, removing two variables, (H) 'good at gathering information' and (I) 'is problem-oriented', because these had fairly low loadings (0.39 and 0.42) in the factor analysis but even lower in the CFA. The five factor model met the recommended cutoffs for four of the six fit indices, only falling slightly short in regard to two others.[1] Based on these findings, the five factor model is considered a reasonable representation of the theory-driven leadership types.

The final model, after adjustments were made to improve the fit, is shown in Figure 8.1, and the final column of Table 8.2 provides an overview of the

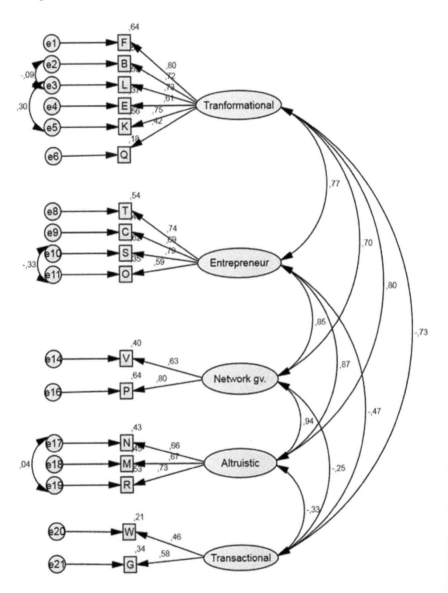

Figure 8.1 The Hypothesized Five Factor Model of Leadership

items included in the five factor model. We conclude that the items, together with the five theoretical concepts, serve as a reasonable framework for exploring the perceptions of leadership styles among senior managers in the three government municipalities of Copenhagen, Rotterdam and Barcelona.

Leadership Types in the Three Cities

Having examined leadership types for the overall sample in search of types that might appear in different places, we now move on to exploring leadership types within each city context. This analysis is focused on a search for types that might appear in each case or might be specific to each of our three cities.

In the analyses that follow, exploratory factor analysis (Principal Component Analysis with varimax rotation, and Principal Axis Factoring with promax rotation and Kaiser normalization) were used to analyse the data for each city (see: Tabachnick and Fidell 2014). The principal axis factor results are shown, as these provide a matrix focusing on the difference between the factors, and the promax (oblique) rotation was appropriate, as the factors were expected to be related to each other. In each case, a scree plot of the eigenvectors showed that three factors were appropriate (based on where the elbow of the graph was located), rather than using all the factors with an eigenvalue greater than one (four for Copenhagen, five for Rotterdam and six for Barcelona). Only factor loadings with a magnitude of .40 and higher are included for ease of interpretation. These individual, city-based EFAs are shown in Appendix B.

The Barcelona analysis (see Appendix B) offers a picture of leadership and innovation, where the network governance entrepreneurial leadership type (called the collaborative entrepreneur) is the factor that explains the most variance, followed by a mix of the transformational and motivator types (called the transformational leader). The collaborative entrepreneur factor explains 30.4 per cent of the variance, the transformational leadership type explains 11.6 per cent and the third factor, which explains 8.9 per cent, is labelled the transactional leadership type. This has a rational leadership approach (see Box 8.1). Barcelona stands out by having this 'rational type' of transactional leadership on its third factor, even though it is the weakest type.

The results of the factor analysis for Copenhagen shows that there is one very strong factor for Copenhagen, which explains 36.6 per cent of the variance and involves a group of variables that relate to interpersonal leadership styles such as commitment, motivation, intelligence and collaboration. This has been labelled the 'dedicated-motivator' (see Box 8.2). The second innovation leadership type relates to the 'entrepreneurial' leadership style, which allows mistakes by employees with a view to promoting learning. This type of leader does not always follow procedures, but is willing to take risks. The third leadership type, labelled the 'the long term planner' relates both to the transformational and entrepreneurial leadership styles, displaying a

Box 8.1: Barcelona Leadership Factors

Factor	*Description*	*Percentage of the variance explained*
The collaborative entrepreneur	Willing to risk mistakes, works collaboratively, committed to colleagues and organization, involves others in key decisions, open to new ideas, good at learning from mistakes, willing to sacrifice self-interest and mobilizing the resources needed	30.4
The transformational leader	Provides intellectual stimulation, displays a long-term perspective, inspirational, displays a visible leadership	11.6
The transactional leader	Knowledgeable, always follows procedures, displays a short-term perspective and is problem-oriented	8.9

Box 8.2: Copenhagen Leadership Factors

Factor	*Description*	*Percentage of the variance explained*
(1) The dedicated-motivator	Committed to colleagues, provides intellectual stimuli, willing to sacrifice self-interest, good at mobilizing resources and gathering information, knowledgeable, inspirational, results-oriented, involves others in key decisions, works collaboratively, is problem-oriented and open towards new ideas, displays visible leadership and takes initiative	36.6

Factor	Description	Percentage of the variance explained
(2) The entrepreneurial leader	Good at learning from mistakes, is the opposite of authoritative, is willing to allow mistakes by employees, does not always follow procedures and never takes decisions alone	7.1
(3) The long-term planner	Displays a long-term perspective and is visionary	5.7

long-term perspective and being visionary. Both these factors explain only small proportions of the variance—7.1 and 5.7, respectively.

The analysis for Rotterdam provides quite a different picture of what kind of leadership is related to innovation in the views of senior administrators. The first factor explains 27.1 per cent of the variance and is labelled the 'the transformational leader', the second explains 10.0 per cent and is labelled the 'collaborative-motivator' and the third explains 6.8 per cent and is labelled the 'long term planner' (Box 8.3). The first and second factors are very similar to the committed-motivator type found in Copenhagen but split into a transformational style of leadership and a more collaborative/network style of leadership. The third type resembles the third factor in Copenhagen but has more characteristics from the transformational style.

Box 8.3: Rotterdam Leadership Factors

Factor	Description	Percentage of the variance explained
The transformational leader	Takes initiative, open to new ideas, is results-oriented, does not always follow procedures, is willing to risk mistakes by employees, is somewhat authoritative	27.1
The collaborative-motivator	Involves others in key decisions, works collaboratively, good at mobilizing resources, committed to colleagues	10.0

Factor	Description	Percentage of the variance explained
	and organization, willing to sacrifice self-interest, good at gathering the information needed	
The long-term planner	Displays a long-term perspective, is visionary, inspirational, and provides intellectual stimulation.	6.8

Table 8.4 Correlations Between Leadership Types and Innovation Capacity

	Self-rated innovation capacity
Altruistic	.352**
Transformational	.436**
Entrepreneur	.434**
Network governance	.418**
Transactional	.094

Spearman rank correlation coefficients, **significant at p<0.01.

In summary, the senior administrators in our survey from all three cities shared a vision of leadership and innovation, based on some combination of motivational, entrepreneurial, network governance and transformational leadership styles. However, there are also some interesting nuanced differences within the three cities. The strongest perception of leadership style, seen to be important for innovation, was an altruistic motivator in Copenhagen, in Rotterdam this was a transformational type and in Barcelona, it was the collaborative entrepreneur.

In addition to understanding leadership types that are important for innovation, we aim to understand the link between these and self-rated innovation capacity. As can be seen in Table 8.4, four of the five types are strongly correlated with self-rated innovation capacity, with the transactional type being the exception to this. The interpersonal type is not as strongly correlated with innovation capacity as the other three types, but the relationship is still significant.

Conclusion

In this chapter, we empirically tested five perspectives on leadership for innovation in the public sector. We have shown that of the five perspectives hypothesised in Chapter 4, four of these could be observed empirically using data from our three cities in different nations. The perspective that was least convincing as a scale was the transactional type, which encapsulates a view of leadership that relies mostly on rational approaches, incentives and strategies to obtain the desired performance, and a clear hierarchical relationship between leaders and other actors. Given the contemporary predominance of other forms of leadership in the literature and in practice, it is perhaps not surprising that this perspective received little support from the respondents to the survey. Future work on leadership for innovation in the public sector might consider trying different items to capture this dimension, in order to determine whether it is simply not very salient, or whether our scale items could be improved.

The second phase of analysis examined whether we could find these leadership scales in three cities with disparate governance tradition and organizational structures, and if so, what differences and similarities could be found. Our study reveals that leading innovation in public sector environments is not perceived to require exactly the same skills in these different cities, despite the respondents in each case being in similar positions in these municipalities. Copenhagen senior administrators perceived that altruism and collaborative and motivational skills were the most strongly related to leadership for innovation. The transformational perspective (visionary, takes initiative) appears to be stronger in Rotterdam and Barcelona, although collaboration and inclusive decision-making were also seen as related to innovation in these cities.

It is clear that the collaborative element is important in all three cities. In Rotterdam it is strongly present in the second factor, and in Barcelona it is a very visible part of the first factor (the strongest), while in Copenhagen it is a major part of the strongest factor. Across the three cities, it seems that leadership style for innovation is mostly perceived as a mix of a transformational leadership style that emphasizes visionary leadership and is inspirational, along with a more collaborative/interpersonal leadership style that provides intellectual stimulation, is willing to risk mistakes by employees and emphasizes working collaboratively. In this sense, our results differ from research on transformational leadership styles reported from the private sector and from the tone of much of the current public sector literature.

Our findings show strong similarities in the selected leadership qualities of the senior managers in regard to innovation. One likely explanation for this could be that despite culture and country specific characteristics, the leadership literature that senior public managers are exposed to through their training and professional development is similar in all three contexts. That is, they all might have read the same texts and ideas about what is (in theory) positively associated with being a successful leader. On the other hand, given that these are all senior managers in municipal governments, they are all likely facing similar challenges to some extent, even though they are in different European countries.

Given the emphasis currently being placed on leading change and innovation in the public sector, we argue that understanding leadership and its role in innovation capacity is an important addition to our examination of governance structures and social networks in preceding chapters. Recent studies are becoming more critical towards the idea of transformational leadership (see van Knippenberg and Sitkin 2013). With this and our findings in mind, we argue that it is time to broaden the perspective of leadership research in the public sector beyond the transformational type and to look for other important qualities such as risk, motivation and network governance skills rather than visionary leadership alone.

Finally, it should be remembered that our data were obtained from senior managers in three cities, based on their views on leadership qualities related to innovation, in relation to their direct experiences and within the set of conceptual leadership choices offered. We cannot conclude whether the leadership styles perceived as the most important are also actually evaluated as successful or unsuccessful for innovation, or whether these are what is actually implemented in these municipalities. Our data do not allow us to confirm that these qualities are what actually spur innovation, and nor was this what we set out to do. What our results do suggest is the existence of identifiable public leadership styles which are regarded as promoting innovation in these three municipal governments. It is also clear that each of the leadership styles, with the exception of the transactional type, are strongly and positively related to self-rated innovation capacity.

The results presented here suggest a need to go beyond the current emphasis on transformational leadership, and to consider other leadership skills that might be just as important for innovation in the public sector. More research in this direction should broaden the variety of styles and underlying attributes which public managers are exposed to as professionals. This should provide a better menu from which they can select when taking on leadership roles that require them to foster innovation.

Note

1 Several recommended measures of model fit were used. For the tested model, it is suggested that the four goodness of fit tests, CFI, NFI, TLI and GFI (see table for an explanation of these), should be close to or higher than .90 to demonstrate an acceptable fit. It is also recommended that the RMSEA be lower than 0.06 and definitely not exceed 0.08 (Hu and Bentler 1995). However, it has been suggested that a score below 0.10 reflects an acceptable fit and below 0.08 is a good fit (see Kline 2010; Byrne 2012). A value of less than 5 for the CMIN/ DF (χ/df) ratio should be obtained (Schumacker and Lomax 2004), and preferably less than 2 or 3 (Ullman 2014). Our model meets these criteria. Furthermore, a value less than 5 for the CMIN/DF (χ/df) ratio should be obtained. Additionally, it is good practice to check modifications of the residuals. Following Figure 8.1, the following unobserved variables was set to co-vary: e10 to e11; e3 to e5; e17 to e18; and finally, e2 to e3. These were all on the same constructs, and we could then co-vary the model's predicted variables in order to modify these residuals (see test results of model optimized 2).

Statistical measures for model fit

	CFI	NFI	TLI	IFI	RMSEA	CMIN/df
Model p-matrix	.86	.82	.84	.87	.800	3.34
Model optimized 1	.89	.86	.86	.89	.085	3.63
Model optimized 2	.91	.87	.88	.91	.075	3.28

CFI = Comparative Fit Index; NFI = Normed Fit Index; Tucker-Lewis Index; RMSEA = Root Mean Square Error of the Approximation; IFI = Bollen's incremental fit index; CMIN/dF = Ratio of Chi-Square to degrees of freedom. PCLOSE = 0.000 (probability level) but this is due to the large sample size of n=365.

References

Byrne, Barbara M. 2012. *Structural equation modeling with Mplus*. New York: Taylor & Francis.

Howell, Jane M., and Bruce J. Avolio. 1993. "Transformational leadership, transactional leadership, locus of control, and support for innovation: Key predictors of consolidated-business-unit-performance." *Journal of Applied Psychology* 78(6): 891–902.

Hu, Li-tze T., and Bentler, Peter M. 1995. "Evaluating model fit." In *Structural equation modeling: Concepts, issues, and applications*, edited by R.H. Hoyle, 76–99. Thousand Oaks, CA: Sage.

Hu, L., and P. M. Bentler. 1998. "Fit indices in covariance structure modeling: Sensitivity to underparameterized model misspecification." *Psychological Methods* 3: 424–53.

Kline, R. B. 2010. *Principles and Practice of Structural Equation Modeling*. New York, NY: Guilford Press.

Nunnally, Jum C. 1978. *Psychometric theory*. Englewood Cliffs, NJ: McGraw-Hill.

Nunnally, Jum C., and Ira H. Bernstein. 1994. *Psychometric theory* (3rd edition). London: McGraw-Hill.

Schumacker, Randall E., and Richard G. Lomax. 2004. *A beginner's guide to structural equation modeling* (2nd edition). Mahwah, NJ: Lawrence Erlbaum Associates.

Tabachnick, Barbara, and Linda S. Fidell. 2014. *Using multivariate statistics* (6th edition). Harlow, Essex: Pearson.

Ullman, Jodie B. 2014. "Structural equation modeling." In *Using multivariate statistics* (6th edition), edited by Barbara G. Tabachnick and Linda S. Fidell, 731–836. Harlow, Essex: Pearson.

van Knippenberg, Daan, and Sim B. Sitkin. 2013. "A critical assessment of charismatic-transformational leadership research: Back to the drawing board?" *The Academy of Management Annals* 7(1): 1–60.

Part III

Conclusions

What Supports Innovation in City Governments?

9 Modelling Innovation

The innovation capacity of any city government is related to many different structural—political, social and economic—factors (the macro-level), a set of organizational structural dimensions (the meso-level) and the individual perceptions of the people who work within it (the micro-level). In previous chapters, we have examined each of these factors (structures, networks, and leadership) and their relationships to innovation capacity on a one-to-one basis. In this chapter, we provide a summary overview of our findings, and then return to the model presented in Chapter 1. We analyse the links between each of structures, networks, and leadership. And we link these to innovation and make some claims about which factors seem to have the biggest impact on innovation capacity in city governments.

Challenges, Innovations, and Innovation Drivers

A summary of the socioeconomic challenges, significant innovations and innovation drivers nominated by the municipalities are shown in Table 9.1. There are some striking similarities in the socioeconomic challenges that are mentioned (demographic changes, economic growth, unemployment, health care and educational problems). The municipalities appear to be facing similar circumstances. There are, however, contextual differences between the cities: Unemployment was mentioned more in both Rotterdam and Barcelona and less in Copenhagen, not surprising, given the differences in their unemployment rates (see Chapter 5). Clearly, demography and other specific contextual factors have an impact on the more particular challenges faced in each city.

These similarities and differences in regard to the important socioeconomic challenges and significant innovations in each of the municipalities have already been discussed in detail in Chapter 5. Some interesting additional insights are provided here in relation to what the most frequently nominated innovation drivers were. Copenhagen was most positive about the impact of internal factors (meetings and administrative issues) as well as external factors (elections and the business elite). Rotterdam staff regarded outside factors (the pressure from national government, media, economic

Table 9.1 Socioeconomic Challenges, Innovations and Innovation Drivers

City	Main current and future socioeconomic challenges (5 most nominated)	Innovations (5 most nominated)	Drivers (5 most nominated)
Copenhagen	1 financial (cuts) 2 demography (growth in size, ageing population) 3 environmental (infrastructure, pollution, securing green areas) 4 political (inclusion business, citizens, users etc.) 5 social equity (poverty, and social isolation)	1 organization development (trust based management i.e. getting rid of time-wasting procedures) 2 citizen outreach (empowerment, involving citizens) 3 IT and organizational development (Digitalization) 4 new service (after hours etc.) 5 new services (empowering weak citizens, i.e., rehabilitation of elderly)	1 municipal election campaigns 2 the municipality statutory committee meetings 3 the municipality advisory committee meetings 4 the business elite of the city 5 pay and promotion system
Rotterdam	1 unemployment/ poverty 2 education attainment/youth (mismatch, school dropout) 3 diversity/ segregation (multiculturalism, social segregation 4 physical environment (housing, pollution etc.) 5 organization of health care (decentralization, budget cuts)	1 digital public service (incl. use of social media) 2 uniform digital management (internal) 3 citizen engagement and consultation 4 collaborative governance (new role for government) 5 organization of public health care	1 contact with and involvement of citizens and community groups 2 the current economic crisis 3 the business elite of the city 4 media attention 5 national government pressure on municipalities
Barcelona	1 assistance to vulnerable people 2 unemployment 3 exemplary management of public administrations	1 new services (sustainable public procurement, payment within 30 days) 2 new service (bus network,)	1 quality of proposals coming from local politicians 2 municipal election campaigns

City	Main current and future socioeconomic challenges (5 most nominated)	Innovations (5 most nominated)	Drivers (5 most nominated)
	4 economic revitalization 5 consolidation of the Barcelona brand	3 new services (smart city) 4 organization (co-responsibility tables) 5 recognition (international events)	3 pay and promotion system 4 values and culture of executive management (not politicians) 5 contact with and involvement of citizens and community groups

crisis) as the biggest innovation drivers. Barcelona nominated external (elections, politicians and citizen engagement) as well as internal (administrative) factors. Rotterdam appears to be much more externally driven than the other two cities, which both report a blend of internal and external factors as driving innovation. It is also the city with the highest level of correspondence between the insiders and outsiders in regard to socioeconomic challenges and significant innovations (see Chapters 5 and 6), which fits with a more outward focus.

Hence, although we see similar (and some different) socioeconomic challenges facing each city, the municipalities responded with different innovations and saw different drivers as supporting innovation. This shows that both the types of innovations and the drivers are contextually determined and different municipalities will need to encourage innovation at the point where it is able to have the greatest impact. In Barcelona this might mean focusing on politicians and the political system, while in Copenhagen it might mean focusing on internal structures and procedures and in Rotterdam, innovation is likely to be externally driven.

Networking, Boundary Spanning and Network Structures

In regard to networking, Barcelona seems to be the most outward focused and most attentive to working with others outside the municipality, compared to the other cities. Barcelona respondents report engaging in the most networking (highest level of external communication) and as having the most boundary spanners in their city. Copenhagen staff rate themselves as doing the least amount of external networking and as having the fewest boundary spanners amongst the three cities. Rotterdam is closer to Copenhagen than Barcelona on both of these measures.

Social networks of interpersonal interactions were also analysed. Analysis of working on projects and seeking strategic information networks (see Chapter 7) showed variation between the municipalities, which reflect their different formal structures, and also some differences in regard to who the brokers are and the patterns of their immediate ties. Table 9.2 provides a summary in regard to the work and strategic information networks that we analysed. Copenhagen's work network has a decentralized structure centred on its seven separate divisions (administrations), while both Barcelona's and Rotterdam's informal networks are much more connected with most people linked into a single network. The informal network structure clearly

Table 9.2 Summary of Network Characteristics for Municipalities

	Barcelona	*Copenhagen*	*Rotterdam*
Work network—% of nodes in largest component	87 (centralized)	54 (decentralized)	71 (centralized)
Work network and external networking	Not correlated with network centrality	Correlated with network centrality	Not correlated with network centrality
Work network—highest level of centrality	Level 1	Level 1	Level 1
Work network—highest level of betweenness	Level 3	Level 2	Level 1 (and Politicians)
Strategic information network and external networking	Not correlated with network centrality	Correlated with network centrality	Not correlated with network centrality
Strategic information network—highest level of centrality	Level 1	Level 1	Level 1
Strategic information network—highest level of betweenness	Level 2	Level 2	Level 1
Strategic information network—brokers' ego networks	Closure (Coleman)	Non-redundancy (Burt)	Non-redundancy and closure
Strategic information network—trust weighted betweenness in brokers' ego networks	Not collected	2 of the top 5 brokers with high trust	2 of the top 5 brokers with high trust

Note: The levels are not identical across the municipalities regarding levels 2/3, and the city samples have different distributions of people across the different levels.

follows the administrative structure. The level of external networking was correlated with centrality in the work network only in Copenhagen. Work network centrality was highest for the level 1 administrators in all three cities, while this varied by level in regard to betweenness.

External networking was correlated with strategic information centrality overall and for Copenhagen, but not for the other two cities. People at level 1 were again the 'go to' people in the strategic information networks. Those with the highest betweenness varied, with the most senior administrators (level 1) being the most central in Rotterdam, while for Barcelona and Copenhagen, the sat in the second tier of the administrative hierarchy. However, this to some extent reflects the variation in responses, with most respondents from Copenhagen further down the hierarchy, more senior administrators from Rotterdam and more politicians from Barcelona.

Examining the brokers in the strategic networks and their immediate ties (their ego networks) revealed a variety of different sub-structures around these important people. In Copenhagen, their immediate networks are non-redundant, with few shared ties to others. Barcelona's brokers appear to have more closure, with many of their ties linked to each other. In the case of Rotterdam, there is a mixture of both of the types that we observed in other two cities. As described in Chapter 3, these reflect the different theories of Ron Burt (non-redundancy and variety) and James Coleman (closure and support). Examining these people with the highest brokerage potential in each municipality, it seems that both non-redundancy and closure are apparent in different locations and in different mixtures. The entrepreneurial view of innovation in the private sector literature sees only brokers with low redundancy in their ties as innovators. A more connected and supported type of broker was observed here. This is further supported by an analysis of the levels of trust in the ties of these brokers, which is very high for some of these in both Copenhagen and Rotterdam (but was not collected for Barcelona).

Leadership

We explored five types of leadership that appear in the literature (in Chapter 4) and found empirically (in Chapter 8) that only four of these appear to be coherent leadership styles related to innovation in the public sector. In addition, each of these four types (transformational, entrepreneurial, network governance and altruistic) was positively correlated with innovation capacity, while the transactional style was not (see Table 8.4).

Analysing the leadership styles for each of the three cities showed that there were some commonalities, but also some local differences in their perceptions of leadership and innovation. For Barcelona, both the altruistic and transformational styles were seen to be equally the most supportive of innovation. The transformational style was the most supportive in Copenhagen, followed by altruistic, and the same two styles were also seen to be

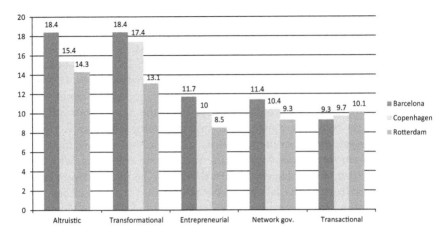

Figure 9.1 Mean Scores of the Leadership Styles for Each City

the most supportive of innovation in Rotterdam, but in the reverse order (that is, altruistic first, followed by transformational). The mean scores for the different styles for each city are shown in Figure 9.1.

We also examined leadership dimensions for each city individually (using a 'bottom-up' approach rather than an approach that proceeds from the theoretical leadership types derived from the literature). In this analysis (see Chapter 8), Copenhagen had a very strong factor based on a combination of altruistic and network styles. For Rotterdam and Barcelona, the strongest factor was more in line with the transformational leadership style, although the network governance style was also regarded as important in both of these cities.

Innovation Capacity and Its Correlates

Throughout this book, we have described some different measures of innovativeness in the three cities that were included in our study. Based on the innovation city index, Copenhagen is ranked as the most innovative of these three (see Chapter 5). When asked about their own innovation capacity, Barcelona staff rated their municipality as having the highest innovation capacity, followed by Copenhagen (see Chapter 6). Rotterdam rated itself the lowest on this. The rank order of innovation capacity, as seen from those outside the municipality, follows the insiders' rankings. The level of correspondence between the insiders and outsiders on the important socio-economic challenges and significant innovations was highest for Rotterdam and lowest for Barcelona.

Amongst these measures of innovation, the best individual-level measure we have is self-rated innovation capacity. Throughout the chapters in Part II of this book, correlations between self-rated innovation capacity and our components were reported. Here they are examined in summary for the three cities in total and by individual city (see Table 9.3).

Innovation capacity (self-rated) was strongly and positively related to innovation drivers, as well as to networking and to boundary spanning. People who see their city as more innovative also judge that they have more supportive contexts, structures and processes for innovation, have more external contact and have more boundary spanners. This is in line with theoretical claims that external contacts and boundary spanning activities support innovation. The strength of these relationships varies across the municipalities, as can be seen in Table 9.3, with the relationship between innovation drivers and innovativeness not significant in Copenhagen (but very strong in the other two cities), while networking was significantly related to innovativeness in that city, but not the others. The presence of boundary spanners was significantly correlated with innovativeness in all three cities.

Innovation capacity was also strongly and positively related to four of the five leadership styles that we examined, with transactional leadership being the odd one out. Transformational, entrepreneurial and network governance leadership were significantly correlated with innovation capacity in all three cities. Altruistic leadership was significant only in Copenhagen, while transactional was significant in both Barcelona and Copenhagen, but not overall. Further, the transactional type did not form a strong scale (see Chapter 8), so little can be said about this relationship.

The picture that emerges from this analysis is in line with the literature: Innovation capacity is linked to having drivers for innovation, doing more external networking and having more boundary spanners present and seeing particular leadership styles as important to innovation. Given that all of these are based on the perceptions of people working in municipalities, this suggests the importance of a positive orientation, which appears to be the strongest for Barcelona. The staff in this city regard themselves and their colleagues as having a greater innovation capacity and also as doing

Table 9.3 Correlations Between Self-Rated Innovation Capacity and Other Factors

	Barcelona	Copenhagen	Rotterdam	Total
Innovation drivers	.375**	-.013	.248**	.151**
Networking	.203	.218*	.101	.242**
Boundary spanning	.347*	.405**	.254**	.362**
Transformational leadership	.335*	.485**	.304**	.436**
Entrepreneurial leadership	.357**	.460**	.382**	.434**
Network gov. leadership	.447**	.515**	.254**	.418**
Altruistic leadership	.218	.354**	.180	.352**
Transactional leadership	.303*	.234**	.005	.092

Spearman correlation coefficients:
*Significant at p<.05.
**Significant at p<.01.

relatively more networking and having more boundary spanners. Copenhagen and Rotterdam are often quite similar on the measures examined, perhaps having a tendency to downplay their level of activity. But Copenhagen leads in regard to seeing its context, procedures and structures as relatively supportive of innovation, as well as leading in the international innovation rankings that we examined for the three cities.

What Supports Innovation Capacity?

Returning to the conceptual model in Chapter 1 (see Figure 1.1), we now move on to an analysis of the relationships between our three components (structures, networks, and leadership) and the relationships between these and innovation capacity. Table 9.4 shows the correlations between boundary spanning, networking and innovation drivers, and between these three variables and the leadership types. Innovation drivers and leadership (four of the five types) are positively correlated, and both boundary spanning and networking and (four of the five types of) leadership are positively correlated. In addition, networking and boundary spanning are strongly and positively correlated, but neither of these are related to innovation drivers.

We used these bivariate analyses to adjust the model in Figure 1.1 and construct a structural equation model to examine these relationships and test the fit of the model. The structural equation model is depicted in Figure 9.2. Innovation drivers (the context, processes and structures that help innovation) was used as the measure of structures. Networking (the amount of external contact) was used as the measure of networks. The leadership styles were included as the measures of leadership.

Because transactional leadership was not correlated with any of innovation drivers, networking, boundary spanning or innovation capacity for the total set of respondents, and our earlier work shows it does not form a coherent scale, we did not include this in the structural equation model. Boundary spanning and networking are correlated, and boundary spanning has a high degree

Table 9.4 Correlations Between Boundary Spanning, Networking, Innovation Drivers and Leadership

	Boundary spanning	Networking	Innovation drivers
Innovation drivers	.053	-.081	
Networking	.216**		
Leadership:			
Altruistic	.333**	.284**	.203**
Transformational	.277**	.236**	.278**
Entrepreneur	.286**	.242**	.192**
Network gov.	.265**	.227**	.253**
Transactional	.055	-.054	.027

Spearman rank correlation coefficients, **significant at p<0.01.

of conceptual overlap with our leadership types. Hence, boundary spanning was not used in this model to maintain conceptual clarity and avoid autocorrelation problems within the model. Innovation drivers and networking were not correlated with each other, so we did not include a path from innovation drivers to networking (see Figure 9.2) for the empirical test of the model.

In addition, while social networks are undoubtedly important to innovation capacity, it is not possible to reduce the complexity of network structures to measures without losing a great deal of information about important whole and ego network characteristics. The patterns of ties that emerge around important brokers are likely to be decisive for understanding innovation, but they cannot be reduced to a single indicator without losing the level of detail that actually helps with the explanation. Because this is what is required for inclusion in this model, the social network structures are not examined here. Instead, they are returned to in Chapter 10, which provides a more detailed narrative about this aspect of innovation capacity.

The model (Figure 9.2) was run using the software AMOS 23. The coefficients shown on this model are for the total of the three cities. The model was also fitted to the data for each city separately, and the coefficients for each of these are shown in Table 9.5. The model has a very good fit in terms

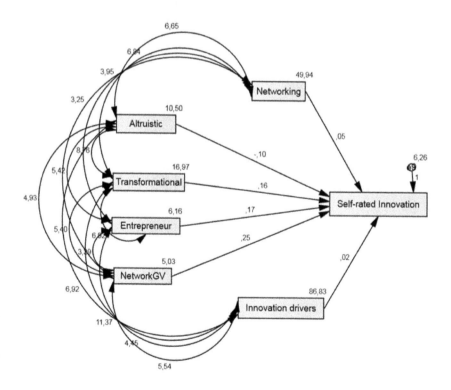

Figure 9.2 Structural Equation Model of Innovation Capacity

Table 9.5 Innovation Capacity Structural Equation Models: Direct Effects and Fit

Self-rated innovation capacity	Network Gov.	Entrepreneurial	Transformational	Altruistic	Innovation drivers	Networking
Full sample	0.25	0.17	0.16	-0.10	0.02	0.05
Barcelona	0.40	-0.15	0.34	-0.18	0.08	0.07
Copenhagen	0.35	0.13	0.20	-0.07	-0.01	0.03
Rotterdam	0.25	0.33	0.10	-0.17	0.08	0.04
Model fit statistical measures						
Measures	CFI	NFI	TLI	IFI	RMSEA	CMIN/df	GFI
SEM model	0.998	0.997	0.952	0.998	0.075	2.818	0.998
Tested model run on subsamples (cities as groups):						
Barcelona	0.987	0.981	0.722	0.989	0.158	2.320	0.988
Copenhagen	0.997	0.995	0.940	0.997	0.089	2.081	0.996
Rotterdam	1.0	0.999	1.0	1.0	0.00	0.300	0.999

Notes: CFI is comparative fit index; NFI is normed fit index; TLI is Tucker–Lewis index; RMSEA is root mean square error of the approximation; IFI is Bollen's incremental fit index; CMIN/df in AMOS is the ratio of $\chi2$ to degrees of freedom. GFI is the Goodness of Fit index.

of eight of the most common fit indices (see the notes following Table 9.5 for an explanation of acceptable fit).

The results from the models show that leadership is the strongest component in terms of direct effects on self-rated innovation capacity. Network governance has the highest coefficients, followed by the entrepreneurial and transformational leadership types, and then the altruistic types. The altruistic type of leadership has a negative effect on self-rated innovation capacity in each city.

The models for the individual cities point to some individual differences in the type of leadership that has the largest effect: For Barcelona, the network governance and the transformational types are the most important. For Copenhagen, the network governance type is clearly the most important factor, while for Rotterdam, it is the entrepreneurial type, followed by the network governance type, that has the largest effect. The direct effects of both networking and innovation drivers are relatively small in comparison. Innovation drivers have a stronger effect in Barcelona and Rotterdam than in Copenhagen, while networking in Barcelona has a bigger effect than for the other two cities.

Conclusions

In this first concluding chapter, we returned to the conceptual model of innovation capacity that was described in Chapter 1 and analysed this empirically. Based on the theoretical framework that we laid out in Part I of this book, we expected that:

- The presence of more innovation drivers, more external networking and leadership that supports innovation would all be positively associated with self-rated innovation capacity;
- Leadership types that support innovation would be positively associated with networking and innovation drivers; and
- Innovation drivers would be positively associated with networking.

These expectations were largely met, with positive associations found between the variables as expected. The exception was that there was no association between networking and innovation drivers (point number 3).

The structural equation models that were fitted for the combined data, and for each of the three cities individually, showed that leadership was the most important contributor to self-rated innovation capacity. The network governance type stands out as very important, although the entrepreneurial type of leadership was the most important in Rotterdam. Interestingly, the altruistic leadership type was negatively associated with self-rated innovation capacity in each of the cities. This is likely to be an effect of its relationship with the other leadership types: Although this type does form a reliable scale in its own right, there is also a high degree of theoretical overlap with the other leadership types. This aside, the finding that different types of leadership appear to be more linked to innovation capacity in different locations points to a conclusion that the leadership styles that support innovation will vary from place to place. In addition, it seems that different styles of leadership can work side by side, and we have few indications that one style dominates and displaces the others in any of the three cities.

The fact that innovation drivers and external networking are weaker determinants of self-rated innovation capacity than leadership, signals a few important things about understanding innovation capacity. First, the role of agency (in this case through leadership) in creating an environment within which people perceive that innovation is supported is sometimes overlooked in studies of innovation capacity. An understandable focus on innovation drivers (and more often in studies of the public sector, innovation barriers) means that leadership is often not considered as an important contributor to innovation capacity. Second, while many studies of innovation describe the importance of external relationships, the findings here indicate that having such contacts doesn't necessarily improve an individual's view of how innovative the organization they work within is.

Related to this last point, is the fact that much research on the relationship between networks (collaboration, external engagement and a range of related ideas) and innovation, is often very unclear in regard to the meaning of 'network', is silent on how it is captured and equally imprecise about how its link to innovation is measured. In this particular case, it may be that a simple count of the frequency of external contact tells us a lot about the amount of time that administrators in city governments are spending talking to people outside the organization, while also telling us very little about the quality of those contacts in terms of gaining new and useful information that might support innovation. We return to this point in Chapter 10 where we further discuss the results of the social network analysis.

Further, the lack of any association between external networking and innovation drivers reveals that what can be understood from examining the frequency of contact outside the organization might be very different to perceptions of the structures, processes and contextual factors that drive innovation. It is possible that being highly engaged outside an organization has little relationship to an individual's assessment of what helps innovation inside it. But it would seem (theoretically) that knowing more about what is going on outside would lead to a better understanding of how structures, processes and contextual factors can be used in support of innovation inside an organization.

Of course, it should also be remembered that many of the measures reported in this book are based on the perceptions (about leadership, what helps and hinders innovation, and their city's innovation capacity) and reported behaviours (external networking) of the administrators who answered our survey (this analysis does not include the few politicians amongst our respondents). We can make no claims about assessments of levels of innovativeness of these cities, or about the generalizability of the findings here to other cities.

This chapter highlights the importance of including leadership and other measures of agency in examinations of innovation, which are often dominated by analyses of structures. It also points to the likelihood that different types of leadership are needed to support innovation capacity in different locations. It also raises some hard questions about the difficulty of researching and modelling innovation capacity in network structural terms. In the next and final chapter of this book, we reflect on what the social network analysis reveals about innovation in city governments. We also examine how we can might extend the use of social network analysis to better understand the important links between networks, innovation drivers and innovation capacity in future research.

10 Supporting Innovation in City Governments

The idea that public sector organizations must innovate in order to meet the ever growing demands on them is now well established. We have, throughout this book, worked towards an understanding of innovation capacity and what contributes to it. We identified some of the main challenges that senior administrators and politicians regarded as important in their municipalities. They included issues like financial cuts, environmental and infrastructure problems and pressing societal issues like educational deficiencies, changing demography and unemployment and economic revitalization. Our respondents also mentioned a wide range of innovations that they regarded as significant in their cities and that should address the main challenges that they faced. These included new services, organizational developments, urban planning and IT developments and citizen engagement.

But anyone who looks at the lists presented in this book will immediately recognize that this is a very temporally specific view of problems and solutions: These challenges are constantly changing, and so are the innovations directed at addressing them. Just two years after we completed the survey, many city government administrators and politicians would be likely to mention immigration (and the need to house migrants in the cities) and climate change as major challenges. And they would also be likely to identify different innovations as the most significant, put in place to alleviate these challenges.

In short, both the socioeconomic challenges faced by cities, and the most important innovations that they introduce in response to these, are constantly changing. Cities need to continually update their policy ideas and the policy instruments that they use, and they need to keep changing the way that they work. People are continuing to move to cities, where most of the increase in economic activity and social and cultural change in any nation takes place. Innovation is not something which is needed sporadically and only to address particular situations as they arise, but instead, there is a pressing need for cities to innovate constantly. Fiscal austerity is not yet over, and indeed, it seems likely to dominate the public sector for a long period of time. It has become urgent in Rotterdam and Copenhagen, which have been affected by a national level decentralization of welfare to the municipal level, and it continues to dominate in Barcelona (and Spain), which is still coping with the consequences of the 2008 financial crisis.

This signals the enormous importance of cities having the capacity to innovate in the years to come. Our aim in this book has been to shed light on the key conditions that will enable them to do so, based around our chosen categories of structures, networks, and leadership. In this final chapter, we summarize the lessons that can be drawn from this research and provide some reflection on them. We briefly re-state our findings which connect the variables in our model to innovation capacity, and we look for the factors that appear to have the biggest impact on the innovative capacity of cities. Then we reflect on our findings about leadership and networks, which are our biggest contributions to understanding innovation capacity. We finish this chapter with a section on what we have learned and what we still do not know.

A Model of Innovation: What Matters the Most to Innovation Capacity?

There are many factors that have an impact on innovation capacity. In this book we focused on three of these, and (as expected) we found that each of them was related to innovation. The context, structures and processes that support innovation (innovation drivers) are directly related to innovation capacity. The amount of networking outside the municipality that occurs is also associated with innovation capacity. And leadership styles that could be expected to support innovation were also positively associated with self-rated innovation capacity. In addition, innovation leadership types were also related to external networking and innovation drivers.

In examining which of these factors appeared to be the most important in shaping innovation capacity, some interesting results arose. First, in each city, leadership was the most important contributor to self-rated innovation capacity. This signals that individual actors and their actions are very important to innovation, in addition to the other factors generally regarded to be important in organizations, such as formal structures, interpersonal networks and a culture that is generally supportive of the creation and implementations of new ideas. Leadership is discussed in more detail in the following section. Second, the level of external networking turned out to be not very important for innovativeness, in contrast to much of what the literature claims about the importance of networks. This is likely to be related to the rather coarse measure of networking that was used. And a different approach to this is discussed in the section on social networks later in this chapter.

Leadership as a Crucial Factor for Innovation

One of the biggest contributions of our study stems from our focus on leadership and leadership styles in city governments. Following the literature on leadership (and network governance), we identified various perspectives on leadership. Thus, we not only looked at transformational leadership, probably the most popular and researched perspective on leadership the past 20 years, but also at interpersonal leadership (renamed altruistic leadership) and entrepreneurial and network governance perspectives on leadership. On the basis of the literature one would expect that transformational leadership, which in the literature is very much connected to change and innovation, would be very important for innovation. The literature also emphasizes that innovation often comes from connecting to other actors and using creativity and the diverse information and resources of other actors to stimulate change. This perspective would suggest that network governance leadership is also an important form of leadership for innovation.

In line with the literature, we found that various forms of leadership are important, and that the network governance, entrepreneurial and transformational leadership styles are all associated with (self-rated) innovativeness. It seems that different leadership styles are employed side by side in supporting innovation. It may well be that the various leadership styles boost rather than exclude each other as is often assumed in the literature. Indeed, our examination of the standard leadership classifications suggests a good degree of overlap in the constituent parts of different leadership types. So, contrary to the expectation that network governance leadership (which involves others in decisions and works collaboratively) might be difficult to combine with, for instance, transformational leadership (which is fairly top down and inspirational), it may be that these different styles actually support each other.

The fact that we see fairly strong correlations between the different leadership styles seems to confirm this assumption. Different leadership activities are probably being employed at the same time, perhaps even by the same people, and it seems that the different leadership activities support each other rather than being in conflict: Network governance leadership secures the necessary connections to the external actors, while transformational leadership creates enthusiasm and spreads a vision, while entrepreneurial leadership secures the necessary resources.

If this is true, then municipalities that aim to support innovation should not only encourage different leadership activities but also employ different leadership strategies simultaneously. This is, however, not as easy as it looks. It requires a balancing act because, for example, a transformational leadership style makes leaders very visible and prominent, which may create tension with the need for leaders to connect actors rather than direct them. So, although using different kind of leadership styles might support innovation, it requires some skill to employ these together, either by having people that can work in different modes or having a range of people with different leadership styles.

Further, there are differences between the cities in the importance of different leadership styles. The network governance leadership style appears to be most important to innovation capacity in Copenhagen. In Barcelona, both network governance and transformational styles are important to innovativeness, and in Rotterdam, entrepreneurial leadership is the most important. This is counterintuitive because the Netherlands (like Denmark) is known for its consensual decision-making and the strong presence of networks. Perhaps entrepreneurial leadership adds something to an otherwise fairly consensual and horizontal approach. This can then be contrasted to Barcelona, the only city where we also found a strong relationship between innovativeness and top-down transformational leadership. There, network governance leadership also contributes significantly to (self-rated) innovativeness. Perhaps every city has a different optimal mix which again emphasizes that there is probably no one-size-fits-all prescription for supporting innovation. Leadership styles interact with the structure and the culture of the municipality and the country, and as we have seen, these vary substantially, as do the challenges they face.

Social Networks and Their Importance for Innovation

Without a doubt, networks hold a special place in the literature that addresses the topic of innovation systems. In contrast to a focus on individual actors with bright ideas, an examination of networks attempts to understand the soft structures that support innovation, allowing new ideas to be sourced and conveyed and innovations to be actually implemented. Networks are crucial, as we have argued throughout this book. But reducing networks to simple counts of the amount of external contact that individuals have does not help us to understand what network structures yield innovation capacity.

The social network analyses in this book demonstrate a number of important points. First, it is clear that informal networks mirror the formal organizational structure of each of the cities. This shows how formal structure shapes opportunities for connecting with others, even in the less constrained (by work obligations) strategic information networks. Structure has a determinant effect on which people are likely to be in contact with each other, and this is important for innovation which is seen to rely on openness and diversity. This is confirmed by the finding that it is the most senior level administrators that are the most central in both types of networks. It matters what position you hold in the hierarchy.

Second, having external contacts is related to being central in the strategic information network (being a 'go to' person). This suggests that there are a set of people (although this only holds for Copenhagen and not the other two cities individually) who are both good at connecting with people outside the municipality and good at distributing information to the many people who seek it from them. They are important actors from the perspective of innovation, as they have access to different information (from outside the organization) and the ability to transmit this internally.

In addition, it is clear that the brokers, who are so important to innovation, reside at different levels in different cities. While this is likely to be partly related to differences in samples from the different cities, it is notable that Rotterdam is very hierarchical in this regard with their brokers mostly at the most senior level. This is not the case for Barcelona and Copenhagen. Further, there is an intriguing difference in the micro-structures of interpersonal connections around the brokers in different cities. While brokers in Copenhagen have little redundancy, in Barcelona there is much more closure, with an individual's ties quite likely to be connected to each other. And in Rotterdam, the brokers are a mixture of both these types.

Even more interestingly, the levels of trust reported in these network ties in both Copenhagen and Rotterdam (we don't have this information for Barcelona) are high, and slightly higher in Copenhagen. Trust could be expected to be high in situations of closure. But despite the low levels of closure around brokers in Copenhagen, trust is high around some of the brokers in this city, as is the case for Rotterdam, where the brokers display a mixture of non-redundancy and closure. The importance of trust in creating a safe work environment in which people are comfortable with taking risks and making mistakes cannot be underestimated in regard to innovation.

We postulate that some of these brokers (with more closure) are uniquely important for innovation in the public sector. They are able to come up with ideas (through unconnected ties that provide different sources of information) and also have the necessary support to implement these (through ties that are linked to each other). Overall, it is a mixture of different types of ties that is needed to provide enough internal support from homogeneous peers, and enough openness to gain new information (e.g., about new technological developments, the socioeconomic situation or citizens' opinions) from heterogeneous actors within and outside the organization, in order to support innovation and continuous development.

These social network analyses enable us to identify the well-connected leaders (senior administrators) and the brokers (at different levels in different cities) with high innovation potential. In practical terms, identifying and recruiting these people into the generation and implementation of innovation should have a positive effect on innovation capacity. They are the people who can help diffuse innovation and overcome potential barriers to implementation across formal organizational structures. The brokers, who are strategically placed to gather information and then disseminate it, are vital to enhancing innovation capacity. They are also playing a role in providing an environment where trust is embedded and risk-taking should be acceptable and even encouraged. Locating these individuals and directing support and training to them should ensure that the potential change-makers are involved and have the capacity to support innovation.

Where to Next? A Research Agenda for the Future

Our theoretical and empirical findings naturally generate a set of questions to ask in the future. We found strong relations between leadership styles, innovation drivers, networking and innovation capacity. Our finding that leadership styles are more strongly related with innovation capacity than the other factors is intriguing. We have learned a lot about what leadership styles are seen as being important for public sector innovation, but there is much more to learn. For example, are there other adaptations to the visions of leadership portrayed in the (mostly) private sector literature that will make these even more relevant to public sector innovation? And what is the relationship between perceptions of leadership that support innovation and leadership behaviour (actual activities)?

Another thought-provoking question is related to our finding that various leadership styles are apparently used alongside each other. Questions that follow from this include how the different leadership styles support or reinforce each other, and whether these different styles are being used by the same or different people. This suggests a need for future research that rests on the collection of data on the activities of individuals and the effects of these activities on others.

Similarly, while we have learnt quite a bit about network structures and characteristics in these cities, there is still much to learn about how network positions are related to particular behaviours and the creation of innovation. For instance, amongst brokers who have a high potential for innovation encapsulated in their brokerage positions, does this potential actually translate into innovation? Do one of the two types of brokers that we observed (with high innovation potential) actually create and diffuse innovation more than the other? Are individuals who are in brokerage positions in these networks applying a different menu of leadership activities compared to their colleagues? And what combination of network characteristics across a whole network best supports innovation? For considerations such as these, we need information on what these individuals actually do and what the outcomes of these actions are. Such information is of course more difficult to collect than self-reported perceptual data.

To make further advances in this area of inquiry, we would need to 'see the network twice' (Lewis 2011). That is, we would have to collect not only the quantitative network information that we have presented here, but also qualitative information about the concrete activities of individuals and how they use their network positions to innovate. This would enable us to draw conclusions about the actual activities of brokers but also other important individuals in the network and provide us with additional information about the strong relationships we found in our research between leadership and (self-rated) innovativeness. Of course, such an approach requires significant effort to collect data about individuals' activities.

As noted above, there also remains an unresolved question about innovation as an output, rather than as a capacity. Although both leadership and social network structure have been shown to be related to innovation, we cannot claim to have proven causality. We certainly can say that there are some clear and significant relationships between leadership, innovation drivers and networking and self-rated innovativeness. But our measure of innovativeness is both perceptual and quite macro, concerning broad judgements rather than being directly related to the activities and services that cities provide. Hence, it is difficult to relate this to the actual performance of cities in terms of innovativeness. Investigating concrete innovation activities, ranking their effectiveness and then relating these to both leadership activities and network characteristics could be a fruitful avenue of inquiry that would further advance our understanding of innovation. This again requires considerably more data collection and a longer period of time, because time is required if an assessment of the effectiveness of an innovation is be gauged.

Our analysis is certainly an advance in regard to understanding innovation in city governments, but it is far from answering every question about the topic. Future research on public sector innovation can build on what we have learnt. Studies that extend this work on leadership styles, including examining the use of different styles in parallel, should further our knowledge of this field. Studies that examine the important micro-structures of networks around brokers and are able to ascertain how these are being used for innovation will move the focus from network structure (potential) to actual behaviour. Research that builds upon the intriguing findings about different types of brokers and the interesting pattern of high trust ties around them would surely be a profitable new direction. It is also one that links the generally quite separate study of brokerage with the idea of safety and risk-taking. Studies that more precisely identify and assess innovation in action, rather than innovation capacity, should also contribute to this growing area of research. This book opens up new avenues for research and suggests a path for some fruitful future directions which also have enormous practical importance.

References

Lewis, Jenny M. 2011. "The future of network governance research: Strength in diversity and synthesis." *Public Administration* 89(4): 1221–34.

Appendix A: Outside Innovators in Barcelona, Copenhagen and Rotterdam

Barcelona (note – no organizational information is used for Barcelona to maintain anonymity)

	Sector	Number of interviewees
	Business	6
	University	6
	University	
	University / Not-for-profit organization	
	Not-for-profit organization	6
	Public organization	5
	Labour Union	1
	Government	1

Copenhagen

Name of organization	Description	Sector	Number of interviewees
CENAPS	Provides service and training in behavioural health field	A private-public partnership	1
Copenhagen University	Research, education, art and cultural studies (active in local city area council)	University	1
Kunst kultur (NGO)	Communication consultant	Private business	1
COWI	Consultant, engineering	Private business	1
FOA	Union for public employees	Union	1

(*Continued*)

FOA SOSU	Union for public employees, social and health care division	Union	1
Frederiksberg Municipality	Neighbouring municipality	Municipality	1
Frivilige center Amager	Local centre for volunteers	Street level volunteers	1
Kommuners Landsforening (KL)	Union for municipalities	Union, public organization	2
Professionshøjskolen Metropol	School for teachers, social and health care assistants	Education, research	2
Roskilde University	Research, education	University	3
Socialstyrelsen	Administration in the Ministry of Social welfare	Government	1
TREDJE NATUR	Architect	Private business	1
Tænketank CURA	Think tank	Private business	1
Ældre Sagen	Interest organization: focus on the elderly	Non-profit organization	1
Aalborg University	Research, education	University	1

Rotterdam

Name of organization	Description	Sector	Number of interviewees
Havenbedrijf Rotterdam N.V.	Port	Public	2
ARCADIS	Architecture/ Engineering	Private	3
Bob Smit Gallery, St. Field of Dreams, RC	Culture	Private	2
InHolland	Education	Public	3
Rotterdam Partners	City marketing	Public	1
Now&Wow Fest	Entertainment	Private	4
Ravesloot BV, Hogeschool Rotterdam	Consultancy, education	Private	8

(*Continued*)

Pameijer	Health care	Public	1
Stichting De Verre Bergen	Funding	Private non-profit	1
Erasmus Universiteit Rotterdam	University	Public	10

Appendix B: Individual City-Based Leadership Qualities Pattern Matrix

Barcelona (n=55)	1	2	3
S Willing to risk mistakes by employees	.973		
P Works collaboratively	.819		
U Takes all decisions alone	−.762		
M Committed to colleagues and organisation	.736		
V Involves others in key decisions	.730		
D Authoritative	−.618		
T Open towards new ideas	.542		
R Good at learning from mistakes	.515		
N Willing to sacrifice self-interest	.511		
O Mobilising the resources needed	.454		
J Results-oriented	.418		
C Takes initiative	.414		
L Provides intellectual stimulation		.819	
F Displays a long-term perspective		.651	
K Inspirational		.598	
E Visible leadership		.581	
B Visionary			
A Good communication skills			
Q Knowledgeable			.772
W Always follows procedures			.759
G Displays a short-term perspective			.623
I Problem-oriented			.563
H Good at gathering information			

Copenhagen (n=157)	1	2	3
M Committed to colleagues and organization	.705		
L Provides intellectual stimulation	.693		
N Willing to sacrifice self-interest	.675		
O Mobilising the resources needed	.669		
H Good at gathering information	.655		

(Continued)

Copenhagen (n=157)		1	2	3
Q	Knowledgeable	.561		
K	Inspirational	.555		
J	Results-oriented	.552		
A	Good communication skills	.513		
V	Involves others in key decisions	.511		
P	Works collaboratively	.487		
I	Problem-oriented	.471		
E	Visible leadership	.427		
T	Open towards new ideas	.425		
C	Takes initiative	.407		
R	Good at learning from mistakes		.569	
D	Authoritative		−.538	
S	Willing to risk mistakes by employees		.529	
W	Always follows procedures		−.441	
U	Takes all decisions alone		−.04	
F	Displays a long-term perspective			.760
G	Displays a short-term perspective	.516		−.715
B	Visionary			.546

Rotterdam (n=150)		1	2	3
C	Takes initiative	.724		
T	Open towards new ideas	.722		
W	Always follows procedures	−.633		
J	Results-oriented	.597		
S	Willing to risk mistakes by employees	.511		
D	Authoritative	.435		
E	Visible leadership			
A	Good communication skills			
V	Involves others in key decisions		.738	
P	Works collaboratively		.683	
O	Mobilising the resources needed		.500	
M	Committed to colleagues and organization		.492	
U	Takes all decisions alone		−.438	
N	Willing to sacrifice self-interest		.437	
H	Good at gathering information		.402	
R	Good at learning from mistakes			
Q	Knowledgeable			
I	Problem-oriented			
F	Displays a long-term perspective			.832
G	Displays a short-term perspective			-.577
B	Visionary			.540
K	Inspirational			.519
L	Provides intellectual stimulation			.401

Index

For Product Safety Concerns and Information please contact our EU
representative GPSR@taylorandfrancis.com
Taylor & Francis Verlag GmbH, Kaufingerstraße 24, 80331 München, Germany

www.ingramcontent.com/pod-product-compliance
Ingram Content Group UK Ltd.
Pitfield, Milton Keynes, MK11 3LW, UK
UKHW021608240425
457818UK00018B/448